Ghost Camps

&

Boom Towns

by
JoAnn Roe

MONTEVISTA PRESS
Bellingham, Washington
1995
Reprinted 2004
Reprinted 2012

ISBN 978-0-931551-19-2
Library of Congress Catalog Number: 95-77844

Other Books by JoAnn Roe:
San Juan Islands: Into the 21st Century (Caxton Press,2011)
Amazing Grayce Roessler (Roessler Estate E-book, 2010)
North Cascades Highway (Montevista Press, 2004)
Stevens Pass (Caxton Press, new publisher 2002)
Ranald MacDonald, Pacific Rim Adventurer (WSU Press, 1997)
The North Cascades Highway (The Mountaineers Books, 1997)
Seattle Uncovered (Seaside Press, 1995)
Stevens Pass (The Mountaineers Books, 1995)
The Columbia River (Fulcrum Publishing, 1992)
F.S. Matsura (Heibonsha Publishers, 1988)
The Real Old West (Douglas & McIntyre, 1981)
Frank Matsura, Frontier Photographer (Madrona Publishers, 1981)
The North Cascadians (Madrona Publishers, 1980)

– *and for children:*
Samurai Cat (Montevista Press, 1993)
Alaska Cat (Montevista Press, 1990)
Fisherman Cat (Montevista Press, 1988)
Castaway Cat (Montevista Press, 1984)

Montevista Press
Bellingham, WA 98229

TABLE OF CONTENTS

CLALLAM COUNTY
Chapter 1 – Carlsborg 1
Chapter 2 – Diamond Point 9
Chapter 3 – Dungeness 15
Chapter 4 – Gettysburg 27
Chapter 5 – Port Crescent 33
Chapter 6 – Pysht 45
Chapter 7 – Twin 55

JEFFERSON COUNTY
Chapter 8 – Irondale 61
Chapter 9 – Port Discovery 75
Chapter 10 – Port Hadlock 83
Chapter 11 – Port Ludlow 93
Chapter 12 – Tubal Cain Mine 107

SAN JUAN COUNTY
Chapter 13 – Roche Harbor 111

SKAGIT COUNTY
Chapter 14 – Avon 121
Chapter 15 – Blanchard 127
Chapter 16 – Clear Lake 141
Chapter 17 – Cokedale 155
Chapter 18 – Hamilton 159
Chapter 19 – Skagit City 175
Chapter 20 – Skagit Queen Mines 179
Chapter 21 – Valumines 187

WHATCOM COUNTY
Chapter 22 – Azurite Mine 191
Chapter 23 – Barron 201
        Eureka Mine
        Mammoth Mine

WHATCOM COUNTY *(Continued)*

Chapter 24 – Blue Canyon & Park 211
Chapter 25 – Glacier 225
Chapter 26 – Maple Falls 239
Chapter 27 – Semiahmoo 251
Chapter 28 – Shuksan 265
     Lone Jack Mine
     Red Mt. Mine

INTRODUCTION AND ACKNOWLEDGMENTS

This book was originally written for the publisher, Sunfire Publishers of Langley, British Columbia, as an extension into the United States of its popular series on ghost towns and mining camps of mainland British Columbia, Alberta, the Yukon, Alaska, and Vancouver Island, a series still marketed in 1995. During the editing of this book in 1994, Garnet Basque, the principal owner of the publishing house, died suddenly of a massive heart attack. Montevista Press decided to publish the book, and possibly others in a continuation of the series for Washington state.

It was difficult to select the towns and camps to be included. The criteria established by Sunfire were that towns must have had a boom and bust economy and mining camps significant development. Small historic towns that always were small towns are not included. However, before knowledge of tiny vanished hamlets and camps is lost, I urge local historical societies to record their histories in society files.

I particularly wish to acknowledge the significant contributions to this book by the pioneers who wrote of their lives and memories for the books, *Jimmy Come Lately* and *Pride of Heritage*, and to others who have left oral accounts filed in the historical societies.

The following people have helped me during research in various ways, for which I am very grateful: Deanna Ammons for consultations about Clear Lake and Eleanor Clough for a tour of the town; John Bullene for sharing his personal papers on Lone Jack Mine; personnel of Clallam County Historical Society; librarians at the Clallam Co. Library for guidance; Fred Hubbard for guiding me to the Barron locations over bumpy roads; Mike Impero for sharing Frances Todd's files; John Munroe for showing me a slide presentation on the Lone Jack & other mines; Betty Pfouts of Jefferson County Historical Museum for guiding me to numerous clippings and unpublished manuscripts; Marjorie Reichardt for consultations about Alaska Packers; Dennis Blake Thompson for keeping me straight about railroads; Chris White of National Park Service at Sedro-Woolley for leading me to information about mining disputes; the staff at Special Collections, University of Washington Libraries, and the ever-suffering librarians at Bellingham Public Library who endure my frequent requests for obscure materials.

IMPORTANT NOTICE

The author and publisher are not responsible for the intrusions of readers onto the sites discussed in this book. Readers are strongly admonished to respect sites that are on private lands, first obtaining the permission of current owners to enter, and to remember that it is a federal offense to vandalize or remove any artifacts from publicly owned lands such as old mining sites located in the national parks and forests.

JoAnn Roe and Montevista Press

Clarifications for the 2004 reprinting:

Page 127, lines 1-2. One can say that Blanchard is at the northeastern corner of Samish Bay or the southeastern corner of the larger Bellingham Bay.

Page 134, line 5. The store owned in the early century by Hinkston subsequently had two other owners, then W.H. Fenno operated it for some years. Fenno also bought the depot from the GNR and later sold it as a community hall.

CLALLAM COUNTY

Chapter 1

CARLSBORG

In response to Clallam County pioneers' need for rail transportation, a wealthy Seattle builder, C.J. Erickson, leased the Port Townsend Southern Railroad (PTSR) from Northern Pacific in 1914. At the time, Port Townsend was probably the most important town of the area. The line had been organized back in 1887 by mostly Port Townsend citizens (L.B. Hastings, Charles Eisenbeis, Sol Levy and others) to go from the Port Townsend to the Columbia River but never got farther than Quilcene, and was sold to Northern Pacific and Pacific Coast Company in 1899. Later the tracks to Quilcene were torn up and installed from Port Townsend to the Port Angeles-Discovery Bay branch.

When Erickson took over the road, he had to replace many of the rotten trestles with earth-fill roadbed. Shipping magnate Joshua Green purchased the PTSR from the Northern Pacific in 1917, honoring Erickson's lease, and extended the tracks through town to Green's steamer dock. Thereafter, freight could come to Port Townsend on Green's Puget Sound Navigation Company and be transferred to the PTSR for points on the Olympic Peninsula. The connection was a boon to the citizens and businesses but it contributed to the demise of several small seaport towns along the Strait of Juan de Fuca, among them Port Crescent and Dungeness.

Erickson's construction business in Seattle absorbed lumber like a sponge does water, and the verdant forests of the Peninsula did not escape his notice. The burgeoning new railroad systems required good ties, too.

Obviously, profits were to be made in milling lumber. Erickson acquired large tracts of fine timber in the Lost Mountain and Indian Valley areas south of Sequim, then built a shingle mill and sawmill, Carlsborg Mill and Timber Company (CM&TC), at a site four miles west of Sequim adjacent to the railroad. As construction began on August, 1915, and a settlement grew up around the mill, Erickson named the new town Carlsborg after Karlsborg, Vastergotland, a town in Sweden at which he had worked.

The site of Carlsborg was adjacent to the railroad tracks that ran along the north border of the 87-acre millsite. The sawmill was designed to cut 50,000 board feet of lumber per day and was later restructured to produce 100,000. The shingle mill was spacious enough to handle four machines, and the sawmill was one of the first all-electric sawmills in the Northwest. This meant that each mill machine was operated by its own motor, instead of being powered from a steam-driven continuous overhead belt.

Simultaneously work went forward on a railroad extending thirteen miles to the timber tracts Erickson had purchased, where the company set up an outlying logging camp for twenty-five men. At the Carlsborg mill the company established a machine shop to service the logging locomotive and other motorized equipment. The millpond was the terminus of the Sequim Irrigation Project ditch.

The Carlsborg Mill and Timber Company.
                              — Courtesy of Port Angeles Public Library

At the mill gate another building of 5,000 square feet arose to house offices, the post office (by 1917), a butcher shop, kitchen and dining room, plus a general store. The company store's inventory included everything from groceries to bib overalls and caulked boots. Twelve bunkhouses were built to house forty-eight single men, as well as a dozen or so homes for married employees.

One of the earliest private structures to be built was the two-story Grange hall with a general store on the first floor and the meeting hall and dining room on the second. The post office operated from the Grange in 1918, and the hall became popular for dances. Soon a log schoolhouse and privately owned homes joined the company enclave.

When the facility was ready to do business, Erickson offered the job of Office Manager to J.A.R. "Jack" Wiborg, then a Dean of the Commercial Department at Adelphia College, Seattle. Erickson added Oscar Fogde, also from Adelphia, as bookkeeper and general office worker.

Like other sawmills, the Carlsborg Mill had ready customers around Puget Sound. Immigrants flooding into the area required homes and business buildings, and the United States Government needed vast amounts of lumber during World War I for its facilities. The shipbuilding branch of Erickson's firm gained a contract in 1917 to build six wooden ships for the federal government (not in Carlsborg).

The town of Carlsborg grew. Among the earlier businesses were Schmuck's Equipment and Supply Company and Emil Nelson's Liberty Theater. The theater functioned as a church, meeting hall, and movie house. In the book, *Jimmy Come Lately*, Oscar Fogde described the background music that was used for the silent pictures of the 1920s. The pianist, George Vautier, had a limited and sometimes inappropriate repertoire. One time, just after a heart-wrenching scene where a daughter threw herself on the body of her drowned father, Vautier broke out with the lively tune, "Ain't it Grand to Meet a Pal from Your Old Home Town."

Alex Wallenius opened a newspaper, the *Carlsborg Review*, on December 15, 1920. After the Grange Hall burned in 1927, the post office moved to a makeshift building near the mill entrance. Gradually the commercial center moved in that direction, too, but the Grange Hall was rebuilt at its original site near the railroad. About this time Frank Knight moved his general store from the fading town of Dunge-

A Harriet U. Fish Drawing

3

ness to Carlsborg. This country store still operates today. The CM&TC naturally encouraged its employees to patronize its own store. Between 1925 and 1930 clerks wrote down the amounts of purchases by employees in even numbers, then issued tin tokens for the change, the tokens redeemable in the company store, of course.

The Carlsborg Tavern and a card room thrived. In the late 1920s, the CM&TC designed a triangular, three-hole golf course on company property near the Dungeness River for the benefit of the employees and families. However, according to John Soderberg, a retired mill employee of Sequim, only a handful of employees ever played the course.

CM&TC's original office and store building, no longer used in the 1930s, was sold to private owners around 1932. The new owners converted the building into a very popular night club called the "Cook Shack". During the 1930s and 1940s it drew patrons from far and near by featuring top entertainers imported from Seattle.

By the mid-1930s, the declining market for lumber caused Erickson to sell the CM&TC mill. An optimistic five-way partnership took over: Victor Soderberg, the general manager; Lou Hubbard of Sequim; Nichols and Trumbull of Port Angeles; and W. Washburn of Neah Bay. The partnership evidently could not survive in the clamp of the Depression, and the mill was sold in 1936 to a Seattle firm that intended to dismantle the mill for scrap. However, lumbermen Lawrence McLellan, Harry O'Donnell, and William Westover of Gray's Harbor stepped in to purchase the mill and reopen it on January 1, 1937, as the Dungeness Timber Co. Unfortunately, this company lasted only two years.

In 1942, the company was acquired by Crescent Logging Company (CLC), headed by pioneer Petrus Pearson, who operated it successfully through the World War II years. During that period most of the output was reserved for United States Government use. Logs for the mill chiefly came from CLC's logging operations along the Soleduck River west of Lake Crescent. Logs were transported by the Port Angeles & Western (PA&W) directly to a Carlsborg mill spur. Mill Superintendent Ed Fleetwood said that "The timber now being logged by the Crescent Logging Company at Soleduck is in such slow growth it has great strength and army engineers are constantly asking for it for structural work." In July, 1945, the government issued an order forbidding the sale of any two-by-fours until a major government order had been filled. Some structural timbers were cut to a whopping sixteen inches by sixteen inches.

The plant's equipment included a nine-foot band saw, a re-saw, ten-inch edger, four-inch pony edger, three planers and two dry kilns, the latter seldom used during this period as most sawn lumber went directly to the railroad for shipment. Also in use were cut-off saws, three Ross lumber

4

carriers, and a locomotive crane for loading. Power was furnished by burning mill waste in special furnaces. In 1945, the mill employed 105 men, so Carlsborg saw something of a boom at the time. Most workers were from the local area with only four transient laborers employed in mid-1945. though. Complying with the war housing needs of the government, the company agreed to house transient farm laborers in the largely empty company bunkhouse.

George W. Pankratz of Seattle acquired the mill in 1947 from owners that then included Joshua Green of Peoples Bank. Pankratz had operated a successful mill on the Duwamish Channel, but it burned down in 1944. Looking for a new location, he saw Carlsborg as a good opportunity to resume business and moved his business there. Business boomed. The returning war veterans sparked a spurt in housing starts, absorbing the output of construction lumber from the Carlsborg mill.

When the 51-year-old Pankratz died suddenly of pneumonia in 1950, George's brother, John S. Pankratz, inherited the mill. The brothers had been partners from 1920 to 1940, and had parted amicably to run their own enterprises. After George's death, John ran both his Seattle mill and the Carlsborg enterprise for a decade.

At that time the Carlsborg Mill obtained many of its logs from the Olympic Peninsula south of Forks and north of Aberdeen. The two largest land owners in the area were the State of Washington and the Milwaukee Land Company (from its acquisitions during railroad construction earlier in the century). The Pankratz operation was the third largest shipper or revenue producer during the 1950s and 1960s for Chicago Milwaukee's rail facilities, as almost all its shipments were "long haul"—lumber bound for cities in the Eastern United States. Cars of lumber were hauled to Port Angeles, placed on a rail car ferry for Seattle, then moved to the regular railroad tracks for final transport to customers. At Port Angeles the railroad maintained a lift mechanism for the cars, because variable tides sometimes made it impossible to transfer the cars on tracks from land to ship. The majority of the Carlsborg lumber, mostly hemlock and white fir, was dimension lumber for homes and small projects. The mill also sold some cedar that went into siding and cut cross-arms for telephone and electric poles. The latter were particularly in demand, for the Rural Electrification Administration moved swiftly to provide electricity to homes and small town businesses.

The log supply from the Forks area was interrupted by the big Forks fire of 1951 that started by a spark from the firebox of a PA&W locomotive laboring up a hill with a full load of logs. The engineer reportedly said, "well, we will get this load to the top of the grade and then go back and put out the fire." But when the train crew returned, the fire was already out of

5

CARLSBORG
Town-site Plan

Drawn by Garnet Basque based on a plan drawn
by John Soderberg in 1978.

Steven's Store

Grange Store

Chicago, Milwaukee, St. Paul & Pacific Railway

Post Office

Baseball
Field

Barn

Pig Pen

Machine
Shop

Office | Storage

Store

Butcher Shop

Dining | Kitchen

Fire

Blacksmith
Shop

Apartments

Shed

Shed

Company
House

Bunkhouse Area

Planers

MILL

N

Company
Houses

Wash House
& Showers

Kiln

control, fanned by a strong wind on that hot summer day. It became a major conflagration that burned along the Calawah River to the edge of Forks. Townspeople were evacuated. The flames swooshed along Highway 101 and scorched timber along the north side of the Olympic National Park. Afterward Pankratz was the successful bidder to remove the burned timber, most of which was only superficially damaged and could be especially processed at the mill. In the process of cleaning up the fire-damaged timber, the company built roads built to federal standards, roads still in use by tourists, among them the Hurricane Ridge and Sol Duc accesses. Meanwhile, Forks residents sued the railroad for damages, forcing it into receivership. In 1954-56, the PA&W tracks were taken up.

Under Pankratz management, with Ed Fleetwood as the superintendent, the Carlsborg mill turned out thirty million board feet of product per shift per year in the mid-50s. About 200 men worked a shift, and mill ran

6

two shifts at least half of the time. The company had its own power plant, since the Public Utility District was not sufficiently completed to provide enough power. The mill actually sold some power to the PUD.

At this time, most mill workers were family men, some living in one of the fifty or more company houses. In later days, private homeowners spruced up the old houses as permanent dwellings.

According to John R. Pankratz, son of owner John S. Pankratz, the town post office in the 1950s was still at the mill, and about a block south of the mill a large two-room schoolhouse operated for grades K-12 in the late 1940s and early 1950s. "I can still remember that bell ringing," said John.

"Our company hired many local Indian men, who were good workers," Pankratz added, "including the then-current chief, named `King George' as his father had been dubbed before him."

Life was quiet in Carlsborg then; there was no tavern and most carousing took place in Dungeness. John remembers that the company had a charge account with the local sheriff to bail out their workers after weekend binges.

Pankratz looked for a buyer toward the end of the 50s. The market had slowed down with a recession, and the old mill was very inefficient, big and labor-intensive, lacking in modern equipment. It had been built for handling the really big logs of the original harvesting of the Northern Olympic Peninsula. With a band saw capable of cutting sixteen-footers, the mill was cutting smaller logs of only four feet or so, and the supply of logs necessitated longer and longer trucking runs. Log trucks were an extension of World War II military trucks and the amount of load carried for a round trip of 200 miles was not cost efficient. The huge Kenworth trucks with Cummins diesel engines were only beginning to appear—vehicles that carried loads of 5,000 board feet of logs or more.

Despite the obsolescence of the mill, Orban Lumber Company bought the Carlsborg mill in May, 1960. Orban had four mills in Northern California and a big distribution center in Pasadena. The gross payroll of the Carlsborg operation was in excess of $300,000 in 1966. Yet, the climbing interest rates of 1967 and the resultant decline in home building caused Orban to close the mill. Orban sold the machinery at auction, tore down the buildings, and filled in the millpond. The area was used as an RV park for many years.

After closure of the mill, many of Carlsborg's residents drifted away. Still, a core of homeowners and essential services remained—post office, general store, school, church, and tavern. Today the town of Sequim is reaching out to encompass Carlsborg; new houses and housing developments move ever closer. The old mill site is being held for potential use as an industrial park.

The small town friendliness remains. In 1984, after Jim Stevenson, owner of the Carlsborg Store broke his leg and then faced the coldest winter in decades, local residents pitched in to help keep things going. They fixed the store heater and water pumps and helped Stevenson with store operations.

The current one-person post office has become a landmark; over the years postal employees have beautified the place by building flower boxes across the front and planting shrubs, adding plants and flowers across the window sills inside. Harriet Fish, Carlsborg historian, said that, as late as 1965, the postmistress cheerfully handed mail to patrons holding the reins of their saddlehorses at the door. She also produced a guest book for strangers to sign at the stamp window.

Chapter 2
DIAMOND POINT

Diamond Point was never a town; it was a quarantine station of the United States Government known officially as part of the Port Townsend Marine Hospital, although it lay across Discovery Bay and several miles of land from Port Townsend. Nonetheless, it was an interesting settlement in Northwest Washington, a historic "ghost site" or camp.

Before the facility was built, there were makeshift health and quarantine provisions at Port Townsend in conjunction with the Marine Hospital. The United States Marine Hospital Service was organized in 1798, its chief duty to care for merchant seamen. Several hospitals were established in various parts of the United States, the cost partially paid by a tax on seamen's wages.

Before actual hospitals were built, seamen were attended by local physicians and their fees presented for payment to the United States Government. Port Townsend became the official port of entry and customs collection point for Puget Sound in 1854, and marine hospitals were under the jurisdiction of the customs service at the time. The exact date of the founding of the local marine hospital is somewhat hazy. However, such a designated marine hospital "service" is credited to Dr. Samuel McCurdy, who came to Port Townsend in 1855 and served briefly (but only two or three patients a month asked for help). McCurdy left the practice largely to an assistant so he could serve directly with the Northern Battalion of Washington Volunteers during the Indian unrest of the period. The Volunteers barely needed his service but he ministered to the Indians on the opposing side during a smallpox epidemic. He returned to Port Townsend and it appears that in 1858, the hospital facility was located in Fort Townsend, a military fort about five miles out of present-day Port Townsend. Later, Dr. P.M. O'Brien built limited facilities for treating patients near his Port Townsend office in 1858, which became known as the first marine hospital *building*. By October 10, 1861, the Marine Hospital under Dr. John Allyn was moved to Fort Townsend again, vacated by military troops that year. The hospital was utilized by an average of seventeen patients per month at the time.

Under customs collector Victor Smith, the patients were moved to Cherbourg (Port Angeles) and a new facility not the Marine Hospital, there to remain until 1866, when the Marine Hospital was moved back to Port Townsend under the direction of Dr. George Calhoun at O'Brien's original site. Calhoun would go on to become the first president of the Washington State Medical Society.

At this time, there were no governmental quarantine regulations; this would come in 1878 after a severe yellow fever epidemic nationwide. Seamen with contagious diseases were "banished" to a decrepit house two miles from Port Townsend aptly called the "pest house." In the book *By Juan de Fuca's Strait*, author James McCurdy wrote: "Here the unfortunate patient was kept under the care of a volunteer nurse, usually an old sailor, and a doctor visited the sufferer when he could spare the time. Under these circumstances, it is not a cause of wonderment that a large percentage of pest-house cases failed to recover."

Quarantine was a city or state matter long before the federal government took over the responsibility. Dr. Calhoun laid out his own regulations soon after taking over the Marine Hospital and carried them out. According to Thomas E. Douglas, a retired physician who researched Calhoun's life, the good doctor boarded ships as soon as they touched dock or even before, intercepting them under way in the Strait, surprising them so they could not throw ill sailors overboard to fend for themselves and thus avoid delays in port. If the ships were infested with rats, which often carried plague by their fleas, Calhoun ordered fumigation with sulphur pots. If contagion prevailed, the entire ship's company might be confined until cleared. The doctor kept track of the disease epidemics raging in various international ports, and a ship coming from such port was particularly examined. Many of Calhoun's ideas were incorporated into the official Quarantine Regulations that went into effect July 1, 1872.

By 1877, the hospital building had been expanded and modernized and could accommodate 100 patients, but the facility was relocated to Diamond Point in the 1890s and the old hospital rebuilt in January, 1896, at Port Townsend.

The records of the Public Health Service in the National Archives indicate that the 50th Congress approved on August 1, 1888, an act authorizing the construction of several quarantine stations, among them one near Port Townsend at the entrance to Puget Sound. The sum of $55,500 was appropriated for its establishment. Mrs. Cassie Pugh sold 156 acres at Diamond Point for the station on July 15, 1892, receiving $3,500 in gold from the government.

Charles A. Sayre, Tacoma, received the contract to build the Diamond Point facility on June 24, 1893, completing the job by late November. Included were the wharf and three hospital buildings or officers' quarters. A disinfection plant followed in the summer of 1894, a warehouse and support buildings thereafter. Dr. A.B. Conover served as Officer-in-Charge of the station as early as December 28, 1893 (he originally worked out of Port Townsend and was the quarantine officer between 1889 and 1894). Dr. William G. Stimpson took over some time between September 21 and October 13, 1894, after the Surgeon General of the Marine Hospital Service declared the station completed. With the addition of later structures, the post included twenty-seven buildings plus miscellaneous sheds.

The quarantine station also owned a boat with which to intercept incoming ships. The first one was the *Cascade,* just a naphtha-powered launch. In 1909, the sturdy *W.M. Wightman* was put into service, a vessel of seventy-two feet length, fourteen feet beam, and powered by a 65 HP engine.

The disinfection plant saw plenty of use. All ships entering Puget Sound had to stop at Diamond Point first. Sailors arriving from tropical ports occasionally brought smallpox or plague. One of the chief causes of smallpox epidemics among the Indians along the Strait was the carelessness of ships' crews. Often they threw smallpox victims overboard or dropped their clothes and effects into the sea, after which the contaminated items or bodies drifted ashore to infect curious natives. Before the disinfection plant was built, a quarantine doctor also reported that, on one occasion, he carried blankets to the beach for burning, went back to the hospital for another load, and found that someone had taken the first load of blankets from the beach.

In a 1963 article for the *Seattle Post-Intelligencer*, Lucile McDonald said the disinfection station processed some unusual articles. "In 1900, inspectors were ordered to stop all preserved eggs, yams, sugar cane, water chestnuts, lily bulbs, dried meats and seafoods, taro, ginger, dried mushrooms and bamboo shoots raised in plague-infested ports or packed in soil for shipment from such places. They had to be disinfected before being sent to their destinations." Most of the foods were staples of the Chinese immigrants. Candy and bread products could not be disinfected so were destroyed, to the disgust of passenger owners.

The diseases to be intercepted included plague, yellow fever, typhus fever, cholera, smallpox, leprosy and anthrax. Ships were fumigated for mosquitos that carried yellow fever, as well as rats for plague. On one occasion in 1917 or 1918, an entire shipload of steerage passengers from the Orient were detained for observation, since there was a cholera epidemic in the Orient. Curiously, the practice of scooping up mud for ballast prior to setting sail spread cholera and plague (the foreign port's tide flats often had become contaminated during an epidemic); when the ships began to use clean sand, the incidence lessened.

According to researcher Lawrence L. Thompson of Western Washington University, Bellingham, quoting from the *Port Townsend Leader*:

"The first case of cholera to appear at Port Townsend was found in the medical inspection of the *Antwerp City*, on July 26 [1895]. While the vessel was fumigated, its crew was held in the isolation hospital for observation. . . . In September, the *Belgic* reported a clean bill of health from Honolulu but, upon further investigation, it was found to have had cholera aboard. The ship's surgeon who 'doctored' the documents was reported to have taken up residence in Japan. About the same time, the *Retriever* arrived from Honolulu. Upon inspection by Dr. Stimpson, the captain was informed that the regulations required any boat coming from an infected port must be quarantined for fumigation, whether or not there was sickness aboard. Over the captain's protest, the *Retriever* was towed to Diamond Point, and detained for five to seven days, while the crew's clothing was disinfected and the vessel was fumigated."

Ship owners were reluctant to stop and encounter the delays, and government officials had to firmly impress upon them the necessity of complying with the law. Customs men sometimes boarded a vessel earlier than health officials and wound up sitting in quarantine with the passengers. On rare occasions an entire ship and crew would sit out a quarantine period.

Around 1894, the Civil War vintage warship *Iroquois* was towed to Diamond Point Quarantine Station's wharf to be used as emergency housing when large groups were quarantined. Later a storm washed the ship ashore, where it partially burned and the rest of its bones were picked clean for salvage.

The doctor with longest service to the quarantine station was Dr. Llewellyn T. Seavey, who began work in 1900 and stayed on until 1929. Dr. Seavey's assistant was Dr. Milton H. Foster. According to Thompson, Foster no sooner arrived on site than a ship, the *Nanyo Maru* arrived January 31, 1900, with plague aboard, first believed to be just beri-beri. Seventeen cases of plague, three fatal, ensued—cases that had escaped notice while the ship was in port at San Francisco. A total of twenty-two grave markers graced a cemetery.

In May, 1912, a special quarantine holding area was specified for Port Townsend Bay, marked by four yellow buoys about a half mile offshore. After boarding and inspection, a vessel could proceed or be sent over to Diamond Point.

The most dreaded carrier was the leper, living death, before the discovery of a treatment for the disease. These unfortunate persons were quarantined for life, a few at Diamond Point.

A feverish controversy arose over the question of expanding the leper colony at Diamond Point—"colony" in 1913 being two men. One was a

12

Spanish American War veteran, John R. Early, who had contracted the disease in the Philippines. He had been intercepted and made the attendant for another case (a man named Govan) already quarantined plus any future cases at the Point. On January 11, 1913, the *Port Townsend Leader* reported that the "Federal Government plans to send two lepers from San Francisco to Diamond Point . . . also one from Spokane." The government had trouble finding transportation for the two from San Francisco, since railroads and steamships refused to allow them on board. It is not clear whether or not the San Francisco victims ever came. Transferred with greater ease was Antonio Valcano from Spokane but, on the last leg of his journey, when people aboard the Sound steamer learned he was on board, they were panicked. The attending surgeon soothed them, saying that it was impossible to catch the disease without personal contact.

It was announced that another leper from Minnesota, Dominic Pittari, was due, and three more from San Francisco, whereupon a number of Clallam County people petitioned Congressman Johnson against making Diamond Point a leper colony, suggesting nearby Protection Island instead, lest the lepers managed to leave. With reportedly only two lepers remaining (perhaps others had died) in April, 1918, it still was not certain whether a permanent isolation camp would be established at Diamond Point. The matter was threshed out at a health conference and seems to have been dismissed.

The government once looked at the facility as a prospective training camp location for World War I, but the problem was—of all things—lack of water supply.

As the numbers of immigrants sharply increased, the authorities at Port Townsend and Diamond Point were assigned the task of preliminary inspection of immigrants prior to proceeding to Seattle. By 1927, however, this only meant a brief boarding, sometimes even while the ship was under way, and—if a passenger had any ailment needing further scrutiny—a notation would be made for further action to be taken in Seattle, and the ship proceeded there. Streamlined procedures were developed for commerce between Canada and the United States.

A crisis developed during 1928 and 1929, when as many as 400 passengers required detention at Diamond Point because of an epidemic of spinal meningitis. Even though the disease was not on the list for quarantine, it was necessary to intercept the patients carrying this dread ailment, most of them from the Philippines or China.

By 1933, it was obvious that a new station must be built due to several factors: the increasing traffic, the poor holding ground in the Diamond Point harbor during strong northerly winds, and—most important—the lack of an adequate water supply. Diamond Point's facility was placed on standby during the time when construction proceeded at Point Hudson, adjacent to the town of Port Townsend, and then was decommissioned entirely.

The station was declared surplus in 1936, and later sold to Dr. Ray S. Crist and Herman N. Simpson in February, 1938. After passing through several owners, the entire spit, fifty-six acres including tidelands was sold on February 14, 1956, to three men, Lloyd Longmire, John Pearce, and Jack Corrock of Diamond Point Land Company, Inc. Later the entire point became a lovely real estate development with an airstrip.

Still remaining are the pilings of the old wharf and a storage building. The surgeon's home, a splendid dwelling with carved fireplace mantels, cherrywood panels, tiles from Italy, and beautiful blue and gold leaf molding around the ceilings, is easily recognizable in the development, a square house with overhanging roof. It was long known as the Milholland House but is now occupied by a private owner, who is very interested in the history of the point and in restoring the interior of the home.

(Note: For a complete history of the Port Townsend Marine Hospital, read Lawrence L. Thompson's Master Thesis on the subject, National Archives, Seattle, or Wilson Library at Western Washington University, Bellingham.)

Chapter 3

DUNGENESS

The North Pacific Ocean is known for its violence and towering waves. On the broad Strait of Juan de Fuca the energy barely subsides, especially during frequent windy periods. It is not surprising that captains of vessels battered by the turbulent waters sought refuge behind a long sand spit that curves northeasterly from the mainland at a point where the shore turns southerly. Spanish explorer Manuel Quimper is the first *known* European to land near the mouth of the Dungeness River. He claimed the land for Spain on July 4, 1790, leaving a wooden cross and a cairn of rocks. Captain George Vancouver was next to record a visit, dropping anchor in tranquil, shallow waters in May, 1792. In his log he rhapsodizes that the nearby land presented " . . . a landscape almost as enchantingly beautiful as the most elegant finished pleasure-grounds in Europe . . . a beautiful variety of extensive lawn, covered with luxuriant grass and diversified with an abundance of flowers. While we stopped to contemplate these several beauties of nature in a prospect no less pleasing than unexpected, we gathered some gooseberries and roses . . . " He also commented on other wild fruits and shrubs—gooseberries, raspberries, currants, sweetbrier, roses. Vancouver named the location New Dungeness, for it reminded him of an English harbor called Dungeness.

A substantial group of Indians, perhaps 1,000 people, lived well in cedar longhouses at Cline's Spit, slightly east of Dungeness Spit, near the site later called New Dungeness, fishing and hunting, fighting and playing as their ancestors did back into the mists of time. Early explorers indicated that their trading friendships were fragile, hostility erupting with little warning. Yet in 1850 a brig captained by Thomas Abernethy stopped to take on provisions and water at New Dungeness. Attracted by the pleasant land Abernethy returned in spring, 1851, to stake a claim (other accounts put this date at 1852 or 1853). Fellow sailors B.I. Madison, J.C. Brown, John Donnell, Jim Connelly and Elisha McAlmond also filed claims at different locations nearby—McAlmond on the bluffs, Madison at the mouth of the Dungeness River, a site later known as Whiskey Flat because Madison sold

15

liquor to the Indians. Donnell became the first settler in Clallam County to prove up his claim and receive a patent March 6, 1866.

The Washington Territorial Legislature separated Clallam County from sprawling Jefferson County on April 26, 1854, designating New Dungeness as the county seat. Elisha McAlmond, who had retired from the sea to enter business, eventually became a justice of the peace, commissioner, deputy United States marshal, probate judge and legislator. He was joined by John Thornton, another early settler, who was elected to the legislature in 1860 during the first general election after serving as Clallam County Treasurer for six years. Ninety votes were cast in that first balloting and, since women did not vote, one may extrapolate that—including wives and children— New Dungeness may then have had a population of about 300.

Incoming goldseekers appeared at New Dungeness and Port Townsend in the 1850s, responding to the Fraser River gold discoveries. The trickle became a flood around 1858, when would-be miners came to Port Townsend and New Dungeness seeking transport to Victoria to obtain licenses to mine from the British government at Victoria (British Columbia Colony was formed in 1858). But such men were merely transient.

Perhaps Thomas Abernethy accommodated some of them; from the earliest days he took cargos of the settlers' produce to sell at Vancouver Island and, in 1853, he sailed his brig loaded with potatoes and towing a boom of pilings to San Francisco, where food and lumber were desperately needed by gold-seekers. On the return trip he brought a yoke of oxen for farmers Joe Leary and Jim Connelly, unloading them at the mouth of the Dungeness River.

Other ships began to call at New Dungeness, not just small craft to cross the Strait or ply the Sound, but ocean-going ships bound for California or Boston. They took on provisions or lumber and sometimes sought refuge from storms in the protected harbor. Unfortunately, Dungeness Bay was shallow and ships could only enter through a narrow passage betweem Cline's Spit and Graveyard Spit.

Extending roughly northeast from the site of New Dungeness, the sandy Dungeness Spit, comprising two separate spits really, was both a dangerous impediment to navigation and a refuge from westerly winds. No wonder, then, that the first light on the Strait of Juan de Fuca was placed there, its beacon beaming a warning to mariners after December 14, 1857. Henry Blake, only twenty years old, was the first light keeper in the ninety-foot tower. When fog extinguished all visibility, the keeper wound up a rope on a large windlass which gradually unwound to toll a large bell. Every few hours the keeper had to rewind the contraption. According to pioneer Hannah Ward Mansen, the tower cracked some years later and the new one was lowered to seventy feet, its present height. Today the light is automated and supervised by the United States Coast Guard. The spit continues to grow from sand washing away from the eroding cliffs at New Dungeness and the curve of the spit from the Dungeness River, and is protected from development. It is the world's largest natural sand spit, extending five and one half miles into the Strait of Juan de Fuca. The tidal flats are a rich resource of shellfish. Far out on the spit in protected coves harbor seals lounge about. One may see bald eagles, but near the base of the spit huge numbers of ducks, geese and lesser numbers of great blue herons and sanderling search for dinner along the shore. The shallow salt water and mild climate create an ideal environment for eelgrass, an important food for waterfowl—especially the black brant.

The plentiful game and wild fowl were a welcome addition to many homesteaders' fare, as more settlers came to New Dungeness, drawn by the mild winters and low rainfall, since the northeast section of the Olympic Peninsula lies in a rain shadow of the Olympic Mountains. Those homesteaders that moved into the dense forests toward the mountains, however, found a dark, damp world which their pathetic clearings barely opened to the sun. On the prairie lands around Sequim and New Dungeness, cattle ranching became profitable with a market across the Strait on Vancouver Island. Some settlers hand-cut cedar shakes and marketed them at Vancouver, but a major drawback was the lack of horses, oxen or wagons for transporting cash crops to the port. Homesteaders were reduced to hacking out crude wooden wheels to make carts.

In 1858, a colorful addition to New Dungeness was settler John Weir, who hunted for a living after homesteading. He wore buckskin clothing and traded meat and hides for supplies at New Dungeness, or sold them to the Hudson's Bay Company in Victoria. He learned the Clallam Indians' language and became their friend. On one occasion he prevented an outbreak of Indian violence. An Indian woman had fallen off a footbridge across the Dungeness River built by the white settlers, and the Indians blamed them for the woman's accident. Upon hearing that the Indians were planning vengeance, Weir walked into their village unarmed to reason with them.

New Dungeness began to take shape. In 1860, Hezekiah Davis came to set up a store. Welcome to the thirsty was a Bill Law who set up the first saloon, which also doubled as a restaurant of sorts where one cooked his own food. John Thornton and a Mr. Owens started another store. When New Dungeness settlers Elliot and Margaret Cline donated land to build a courthouse and jail, the county records were moved from a temporary storage place into the new courthouse.

The town grew to include William King's blacksmith shop, restaurant, hotel, two saloons, a general store, a Good Templars' Hall, and sturdy, simple homes. A typical dwelling was built of logs, had a fireplace and chimney of

17

clay, a clapboard roof, and a door of split cedar on wooden hinges, the wooden latch raised by a buckskin thong. According to an item from *Jimmy Come Lately*: "When Captain McAlmond built one of real lumber throughout, actually lathed and plastered inside, with real boughten doors and a cornice around the roof, there was a general feeling that the county had taken a long stride toward the opulence and luxury of the old world. The captain was elected justice of the peace out of pure deference for his superior attachments."

The county commissioners levied a two-mill tax to build schools. The first school was established in a log house on a farm owned by Thomas Abernethy, followed by a properly built schoolhouse in April, 1862, at a different location. In 1902, teacher H.E. Risley received a salary of $65 a month plus living quarters, conditional upon Risley's assumption of the janitor's work. It was inferred that Risley's wife should also help with the school children. However, that was in Dungeness, the second site for the town, the plat filed March 18, 1892.

Elliott Cline

— Photo Courtesy of Port Angeles Public Library

The renowned pioneer, James G. Swan, liked to hunt near New Dungeness. He worked off and on at Port Townsend, helping his friend, G.L. Gerrish, in his store. Since Gerrish also had land on Sequim Bay, he invited Swan to accompany him for a hunt there in 1861, traveling through high seas in a canoe with four Indian companions. Swan shot a partridge, two snipe, and two ducks on the hunt, but was as taken with the scenery and vegetation as the hunting. Later Swan partied with the local people. In an article for the *Seattle Times*, January 22, 1961, Lucile McDonald said Swan declared: "I found the Dungeness people very hospitable and numerous invitations were extended to me. We made preparations for a shin soup today, but it got burned so that it was spoiled. Skip Fitzgerald and myself consequently killed a pig. Some Indians came up from Sequim and were very glad to eat the burnt soup, and we made a supper of pigs' liver. During the evening the Indians played games something like pawns or hide and seek and a game where one goes out and the rest cover themselves in shawls and blankets. Then the one outside comes in and guesses the names of those covered. If he guesses right, another takes his place, and so on. Another game is played by sticking sticks in a crack in the floor. The person blinds his eyes, then guesses as another points with a stick how many are upright and how many sticks are down."

There were few conflicts between the Indians and settlers, but in 1868, frightened settlers were spectators at a inter-tribal massacre on Dungeness Spit. According to Mary Lou Hanify in the *Port Angeles Evening News*, 1971 Visitors Guide, a party of eighteen Tsimshian Indians were homeward bound in their large canoe to Fort Simpson, British Columbia, on a foggy September 21, 1868. The men of the party had been picking hops near Puyallup and had $500 or $600 in gold, plus bright blankets and trinkets, all carefully noted by watching enemies, the local Clallam Indians.

While the Tsimshians were asleep on Graveyard Spit, camping out for the night in a large tent, twenty-six Clallams crept up to cut the tent ropes, collapsing it onto their victims. Without mercy they clubbed and speared all of the Tsimshians . . . so they thought. But one woman feigned death, even as rings and earrings were torn from her, and crept into the salt water. She made her way about a mile to the Dungeness Lighthouse. Here Henry Blake answered a feeble rap on his door, and the poor woman, pregnant, too, fell inside. Blake and his wife dressed her wounds and, when the Clallam Indians stormed to his lighthouse dwelling (they discovered her tracks), Blake stoutly refused to give up the Indian woman and retreated to his rather impregnable brick lighthouse. The Indians finally went away.

Indignant settlers could do nothing, but they did bury the victims in the area now known as Graveyard Spit. James G. Swan was then the United States Commissioner and over a period of time, apprehended all twenty-six of the Clallams and turned them over to United States justice. The men were placed in irons at hard labor on the reservation. Eventually the pregnant woman was well enough to travel and went on the Hudson's Bay Company steamer *Otter* to her home in Fort Simpson, bearing many Tsimshian possessions that had been recovered from Graveyard Spit. The large Tsimshian canoe was also recovered. Captain Andrew Abernethy refitted it with sails and used it to transport produce and supplies to and from Victoria.

Not much later, the pressure of increasing population of the Dungeness area caused the Indians to move their village several miles southeast to Jamestown.

Maritime traffic increased at New Dungeness, especially to load pilings and other lumber. No roads yet served the community, and travelers

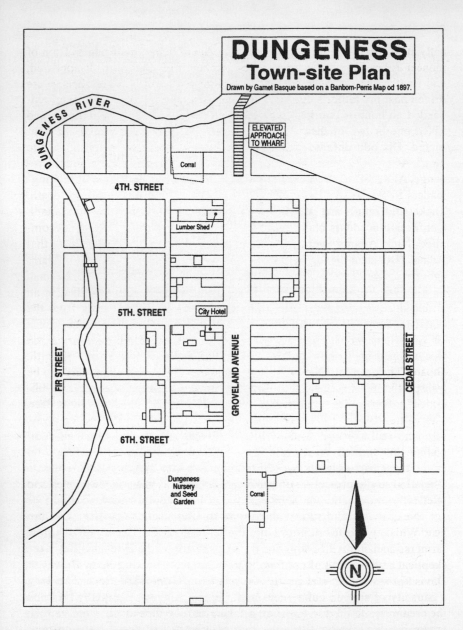

DUNGENESS
Town-site Plan
Drawn by Garnet Basque based on a Banborn-Perris Map od 1897.

DUNGENESS RIVER

ELEVATED
APPROACH
TO WHARF

Corral

4TH. STREET

Lumber Shed

5TH. STREET

City Hotel

FIR STREET

GROVELAND AVENUE

CEDAR STREET

6TH. STREET

Dungeness
Nursery
and Seed
Garden

Corral

N

went by canoe or the government boat *Active*. Tom Ballister hauled produce to Victoria to sell for the farmers.

In the 1860s life seemed peaceful enough until some deserters from the British Navy came to the area, formed a gang and began to systematically steal from the settlers. According to Allen Weir, a historian and son of pioneer John Weir: "Hen roosts were robbed, pigs and corn disappeared, and finally matters were brought to a climax when a band of sheep were driven past my father's door in broad daylight, and the thief was taken red-handed an hour or two later where he had driven the sheep into a barn and killed one or two of them." The thief, Jack Tucker, was arrested and convicted. His odd defense was "that the blamed sheep were trying to bite him." After thirty days he was released, but he and his gang sought revenge. After further trouble, a group of vigilantes escorted three of the ringleaders to the county line, telling them not to return, under pain of death. Tucker did return and was found shot to death by an unknown assailant. Conflicting accounts claim that the charges against Tucker and an accomplice, Nick Adams, were false. Lending credence to this version is that Adams later sued the vigilantes who murdered Tucker and gained civil damages for damages to his own reputation. Former Port Angeles mayor, Norman Smith, believed in Tucker's innocence, and the events he described in an article in the Port Angeles Evening News (1950) differ sharply from the other accounts. Smith said that, when the embargo on live cattle (not a sheep matter) was in effect, Captain D.B. Finch of the ship *Eliza Anderson* was stopped by British authorities and turned back with a load of cattle aboard. They put into New Dungeness and the cattle were slaughtered to be transported as dressed beef. During the procedure some local settlers "liberated" a few cattle, which ran into the woods and became as wild as deer. The cattle became targets for hunters. The Civil War, 3,000 miles away, was very real to many settlers, more Southern than Northern in their sympathies. When Jack Tucker and Nick Adams shot one or two of the wild cattle, these two—Union sympathizers—were warned to leave the country. They fled to the protection of Victor Smith's family near Port Angeles and later returned, whereupon they were ambushed and Tucker was killed.

Near 1870, Alonzo Davis immigrated from British Canada to a farm near Whiskey Flats, bringing with him a small herd of Jersey cows. Most farmers, accustomed to big, sturdy Durham cattle imported earlier, were skeptical of the worth of the fragile-appearing, doe-eyed Jerseys. However, Davis knew what he was doing. His brother Hall developed large vats with a capacity of sixteen cubic feet, in which the milk was allowed to set and the cream rise to the top for butter-making. Two muscular men churned the cream into butter with large paddles, added salt and pressed it into two-pound rolls. It was packed for shipment in crates holding about twenty rolls to lumber camps and trading posts, marketed under the label "Gold Edge." Later inventions of machine-turned churns and a cream separator facilitated butter-making and eventually the Dungeness-Sequim Cooperative Creamery was formed.

All was not work. The town hosted an annual Fourth of July picnic, dances, roller skating contests, sleighing parties at infrequent times of snow, clambakes, smelting parties (where residents caught smelt with their bare hands from hordes migrating toward shore), and baseball games.

Toward the end of the decade New Dungeness began to fade. A wagon road connected New Dungeness with the larger Port Angeles. When the Puget Sound Cooperative Colony swelled the numbers in nearby Port Angeles in 1887, petitioners placed the question of the county seat's location on the ballot in 1890, and Port Angeles won over Port Crescent and New Dungeness. Some said the election for removal was illegal, because the New Dungeness county seat was in an official building designated and owned by the county (Port Angeles's building apparently was not). However, the decision stood. About twenty-five Port Angeles citizens rode into New Dungeness to help load the county records into wagons. Anticipating possible objection from New Dungeness folks, the Army sent soldiers to the site; however, no objections were raised.

In the 1890s the bay at New Dungeness had become so shallow that ships coming into the harbor became stranded at low tide. Townspeople essentially picked up their belongings and moved eastward about a mile and a half in 1891. Now "New Dungeness" often was referred to as "Old Dungeness" or "Old Town," and the new town was simply "Dungeness."

Dungeness Trading Co. – Photo Courtesy of Port Angeles Public Library

22

The prime mover of construction of a new 4300-foot dock out to deep water was C.F. Seal, president of the Groveland Improvement Company (GIC). He bought the Farmers Mercantile Company of the original town, moved it and renamed it Dungeness Trading Company.

The GIC basically was a real estate promotion firm. Advertising urged newcomers to come to "The most prosperous place on the Sound, surrounded by richest farming country. Dungeness the Beautiful. Come Now." Seal made it a point to meet arriving boat passengers.

C.F. Seal built a handsome home he called "Groveland" on the main street of town, past which tramped teams of horses pulling wagons to the dock. The house had a pergola, sunken gardens with a rustic bridge, and greenhouses. He entertained well-dressed guests in the spacious rooms.

In the book *Jimmy Come Lately*, a 1902 manifest listed a typical incoming shipment of "barrels of whiskey, grass seed, seed wheat, stove pipe, sugar candy, a horse, glazed windows, twelve milk cows, a crated rooster, tombstones, a piano, a live pig, fireworks, ice cream, a sewing machine, butter wrapped, milk tank, crated ducks and school crayons." As the Indians were very fond of black molasses (from Hawaii, no doubt), the shipments included hogsheads of the sticky stuff.

Outgoing freight was largely agricultural—eggs, butter, apples, wool, etc. Butter was a major cash product.

A few Chinese men moved into Dungeness, operating laundries or growing crops. Pioneer George Hansen said that, during their New Year celebration, they cleaned house and set out bowls of candy and leechee nuts, leaving their houses open so anyone could enter and help themselves. Among the Chinese who came and went were Wong Tong, a vegetable grower; Wash Tong, who operated a laundry; and others who worked in the logging camps. Bow Shee, a potato farmer, stayed until his death in the Dungeness area.

Buildings arose at the new site, including a three-story brick hotel owned by Elias Cays, Gunder Halverson's blacksmith shop, Knight's mercantile store, a saloon or two, Woodmen's Hall, the Dungeness Trading Company, Clapp's store, Joe McKissick's photo shop, Noble Turk's store, City Hotel, a drug store, bowling alley, and numerous new residences. In 1892, a handsome two-story schoolhouse topped by a belltower was completed. After housing generations of rowdy students, the school building is today a community center and on the National Register of Historic Places.

R.C. Wilson and G.K. Estes established *The Dungeness Beacon*, June 24, 1892, with Joe Ballinger as editor. The name of the newspaper changed several times and was absorbed in 1903 by *The Tribune-Times*. The *Beacon* was noted for its lively prose and local news and was delivered by a horseback rider. One wonders what the details were of a cryptic notice in the

23

Dungeness School.   *– Photo Courtesy of Port Angeles Public Library*

February 17, 1893, *Beacon*: "William McKinney wishes it understood he is not married at present as reported last week."

Logging of the verdant stands of timber increasingly attracted financiers, large and small. Back in 1857, Joseph Benson Roberts came from Olympia to log along the Dungeness River, simply cutting the trees and rolling the logs into the river to be floated out to ships bound for San Francisco. Later in the 1860s, the Port Discovery Mill was the prime consumer of logs from the Dungeness area. Some Dungeness residents walked all the way to Discovery Bay for their daily work, a distance of about eighteen miles. In the early 1870's an unidentified logging company built a "railroad" from poles and timbers over which to ship logs to Jamestown for rafting. Later loggers were C.F. Clapp and William Long. About 1895, John Wilder logged at the base of Dungeness Spit. His outfit consisted of a pole road and a chute from bluff to bay for transport of logs. Later the larger logs were moved by cumbersome steam tractors. N.E. Peterson with his sons Blaine, Oscar, and Goldy, formed Pacific Logging Company in the Dungeness/Sequim area. renamed Dungeness Logging Company. Two and three decades later logging on a grand scale was continuing all over the Olympic Peninsula, as logging railroads made it possible to snake the logs out of areas not adjacent to streams.

24

Buoyed by shipments of logs, lumber, shingles and agricultural produce, the shipping activity from the new dock was brisk, sustaining the town for at least three decades. Teams pulled wagons to the warehouse at the end of the dock to stockpile products until a full shipload accumulated. Perishable produce went out every day by mailboats, schooners and private sailboats. Living in Dungeness from 1917 on, Aline Christensen remembered that her grandfather, Captain A.W. Horn, an owner of the Strait Steamship Company, frightened her by driving her onto the dock behind a spirited team of Kentucky-bred carriage horses.

After mere subsistence ceased to consume all their time, settlers soon organized baseball teams and a brass band, and held church socials (Methodist) and Fourth of July celebrations. At times, steamers put in to run excursions as far south as Seattle or out to Neah Bay at the mouth of the Strait. Traveling theater groups included Dungeness on their schedules. Horse racing was a big favorite with locals and guests, and the Beacon declared one year that the "Steamers Willapa, Garland and Monticello will run excursions from Seattle, Hadlock, Townsend, Port Williams, Port Angeles and all way ports from Neah Bay to Dungeness. [This fleet of steamers serving islands and isolated mainland towns was dubbed the `Mosquito Fleet.'] The Brass Band will meet all steamers and escort visitors to the grounds. The Park and Race track is only one block from steamboat landing."

Although Dungeness citizens clamored for a railroad, it was not to be. Among the paper-only railroads that were touted in the early 1900's was the Tacoma and Northwestern, which would have gone through Dungeness. As early as 1893, C.F. Seal for the GCI offered to donate 300 lots of Dungeness if "the railroad," any railroad, no doubt, would come through his town. Through a series of mergers that combined bits and pieces of trackage and terminals, the Chicago, Milwaukee and St. Paul Railroad gained a practicable route and by 1916, two round trips a day went from Twin (Twin Rivers) to Port Townsend. Unfortunately, the more direct route lay through the hamlet of Sequim, five miles inland from Dungeness. Adding another death knell to Dungeness was the eventual completion of a county road, also through Sequim.

Once more, merchants of Dungeness picked up their businesses and moved south to Sequim. As a shipping center, Dungeness was doomed when rail and auto freight began to supplant coastal maritime freight. Fires in 1914 and 1915 destroyed most buildings on the west side of Groveland Avenue, the main street, and portions of the east side. The hotel burned in 1929, and Dungeness Trading Company's building in 1937.

Meanwhile, ships continued to use the sturdy dock for loading dairy products from the Dungeness Creamery and other sources until 1941, when the creameries turned to auto freight. The swirling sand took over and created about a half mile of new Dungeness townsite, where the famed Three Crabs Restaurant still stood in 1995. And straggling out to sea, the two lines of decaying pilings are perches for gulls and other seabirds today. C.F. Seal's lovely home became Groveland House, a Bed and Breakfast establishment and general store. The Dungeness Tavern occupied the old creamery building. The old school remains in good repair, is listed on the National Register of Historic Places, and rings with activity as a community center. Other small homes suggest antiquity, but new stores have opened along the main street of town as the town gains popularity as a retirement community.

The original settlements of Whiskey Flat and New Dungeness are marked only by a couple of apple trees planted in 1852, a pear tree that has survived, and the imposing home of Elijah McAlmond has been maintained and is occupied privately. It is listed on the National Register of Historic Places and is assumed to be the oldest occupied dwelling of Clallam County.

Chapter 4
GETTYSBURG

The first known activity around Gettysburg, five miles west of Port Cres cent, came in the late 1880s, when George Myers and W.E. Van Allen Company logged at the mouth of the Lyre River, employing about twenty men. The company built its main skid road along the Lyre River and over to what came to be known as Getty's bay; another came from the timber stands on a high hill near the river. Many a logger got his start by "greasing the skids," a job that required him to walk along the skid road, dabbing hot tallow on the logs from a five-gallon can.

The company constructed a chute several hundred feet long from the hill to the flat below to move the logs. The logs were barked and stripped on one side to make them slide more easily down the chute. From the end of the chute oxen towed the logs to the water's edge.

Oxen used in the woods were equipped with special shoes to guard their feet against injury. When the ox was to be shod, the blacksmith placed leather bands under the animal's belly and attached them to a sling of strong poles six to eight inches in diameter and bolted together. A winch-like de vice tightened the leather bands to lift the ox slightly off the ground. The blacksmith then lashed the animal's foot to a special platform and applied the shoe. An ox shoe consisted of two parts, one part for each half of the hoof. If the hoof was injured from foot rot or otherwise, the blacksmith seared the spot with a red hot piece of flat iron, then poured boiling hot tallow between the two parts of the hoof. Generally the injury healed in a few days.

Not long after the Myers-Van Allen operation began, Robert N. Getty, a prosperous Pennsylvania farmer and lumberman, came to homestead a huge chunk of land along the northeasterly-facing cove, protected some what from incoming swells on the Strait. He opened a general store, ob tained a post office, and called the place Gettysburg. To encourage the log ging firms to build skid roads to Gettysburg as a shipping port, Getty helped to construct a log breakwater for the bay.

Getty's effort to attract substantial logging firms was successful in 1891 when Winfield Scott Miller, Justice of the Peace, handled legal mat-

Logs being boomed at Gettysburg.
— *Photo Courtesy of Port Angeles Public Library*

ters for the sale of timber by a Miss Downie to the firm of Stephen Hall and William Bishop. This pair had been working farther west around Pysht in the 1880s. The substantial operation employed at least eighty men, who bragged that they had the best-fed camp in the Northwest.

Log crews usually furnished their own blankets. In a typical crew's quarters, bunks were built around the ends and sides. The building was heated by an open fire in the middle topped by a large funnel to vent smoke through the roof. A logger's average pay in the late nineteenth century was $2 a day plus shelter and food, always abundant. In the kitchen forty-pound hams were skinned and sliced. The skin rinds were burned to produce a very hot fire in the cookstove for ham, eggs, etc. A typical breakfast might be ham, eggs, pancakes, pie and cake, bread and coffee.

Although they probably used oxen originally for dragging out logs, Hall & Bishop (H&B) soon built three miles of railroad to bring logs from forest to sea, using a highly unusual method of creating the trackage. They cut trees parallel to the ground on the right-of-way, placed hemlock logs crosswise, and laid down the rails on other logs flattened on one side.

In an 1891 directory, Gettysburg listed fifty-three men (no doubt heads of families). H&B employed eighty, some of whom lived at Gettysburg and others in outlying camps. Counting wives and children (though many men were single) perhaps as many as 200 people lived at Gettysburg at one time.

Whether brought to the bay by rail or skid road, the logs had to be shoved into the water at high tide—no matter what time of day or night that might occur. The logs were formed into a boom about 100 feet by 50 feet, using lengthwise sections, as well as cross-sectional logs for stability. Generally four or five such booms were fastened together and towed to the mill by tugboat.

Apparently a second firm, Mohrdick and Wolf (Wolf left the partnership in December of that year) operated out of Gettysburg, because the *Dungeness Beacon* of November 11, 1892, reported that "a boom of logs containing 500,000 feet of timber was towed into the harbor [Dungeness] for Mr. Peter Mohrdick of Gettysburg. The logs are to be sold at the Port Hadlock Mill." Little else is known about this Gettysburg firm.

Not only did pioneers log the forests, but also the flats just inland from Gettysburg supported enormous crops of vegetables, enormous in size as well as quantity. Homesteader Michael Minnihan set out 2,000 cabbage plants in the spring of 1891. The heads grew as large as twenty pounds. Rutabagas of fifteen pounds, potatoes of four pounds, and oats seven feet tall sprang out of the fertile ground, but Minnihan and his fellow homesteaders were unable to sell the produce. Unlike Dungeness, where merchants had established a trade system to supply Victoria, no market for the magnificent crops existed at Gettysburg. Nevertheless, out of the equally splendid timber, the homesteaders built substantial log homes and lived well without much cash money.

In response to growth, Getty built a new store and the Gettysburg Hotel. The hotel building was twenty-four feet by thirty feet, two stories high with a one-story addition sixteen feet by twenty-four feet. The store, post office, dining room and kitchen were on the first floor and sleeping rooms on the second. Getty, the one-man town owner, also built a new boat house and warehouse. On March 17, 1892, he dedicated the new buildings with a big party that included dancing and supper. Some of the guests came on horseback from Port Angeles and Port Crescent and had to stay overnight because roads were so muddy. Clallam County Sheriff William Gould, Ex-Mayor Willard Brumfield of Port Angeles, John W. Troy, W.W. Dedman of the *Democrat* newspaper, R.A. Grimes, William Ritchie, Ken Church and J.H. Myers arrived a day late.

Getty donated land for a schoolhouse and a cemetery. The Democratic Club organized March 5, 1892. A Sunday School organized by the Tacoma Congregational Church opened with thirty members.

Before 1892, mail came to Port Crescent for the entire area. That year the local steamer *Garland* added Gettysburg to its list of ports. Captain

Hansen, a partner and operator of Getty's hotel, rowed a dory out into the Strait to meet the steamer just off Gettysburg to pick up mail, freight and passengers. The postmaster or his helper also tended the handlit light on the buoy east of the Lyre River. The buoy guided boats and ships into the harbor and was a navigational light for larger ships plying the Strait. It was 1908 before a road connected Gettysburg with Port Crescent. Travelers had to walk the beach or struggle over a crude trail with mudholes so deep one almost sank out of sight.

Gettysburg loggers had a case of whiskey delivered by mail boat to Port Crescent at intervals. One logger was elected to walk the beach from Gettysburg to Port Crescent to fetch it. Sometimes his companions in Gettysburg, impatient for the liquor, met the messenger at the mouth of the stream that came to be known as Whiskey Creek.

H&B was asked to provide the logs 100 feet long, twenty-four inches in diameter at the top, used for the arch at the 1893 Chicago World's Fair. It took two logging cars to ship them. Some parts of the railroad's right-of-way were widened and curves modified to transport the logs.

H&B moved their operations farther west around 1900 after depleting timber near Gettysburg. The Thompson Brothers Logging Company logged for a time out of Gettysburg. The 1911-12 *Polk Directory* listed sixty-five

An 1897 Climax No. 1 locomotive used by Hall & Bishop.
— Photo Courtesy of Port Angeles Public Library

30

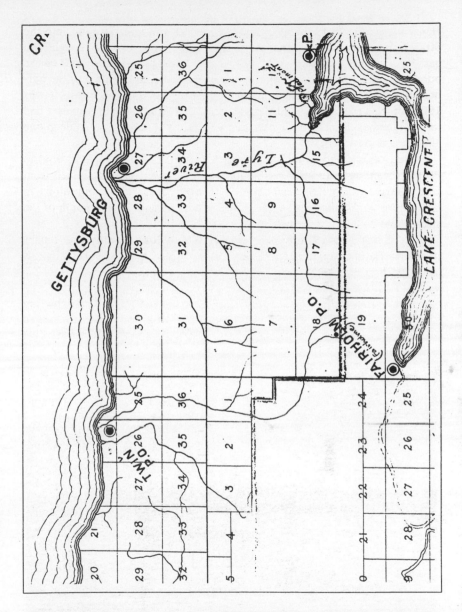

people residing in the town. The Gettysburg Hotel had burned in 1908. However, when the Thompson Brothers moved on, the Green Lakes Shingle Mills Company opened operations on the east bank of the Lyre River near Gettysburg, with William D. Mackie the manager. The shingles probably were taken out by ship. During that time, when Mackie's daughter-in-law was due to have her baby, she boarded the steamer *Bellingham* for Seattle. After having the child enroute, she named the child Winnifred Bellingham Mackie. No one seems to have named a baby "Willie," though, after the boat *Waialeale*, a boat settlers referred to as "Weary Willie."

A handful of people enjoyed the isolation. Undaunted by the remote location, Mrs. Ida Barker Simmons, built a small dam and installed a large wooden water wheel to power her commercial laundry operation, remaining in business until 1921. Many men farmed part-time and cut shingles or shakes.

The town of Gettysburg lurched along by fits and starts. Michael Earles and his Puget Sound Mill and Timber Company built a railroad spur in 1914 to log timber in the vicinity. Claus Skavdal logged at the mouth of Whiskey Creek. A Mr. Wallitner operated two shingle mills in the vicinity for a time.

However, the railroad and county road, both running parallel to shore about five miles inland, usurped Gettysburg's seaport business, and people moved away. The post office was discontinued in 1920. Today only one family lives on that beach at Low Point, and no one would ever know that once a bustling small settlement thrived as Gettysburg.

Chapter 5
PORT CRESCENT

One of the loveliest harbors on the Strait of Juan de Fuca, Crescent Bay embraces a seemingly tranquil harbor, with Clam Horn on the west, Tongue Point on the east. Waves lap at the edge of a curving beach, marshy in places where Salt Creek meanders into the bay, sandy in others, while the land rises gently to the south and precipitously to east and west. Adjacent to the bluff containing Clam Point is Agate Beach, an exposed small cove where agates, moonstones and jasper often were found in early days. The Strait is only nine miles wide at this point, and later entrepreneurs visualized a major seaport and ferry port at Crescent.

However, the first known white people came in the 1860s to the lovely spot from Fort George, a Hudson's Bay post. Perhaps they had been voyageurs or trappers. Ralph Samuel Snecal, Baptiste Poquette, and James Frank trapped river otter, mink and other animals near Crescent Bay, selling the furs to Hudson's Bay. They staked out adjacent claims, found wives and started families. Snecal (and perhaps the others) started to log the area, creating a log slide to maneuver the big logs into water for transport to the Puget Sound mills. Later he used a skid road and oxen. In 1868, Snecal married Sophia from Port Simpson, British Columbia, a half French, half Indian woman who had come with her parents to Dungeness in 1862. When Snecal died, Sophia married a Gust Coleman, divorced him and married Severn Johnson, becoming known thereafter as "Grandma Johnson" because she affectionately mothered the new settlers, doctored them, gave them hay, delivered their babies, and told stories of her exciting past life in Canada to the children.

A few additional settlers came to Crescent Bay—John Mohrdick, Fred and George Raney, Thomas Allen Miller, Fitch J. Hart, and Winfield Miller, Sr. The families intermarried and lived quietly. As early as the 1870s Thompson and Paine logged at Crescent Bay for the Port Discovery Mill. In 1880, Charles Wintworth Thompson, with the financial cooperation of Cyrus Clapp of Dungeness, logged with twelve oxen and two men around Crescent Bay, rafting the timbers for towing to Port Discovery Mill. Somewhat to the west was the larger Hall & Bishop operation, the company building puncheon road (skid road) to get the timber out to Gettysburg's bay. Population at Crescent was static; the town slept along.

Then came news of railroads building northwest from Tacoma into the Olympic Peninsula. Speculation was rampant, because timber cruisers were stunned at the size and quality of the timber stands and—with railroads to get the logs out—well, there were fortunes to be made. A convenient harbor was important. In 1889 or 1890, a promotional firm, the Port Crescent Improvement Company, was born, their articles of incorporation filed March 1, 1892. Chief officers were Cyrus F. Clapp, John Lutz, A.R. Coleman, and Canadians Theodore Lubbe and Edward McQuade. The company believed Port Crescent would be the terminus for the Northern Pacific, as the Victoria, Port Crescent and Chehalis Railroad Company, connecting Port Crescent with Gray's Harbor and extending by ferry to Vancouver Island. They envisioned a stream of logs arriving at Port Crescent for loading onto foreign ships.

In the middle of all the grandiose dreams, Port Crescent made a bid for the county seat but lost to Port Angeles which took it away from New Dungeness.

To be ready for the boom, the company laid out an ambitious townsite; some maps show platting all the way to today's town of Joyce,

Port Crescent.

– Photo Courtesy of Port Angeles Public Library

34

four or five miles south. The main core itself was significant—20,000 lots on 166 blocks laid out in a neat rectangular pattern. The central avenue reached south two miles from the bay and was graded for wagon traffic. The avenue even had sidewalks.

As engineering for the wharf began, the builders soon discovered that the tranquil-appearing bay was treacherous. Just under the surface extending northeasterly from Clam Point was a substantial reef; in turn, a shorter underwater obstruction created a hazard from Tongue Point, leaving only a narrow, safe entrance for larger ships. The developers made ambitious plans to construct a breakwater 1,200 feet from shore, taking advantage of the natural reef. Then they would blast open the passageway farther, and attract those larger ships.

Equipment arrived from San Francisco on the schooner *Jenny* February 18, 1891, consisting of a 30 HP boiler derrick and drum that could lift one ton on a single line, and other machinery. Blasting already was under way to tunnel into the westerly headland for fastening the breakwater to the shore. Handling explosives was not for the faint-hearted, as the newly-formed newspaper, the *Port Crescent Leader*, reported:

"Mr. DeLong was lying flat upon his stomach occupied in the delightful task of filling the blast-hole full of No. 2 giant powder—each stick containing 40 per cent of nitro glycerine. He would take a stick, gently encircle it with his knife blade, break it in two in the middle, and then, after slitting the paper wrapper on both sides, gently place each half-stick as far back into the hole as possible by means of a tamping rod. A half dozen sticks of powder were crammed into that hole, a 'five-minute' fuse was properly inserted, and the whole securely tamped. A man then came with a red hot iron to light the fuse while everyone got out of the way." Within a week the first tunnel was thirty-five feet deep.

Following breathlessly every moment of progress, the *Leader* cheerfully boasted on March 12 that it was "the extreme western port of Puget Sound, and THE FIRST DEEP-WATER HARBOR north of San Francisco without a bar, a shoal or a sandbank. It will accommodate 120 ships at cable length, besides 100 more alongside wharves. A short and clear waterway of 43 miles to the ocean, enables ships to dispense with the heavy charges necessarily incurred for tugs and pilots on the Columbia river and the upper ports of Puget Sound."

The banner pronouncement, really an advertisement by William Newton, Real Estate Broker of Port Crescent, went on to claim that its unique geographic position secured for it the attention of The Northern Pacific Railroad Company which decided to adopt it as an OCEAN TERMINUS.

"The President of that corporation, Mr. Thomas F. Oakes, of New York, and other influential officers of the Northern Pacific, are Trustees of the

Victoria, Port Crescent & Chehalis Railroad Company, with a Capital of $4,000,000. This line will run from Port Crescent westward of the Olympic Mountains and connect with the existing Northern Pacific system now being extended to Gray's Harbor. The clearing of the first section of the Right of Way from Port Crescent is now in progress, and the president states that construction of the line will begin at both ends early in the spring, and BE COMPLETED BY THE CLOSE OF THE YEAR. An essential feature in this project is the ferrying of solid Northern Pacific Trains over to Port Becher, on Vancouver Island, and thence, along a line to be also built by the Northern Pacific, into the City of Victoria, B. C."

To be sure, work was going forward on the Canadian side, too, for the *Leader* reported on February 26, 1891, that the telegraph cable was being extended from Becher Bay to Port Crescent.

International visitors to the site had expansive words. The famous English publication, *Blackwood's Magazine*, quoted one Captain Andrew Haggard as saying that " . . . before long a steam ferry will run across from Port Crescent, at the narrowest part of the Strait of Juan de Fuca, a distance of only nine miles." The editor, Lee Fairchild, of *Pacific Magazine*, Seattle, said there were few, if any, lovelier places than Port Crescent: " . . .The quiet vale and the green slopes; the eloquent sea perpetually piling on the shore her blue billows, that phantom-like roar of . . . unseen waves of sound . . . the far blue range of mountains."

To transport heavy machinery to the breakwater site, workers constructed a trestle. Within a few months work was proceeding feverishly on the breakwater, using three engines powering swinging derricks. By April 23, 1891, the breakwater extended 250-300 feet seaward. The Port Crescent Mill Company's new sawmill arrived on the schooner *J.C. Brittain*—two big boilers, a large planer, and a single mill with all necessary equipment. The mill workers began cutting clear cedar. The steamer *Hermosa* stopped at Port Crescent's new dock three times a week, a surprisingly luxurious ship with a bridal suite and a piano in the main saloon.

Originally the harbor development plan called for blasting out a wider and deeper channel between the Tongue Point reef and the end of the new breakwater, eliminating part of the existing reefs. Unfortunately, when matters progressed to that point, the explosives failed to do their job and, despite the extensive work already completed, the Port Crescent Improvement Company abandoned the idea of creating a deepwater harbor for seagoing ships. One only has to see the harbor to realize that it never was spacious enough, anyway, for the numbers quoted in Newton's glowing advertisement. Nevertheless, investors had been attracted to the town, which seemed to promise expansion, and continued undismayed to complete their buildings. In 1891, the town had two saloons, the Markham House, a modern hotel for the time (it even had bellhops), the Port Crescent Hotel, a few stores, a cobbler shop, livery stables, and all the amenities of a frontier town.

An interesting sidelight made the papers in 1891, when a New York explorer said he was organizing an expedition into the Olympic Mountains (parts of which were unexplored) in search of cannibals and other things. He was quoted as saying he would "unravel the dread mysteries of the section and lay bare before the wondering gaze of the world the awful secrets and hideous orgies of the tribes of cannibals, with whom timid rumor has populated this country."

Undaunted by such horrible rumors, small shipowners began to call at Port Crescent's wharf. Noteworthy was the first *Lady of the Lake*, a launch destined to be hauled over a crude road to Lake Crescent, even then beginning to attract tourists. But Port Crescent then was a town more on paper, built on promotional oratory, than one of substance. After failure of the breakwater and railroad bid, plus defeat in the effort to claim the county seat designation, the town faltered. The logging railroad did not materialize, though much of the surveying was completed. The severe depression of 1893 nationwide caused capital to dry up, and Port Crescent languished, too. The settlement was destined to flare and fade two more times before dying entirely.

About 1892, Port Crescent had been noticed by a young logger, Michael Earles, who—with a partner, Jim Donohue—logged at Clallam Bay and built a little mill. When it burned, Earles went south to work in Maple Valley, King County, where he met another logger, Ed Gierin. These two teamed up with John Earles, Michael's brother, to form Seattle Logging Company, which later became the Puget Sound Mill and Timber Company (PSM&T) with some additional backing by Cyrus Clapp. Earles also had an interest in another mill in Bellingham.

In 1897, the company repurchased a large block of timber near Crescent Bay from Cyrus Clapp of Dungeness, who had logged there earlier (one speculates that perhaps Clapp contributed the timber as his investment in the new company). Michael Earles was the general manager, Ed Gierin the logging superintendent. A friend of Earles, Shorty Owens, was active in management. The old businesses came back to life; Markham House became the company headquarters and also a rooming house for the executives and higher-paid employees—the accountants, locomotive engineers, mechanics, managers. There were a dozen or so company homes for married employees, plus bunkhouses or shacks for single men.

In the beginning of operations, logs were lowered by cable car over a steep bluff which fronted on the harbor. Soon the contraption was replaced by a narrow gauge railroad which switchbacked down the hill to the western part of the bay and onto the sturdy wharf. (The first railroad had wooden rails with iron straps.) The firm added a warehouse on the wharf and built a machine shop for servicing the five logging locomotives. The logs were dumped into the bay for rafting, then company tugs, the *Augusta* and *Wallowa*, towed them to mills in Bellingham. Later Earles built what was locally known as "The Big Mill" at Port Angeles, ten miles east.

At first the logging methods were primitive. Oxen or horses dragged a cable into the woods, loggers attached a downed log, and a donkey engine dragged it back to the yarding point. Later horses were replaced by more sophisticated machinery. The logging railroads, as mentioned earlier, snaked through the woods to transport the logs to water.

Most of the loggers were single and often transient; companies said it took three crews to keep enough manpower to keep two full crews working at one time. Calling themselves "timber beasts" since their earliest living conditions were more fit for beasts than men, the entry level logger (the man who drove the horses, usually) made about $2.25 a day, working up to about $100 month for lumberjacks and $115 for camp foremen. Teenage "flunkies" sometimes earned less than $25 a month. Bunkhouses and individual shacks often were built on skids so they could be loaded onto flatcars and moved close to the current work site in the woods. Men provided their own bedrolls but were fed and housed by the company. As companies improved the food and housing, men tended to stay longer, of course.

The loggers let off steam at Port Angeles, usually, although on Christmas and the Fourth of July they might travel all the way to Seattle for a spree. Most purchases were in company scrip at designated stores.

Earles divided his time between Seattle and Port Crescent. He had two sides to his personality—his "down-home" logger look and his polished corporate demeanor. He preferred the bright lights of the main office in Seattle but, when he came to Port Crescent for awhile, he let his hair and beard grow and slouched around in old clothes. He was a dedicated poker player and engaged fellow travelers on the boat from Seattle in non-stop games, sometimes bypassing Port Crescent and playing on into Neah Bay.

In 1898, Port Crescent gained a new business when the United States Weather Bureau moved its local main office there, the office consisting of instruments and a telegraph system operated by one or two men.

By 1907, the PSM&T was running seven locomotives. Logs were cut to thirty foot lengths for transport during the narrow-gauge period, and up to forty feet thereafter. Occasionally extra-long lengths were ordered especially for booming or for spars. The crews utilized a flexible transport system that accommodated the different lengths, known as "disconnected trucks." No flat car as such existed during the narrow gauge period. Instead there was a set of two axles and wheels, each `truck' with a hand-brake, and a "bunk," a transverse piece of wood or metal to support the logs. In this manner, the length of a 'car' could be varied to suit the length of the logs. Chains connected the two ends of the segment of disconnected trucks. The braking systems certainly were needed to slow the steep descent from bluff to water. Logging jacks and wood blocks were used to tilt the loads of logs off the train into the booming area between the dock and Clam Point. Tugs then towed the booms away.

The operation included about 200 men in the log camps, eight or ten railroad operators, and fifty to 100 persons in management. With wives and children of some employees, the population of Port Crescent was estimated to be 500 or 600. If logging was curtailed in winter, some men moved on; also, during midsummer, when forest fires were a serious danger, companies shut down operations for weeks, and some employees moved on to other jobs.

Port Crescent had a sense of permanence, of community. It had a school, although it was in session only in fair weather from April to October. PSM&T built a small hospital and engaged a doctor. Residents scheduled fishing trips, clamming, coon-hunts and dances at the Markham Hotel. To get musicians the railroad operator might fire up a locomotive and pick up Port Angeles groups at Salt Creek. Song fests were popular; loggers loved to sing the old hymns . . . with gusto, loudly.

Earles got the idea of hiring the Joyce brothers, his brothers-in-law, to clear land where he thought rice would grow. He brought in Japanese to do the clearing, but the loggers were unkind to the foreigners and with so many problems, Earles changed his mind about growing rice.

An outlying logging camp was established at Joyce named for Joe Joyce, after the arrival there of the Seattle, Port Angeles & Western railroad tracks (Chicago, Milwaukee, St. Paul and Pacific Railroad assumed complete control of this line in 1915, a wholly-owned subsidiary), which were laid on west to Colville, Ramapo, Shadow, Majestic, Deep Creek and Twin, all settlements or camps surrounded with grand Douglas fir and cedar forests. Locomotives were converted to standard gauge in Port Angeles, and the narrow-gauge rails removed. Port Angeles, Joyce and the logging camps to the west were joined by standard-gauge rails.

With the removal of narrow-gauge and the severing of Port Crescent's tie with the rest of the Peninsula, the town soon faltered. Earles ceased his Port Crescent operations after his new "Big Mill" at Port Angeles was completed, and began logging over toward Twin during the World War I demand for spruce. Off the beaten path since the new, standard gauge railroad ran considerably south of the town through Joyce, Port Crescent essentially became just an extra large logging camp. Within months, most businesses picked up their belongings and moved to Joyce or called it quits. The post office moved to Joyce with Joseph M. Joyce becoming the postmaster, operating out of the Joyce General Store (the store still operates). Then the county road was built west from Port Angeles to Neah Bay, going through Joyce. Out of the mainstream, Port Crescent was dismantled, building by building, after the Earles' enterprises departed.

Despite his energetic performance, Earles was often ill and traveled to try the curative powers of Sol Duc Hot Springs beyond Lake Crescent. He credited the waters with restoring his health, fell in love with the place, and bought the rights to the springs and adjacent land from the heirs of Theodore Moritz, original owner, in 1910. To access the property, he had to build a road from the west end of Lake Crescent (Fairholm) at a reported cost of $75,000-$100,000. All materials to construct his planned four-story inn were delivered by a complex route: by ship to Port Crescent, on the logging railroad to the end of the line, by wagon to Lake Crescent, then aboard a small steamboat to Fairholm, and on wagons again to the springs.

Despite the difficulties, contractors Kuppler & Sons constructed the Sol Duc Hot Springs Resort complex within two years. The four-story rustic inn had 164 rooms, all furnished elegantly with imported tapestries and paintings. Mr. Zimmerman of Frederick and Nelson, Seattle, supervised the interior decorating.

The imposing front of the structure was built of upright hewn fir logs. Walls of the lobby (forty feet by eighty feet in size) were covered with burlap, the upper half golden brown, the lower dark green, separated by white molding. Immense pillars supported the ceiling, white with gold trim. The same motif was carried out in the dining room and alcove built especially for musicians. The second-story rooms sported balconies six feet by nine feet. All roome had hot and cold running water and phones; many had private baths. Since the mineral springs were said to be good for many ailments, Earles built a three-story sanatorium with thirty bathtubs, an operating room, medical and x-ray equipment, and beds for 100 patients. A Seattle friend persuaded Earles to bottle the water and sell it for a time, since it contained iron, potash, silica, magnesia, soda and other minerals.

Tennis courts, a gym, golf course and other buildings followed. Earles invested about half a million dollars to make everything first-class, for this spa was for the rich and famous. Rates were $3 a day American plan, and cheaper cottages were available for families who could not live luxuriously. When the resort was in full operation, passengers enjoyed a voyage from Seattle to Port Crescent, then traveled to the lake in Stanley Steamers, boarded a lake steamer to Fairholm, followed by still more road travel (before the Steamers, wagons sufficed). The adventure into the wilderness ended at Sol Duc, where one dressed formally for dinner and the table service was sterling and china. The chauffeurs, maids and governesses ate separately.

Michael Earles himself enjoyed his magnificent resort in the Olympic Mountains, rounding up well-heeled cohorts for all-night poker games.

Tragically, the place burned in 1916, the fire starting in the attic and spreading swiftly. Employees gathered sterling tableware in tablecloths and ran to dump it in the nearby creek. Nevertheless, the fire was so hot that it still melted the silver into one big lump. A macabre twist was that the inn's player organ stuck and played Beethoven's Funeral March throughout the three-hour blaze that destroyed the hotel but left the sanatorium.

A dejected Earles did not rebuild his dream resort. Thirty rooms of the old sanatorium operated for a time as Buena Vista House, then it, too, burned in the late 1920s.

All but deserted, the remainder of the town of Port Crescent died by fire, too. A careless beachcomber left an untended log fire on Crescent Beach, which spread into the oil soaked ground of the old oil house, ate its way along the boardwalk to the hotel and torched that structure. By fire and disintegration, the old buildings totally disappeared.

The attractive location, handy to the mouth of the Strait and the open ocean, rose like the proverbial Phoenix bird once again in the 1940s. "Rose" is hardly the word, for a deadly serious defense unit was installed within Tongue Point, the eastern headland of Crescent Bay. After Pearl Harbor and the declaration of World War II, the United States War Department approved a modernization of all defense units near the mouth of the Strait and designated new ones. Among them was a battery to be installed at Tongue Point, the area to be named Fort Hayden or Camp Hayden.

Colonel James H. Cunningham, later a Brigadier General, directed the updating of facilities, and was in command of the Puget Sound Harbor Defenses and the Northwest Defense Sector. This comprised a huge area including the northern part of the Olympic Peninsula and the northern portion of Puget Sound. Curiously it also included the harbor defenses of the mouth of the Columbia River, 200 miles distant. A Canadian counterpart worked closely with Cunningham to create defenses across the Strait.

Since the crucial Strait of Juan de Fuca was the responsibility of both countries and was vulnerable to enemy naval attack, a Harbor Entrance Control Post was established on a hill overlooking the Strait, manned twenty-four hours a day. The United States Navy installed underwater detection facilities. On the American side a major gun installation was put in place west of Port Angeles, and a new fortification at Striped Peak above Port Crescent. Beaches attractive to potential offensive landing craft were protected by wire and artillery.

The Fort Hayden Military Reservation comprised over 500 acres. The U.S. Army fortified Striped Peak atop Tongue Point with two six-inch and two sixteen-inch batteries, beginning work in May, 1942. The large guns

Remains of a gun emplacement in 1994.

— *A JoAnn Roe photo*

formerly were from a battleship, shipped from the East Coast to Seattle by rail, then hauled to Crescent Bay by barge. The sixteen-inch guns were the largest ever produced in the United States and fired projectiles weighing more than a ton to a distance of thirty miles. Each gun and loading mechanism was on a turntable capable of moving a small locomotive. Buried between the two large guns was the Fort Hayden power plant with its three Worthington diesels serving the installation. The installation included airconditioning and heating systems to keep the stored projectiles under controlled temperature and humidity. A whole underground city was carved out—bunkrooms, mess hall, recreational facilities. The men could move around without ever being exposed to enemy fire.

Captain Walter F. Winters, Plans and Projects Officer under Cunningham, was given most of the responsibility for supervising the Striped Peak (Camp Hayden) and other artillery projects along the Strait. In a report quoted in Gregory's *Keepers at the Gate*, Winter said:

"Work on the Striped Peak 16-inch battery was the first one started and it was completed, being the only one in the whole modernization program to be built. This was a massive project and a real test for the Engineers. For example, the tube of a single gun weighed something like 300 tons and this had to be moved up a steep mountain side to an elevation of about 2,000 feet. To give you some idea of the massive proportions of this fortification, the bomb proofing over the guns and the plotting room was 15 feet thick of solid concrete. The ammunition galleries were hundreds of feet long and each gun was 300 to 400 feet apart."

As early as August, 1943, though, intelligence reports indicated that the Japanese had lost the ability to strike the Pacific Coast, and work on other planned posts was suspended. Fortunately, the guns never had to be fired, other than one target practice after installation. When World War II was over, the guns were manned for a time until the development of missiles and sophisticated delivery systems made gun emplacements obsolete.

The wharf built to serve the camp was removed. Everything else moveable was dismantled. The gun barrels were made of laminated steel and had to be sliced into pieces with a torch for removal. One gun resulted in 500 tons of scrap!

Fort Hayden itself was phased out officially in 1949. The Port Crescent plat was vacated by order of Board of Clallam County Commissioners in 1958. Not one building is left from Port Crescent's three lives. Camp Hayden's land at Tongue Point was acquired to become Salt Creek Recreational Area under the Clallam County Park Board, and commands a striking view over the Strait for campers. The gun emplacement sites are still there, and sample projectiles are on exhibit.

The site of Port Crescent town has a privately operated campground and a couple of residences. No trace of the former towns exists, except for a row of low pilings marching across a marsh, part of the former railroad, no doubt. The land encircling Crescent Bay is private property.

Chapter 6
PYSHT

At the mouth of a small river winding north into the Strait of Juan de Fuca a small Clallam Indian settlement had thrived for generations, when white people straggled into the area. Heavy forests lay in the wedge-shaped extreme northwesterly corner of the United States, drained to the Pacific by the Quillayute River and to the north by (among others) the Pysht River. There are several versions of the derivation of the curious name, perhaps the most likely the Indian language word sounding like "Pishst," a place "where the wind blows from all directions."

The pioneer logging company, Hall & Bishop, worked the area lightly in the 1880s, dragging the logs to booming grounds on the Strait. However, the harbor there was shallow, exposed to fierce northwesterly winds, making a supply route hard to maintain, so Hall & Bishop moved operations to the gentler Gettysburg Bay farther east.

Despite difficult access, homesteaders claimed land along the fertile deltas of the river. First was Harry Martin. Then a Mr. Gordon opened a store and hotel near the beach at Butler's Cove and gained a post office designation in the 1880s. A few years later, Gordon's hotel burned and he moved on to Alaska, although another man continued with the store and post office. Broclay's Hotel operated at the east end of the beach area, and managers maintained the telegraph office for the line from Port Angeles to Tatoosh Island. In 1890, two brothers, Aman and Joe Stange, and their families from Indiana came to seek homesteads. A small girl when the families came, Gertrude Stange (Mrs. Antone) Fernandes remembered in 1971 that their ship could not land at the shallow Pysht harbor; Indian canoeists came to take them and their belongings from the ship to shore.

Until a rough puncheon road (crosswise logs placed over the muddiest part of a trail) was carved out to Clallam Bay, a larger settlement to the west, the only access was by water or foot trail.

In the isolation settlers' families had to be resourceful. Yearning for a little cash money, teenage Gertrude trapped furbearing animals—skunk, fisher, bear, bobcat, raccoon, mink, cougar, and otter (a difficult catch). She

45

was credited with catching the largest known cougar in the area, measuring nine feet from nose to tail, and a rare timber wolf. She also fished for steelhead with a set-net in the Pysht River.

After her marriage in 1909 to a handsome newcomer, Antone Fernandes from Blyn, Gertrude (and her husband) had the mail contract between Pysht and Clallam Bay. Gertrude chiefly handled this task, using a saddle horse over the rough trail. The Fernandes' descendants still are influential in the area today.

R.C. Warner, assigned to maintain about thirteen miles of the telegraph line to Tatoosh Island, arrived in Pysht about 1907. The weather station on Tatoosh at the mouth of the Strait was crucial to maritime shipping, sending a current weather report each day at 7:00 A.M. During bad weather Warner patrolled his section of line twice a week to check for breaks due to falling limbs, for the telegraph line was merely draped on trees about twelve feet off the ground.

John Huelsdonk, the legendary "Iron Man of the Hoh," was an infrequent visitor to Pysht. He had a ranch back in a remote valley of the Olympic Mountains and drove his cattle herds over old game trails to Pysht for marketing. An interesting sidelight of the Huelsdonk family enterprises was that the teenage daughters sought out and captured baby elk to ship to zoos or to stock other forest ranges.

However, little growth ensued until the outbreak of World War I. For the first time in history, aircraft were used for reconnaissance and actual combat. Light, strong and with a straight grain, spruce was favored for the long spars in the wings of airplanes. Free of pitch, spruce also was used for making violins and fine paper. The best spruce grew in Northwest Washington and Southeast Alaska, and the trees were LARGE. The famed naturalist, John Muir, mentioned measuring a tree trunk five feet in diameter, another at six feet three inches.

The chief logging firm to respond to the demand for spruce in the Pysht area was Merrill & Ring (M&R), which seems to have been a model forest business. In 1880, Thomas Merrill, Jr., came from Michigan, where his father operated a logging concern, to look for prime timber while his brother Dwight (usually called R.D.) went to work out of Hoquiam in 1898. R.D. Merrill said in an interview with Lucile McDonald that his brother " ... found this belt of Douglas fir in the forests drained by the Pysht River. We bought up old homesteads and timber claims and by 1908 the firm owned 23,000 acres. Later, several thousand more were acquired."

Prime spruce also grew in the general area. Since the firm was not ready to harvest all this timber, the owners appointed a tree farm manager to monitor the lands. In midsummer 1915, William Chisholm, company manager of M&R (with offices in Seattle since 1903), sent Harry Hall to set

Merrill & Ring headquarters, 1916.

up a logging operation in response to increasing demand for lumber.

When Hall went ashore at Pysht, little remained of the earlier settlement. Company employees offloaded tents for a temporary brush-removing crew (called swampers) and for a consulting engineer, who spent a month or two making soundings and maps for preparation of a dumping ground for the logs, a booming area in the shallow harbor. Hall supervised construction of a tent camp to house forty workmen, built a sturdy foot bridge across the Pysht River, and began clearing for a railroad that was to haul logs to the beach. Early employees included Bill Burnette, Tommy Irving, Guy Decker, Jack O'Leary, Elmer Ronalds, Rudy Dimmel, and Gus Stange, relative of pioneer Gertrude Fernandes. Bids were accepted for road work and construction of a set of permanent camp buildings. One of the contractors was Filberg and McQuade, with R.J. Filberg going on to superintend a logging operation at Comox, British Columbia, and eventually to become Chairman of the Board of McMillan Bloedel Limited.

Work progressed nicely until January, 1916, when an unprecedented five-foot snowfall stymied operations. Workers could not even leave camp. Men cleared snow from the tents to prevent collapse and tunneled paths between snow banks. Necessary communication to Clallam Bay was maintained with Filberg's big team of draft horses; with the snow breast high, even they could not travel long without resting.

As spring came, the Pysht River flooded from the melting snow and, as soon as the river went down, the workmen, restless from winter confinement, eagerly went to work laying ties for the railroad. A tug maneuvered a scow of wet ties quite far up the narrow river, and the railroad's path began to march toward the forest. As the railroad progressed, woods machinery began to arrive—two Lidgerwood skidders, two big and several smaller steam donkeys. With trackage in place, M&R sent in a locomotive with an engineer and by 1917, logging began.

That summer a big suction dredge was towed to the harbor to begin deepening the harbor for the booming grounds. The Kuppler Brothers of Port Angeles constructed the permanent camp buildings, including a cook house, bunkhouse, shop, office, superintendent's home, a guest house for visiting dignitaries, and a company hospital. In 1917 a movie house was added.

Whereas many logging outfits of the time barely provided decent shelter and food for their men, M&R's camp was a model for others to follow. The painted crew's quarters were neat and had good sanitary facilities. Cooks

Elaborate wood trestles supported heavy log trains.
— Photo Courtesy of Port Angeles Public Library

served plentiful, hearty food. Crews responded with loyalty and stayed longer than the usual transient "timber beast."

Harry Hall remembered with pleasure the monthly dances held at either Forks or Clallam Bay. The musicians came from Port Angeles and, if necessary, a logging locomotive went to pick them up.

Not all companies were as forward-thinking as M&R in labor relations. After July 4, 1917, the International Workers of the World (I.W.W.) went on strike, asking, among other things for decent accommodations in the logging camps. The strike dragged on and on, tying up production at M&R along with other owners. Some mill owners were accused of holding back available wood to increase prices. The output of lumber for World War I swiftly dwindled. The Allies requested a monthly production quota of ten million board feet to be developed by October, 1917, and the total production of spruce in 1917 was a mere three million, only 10% fit for aircraft use.

At Washington, D.C., officials took action. After a conference with General John J. Pershing and Chief-of-Staff General James G. Harbord on May 7, 1917, Captain Brice Disque was sent undercover to the Northwest to assess the labor/management situation. He reported that things were bad and apt to get worse. Promoted to Colonel, Disque was given the command on November 7, of a new military unit, the Spruce Production Division (SPD), with offices at Portland, Oregon. Vancouver Barracks at Fort Vancouver was the main center for training and assigning soldiers forest labor. Disque had a free hand in creating an efficient organization and divided the Northwest spruce operations into six districts: Puget Sound (offices in Seattle and including Clallam County), Grays Harbor & Willapa Bay, Vancouver, Clatsop, Yaquina Bay, and Coos Bay, the three latter districts along Oregon's coast.

The contingents of soldiers were dispersed to new camps, if necessary, but more often, to existing camps, including the M&R at Pysht. During the height of spruce logging, it is estimated that as many as 500 people lived at or near Pysht, civilians and soldiers. Thousands more lived in camps nearby.

In September, 1917, the SPD was increased to 1,317 officers and men, and on May 23, 1918, to 28,825 men. At first, the Spruce Division accepted only men who were above draft age, not over forty years old, in good physical condition, and preferably with logging or lumbering experience. By summer of 1918, the soldiers could not enlist in the Division if they were classified as draft status Class 1, with some exceptions. But the Division could take others with draft classifications as high as 4, if they were able to do the work. The soldiers received the going rate for their work, from which was subtracted their Army pay and $7.50 per week for bed and board. Responding to this call for experienced woodsmen to join the forest corps, some loggers did not wait for a draft but volunteered, seeking to bring their experience to bear on the problems.

The concept of soldiers directly assigned to work in the woods met resistance from both the striking union and lumber managers. Unions initially viewed the plan as simply strikebreaking, while the lumbermen feared drastic restrictions on how they operated and the prices for lumber. Colonel Disque, a consummate diplomat, listened fairly to both groups, then appealed to the patriotism of both factions, pointing out the necessity of drastic action if the Allies were to triumph. He also pointed to advantages for both labor and management—for labor, the eight-hour work day, better camps, and such; for management, protection by a soldier cadre against sabotage, stability of the work force, and the possibility of expansion of their businesses. Disque was successful in gaining the cooperation of all concerned, and his work affected labor-management relationships long thereafter. Especially unique was the organization resulting from the labor-management negotiations, the Loyal Legion of Loggers and Lumbermen (LLLL), a sort of union comprised of both laborers and company management. Despite initial shock at such a revolutionary idea as cooperation between these two groups, almost all the owners and over 100,000 laborers signed up, a "marriage" that endured until the Great Depression.

Now the logging effort could at least begin; it was difficult at best to extract huge spruce logs from dense stands of other evergreens. The terrain was precipitous, and as much as eleven feet of rain fell on this section of the Olympic Peninsula. Under Disque and others, selective logging was attempted, now widely practiced but then seldom done. To get the huge trees out, the SPD developed a new method of reducing their size, riving (splitting) them into about six sections for transport. On the soft ground the access roads for trucks had to be "paved" with wood—two tracks for the truck wheels comprised of two planks wide on each side with a piece going across underneath for stability. The SPD had over 100 Ford cars and ambulances to move lighter supplies and machinery.

Clearly the railroad was a more viable solution to getting the logs out, especially without having to pre-size them. The Division planned to build 173 miles of main line and 181 spurs, seven of the railroads in Washington and six in Oregon. One was the Olympic Spruce Railroad No. 1, stretching near Pysht from Disque Junction, west of Port Angeles, to access the Hoko River area, plus spurs along the Pysht River and elsewhere.

In May, 1918, a cost-plus contract was let to a New York firm, Siems, Carey-H.S. Kerbaugh Corporation, to deliver 250 million board feet of spruce "flitches" (twenty-two-foot lengths of delimbed spruce) by November, 1919. To meet their promises, the firm would have to build 175 miles of railroad and two big sawmills. Location surveys began without delay, placing the

A U.S. spruce logging camp near Lake Pleasant.
— *Photo Courtesy of Port Angeles Public Library*

line, an extension of the Seattle, Port Angeles and Western Railroad that terminated near Joyce, in a southwesterly direction through the Lyre River Canyon, along Lake Crescent, across the valley of the Soleduck River and on to Lake Pleasant. It would access some of the finest spruce stands in the world. The effort began with twenty camps or more and 6,000 workmen.

The line required boring two tunnels and four bridges, two with trestles, two truss spans, and paths along rocky cliffs to be blasted along some sections. Track laying began on September 20, 1918, and despite washouts and rock slides, was completed to the west end of the main line at Lake Pleasant on November 30, a herculean feat. Crude roads had supported a fleet of trucks, large and small, to supply the railroad construction camps. Concurrent with the main line railroad construction, Siems, Carey-H.S. Kerbaugh Corporation worked on a twenty-two-mile loop railroad that meandered through the heaviest spruce stands fifty miles west of Port Angeles near the Hoko and Dickey Rivers. Also, the first government sawmill at Lake Pleasant was framed in and the mill machinery ordered. A town mushroomed along Lake Pleasant to serve the mill builders, the logging and railroad operations. On June 15, 1918, even as employees "camped out" in primitive conditions, William F. Carey, the contractor's resident manager in Seattle, contacted the architectural firm of Bebb and Gould to urgently lay plans for an entire new, respectable town on Lake Pleasant for an anticipated 700 residents. It would include a cutting mill, railroad shops, bunkhouses, hotel, hospital, recreation hall, private residences, and provisions for a permanent town. However, the futuristic and attractive buildings planned never materialized, as the project was abruptly cancelled in October, 1918, just twelve days before the World War I Armistice.

With apparent remarkable efficiency and dispatch, the Army completed the spruce operation after spending at least 10 million dollars. The operation brought together some of the nation's leading engineers, architects, contractors, and lumbermen, including: Chester P. Siems, president of Siems, Carey-H.S. Kerbaugh Corporation; B.B. Kelliher, chief engineer for the Spruce Railroad No. 1, a Canadian with railroad design expertise; Ed Donlan, a Montana Senator who initiated logging operations on the loop railroad; C.C. Tinkler, superintendent for the loop railroad; and Richard R. Kilroy, Welfare Department Manager. Spruce Railroad No. 1 was completed in an incredible six months. The joining of labor and management, the LLLL, had achieved a miracle, and said so in their monthly publication, January, 1919:

"The 36 miles of main line construction through the tunnels of forest and of solid rock, over spidery trestles, around dizzy, rocky curves, through the 180 inches of annual rainfall, is being completed practically within five months! It is the most remarkable speed feat in the history of American railroading."

Like the cliche of "always a bridesmaid, never a bride," the SPD was all prepared but never produced spruce. With 150 million board feet of felled logs at various staging areas enroute to the yet incomplete mills, on November 11, 1918, World War I was terminated with an Armistice.

Operations of the SPD ceased immediately. Just one day after the Armistice the order came to cut no more trees. The soldiers were moved out, starting December 1. It was none too soon, for the mud, rain, and chill of the area had caused epidemic deaths from flu in the logging camps. Truckloads of the dead were taken out at the height of the infection.

Seven hundred men stayed on another month or two to complete a small portion of the railroad to Lake Pleasant. They, too, departed by midJanuary. Everything was dismantled as efficiently as it had been built, with the machinery sold out of the Vancouver Barracks later on. Life at M&R's logging camps returned to normal speed.

While the government effort itself, miraculous as it was, did not produce any lumber before war's end, the private companies utilizing soldier workers did increase spruce production during those critical years from 2,887,623 board feet monthly to 22,145,823, aided by the Division's completion of branch railroads into the timber.

M&R, with its own private labor corps, continued its logging operations, taking out a reported ninety million board feet of timber annually on seventy-five miles of railroad track.

Among the loggers remaining on the job were some colorful characters. "Haywire" Tom Newton, a tall, blonde Norwegian arrived at age thirty in 1914, and soon went to work as head highrigger for M&R. A good logger, he was also a daredevil who scorned safety harness when working. He went up 150-200 feet to top a tree and hung on manually as it whipped back & forth after the top detached and fell. Once he did fall 120 feet but landed on his feet in mud, unharmed. Quite an exhibitionist, he walked through blackberry bushes barefoot on a dare and climbed hand over hand up the 125-foot guy wire of a rigged spar tree. He loved mountain climbing and was so fearless that he terrified companions by standing on narrow ledges or the edge of sheer precipices. He lived through his stunts but died at Grand Coulee Dam in 1934 when a crane tipped over, spilling him into the river.

M&R continues to cut timber on its lands near Pysht on a sustained annual harvest basis. Instead of hauling logs from the forest by railroad and/or booming logs at the mouth of the Pysht River as it did in the earlier days, the company uses trucks to transport logs to market. Since 1944, the firm has concentrated on planting the next crop of trees as timber is cut from each plot—beginning its replacement efforts years before the law required operators to do so. In fact, the firm started replanting experiments between 1921 and 1926, planting seedlings of California redwood, eastern white pine, Norway pine, and black walnut trees from Virginia. Unfortunately, the deer ate the black walnut seedlings and the Norway pine died out.

R.D. Merrill was a modest man who shunned publicity; however, he told writer Lucile McDonald that he always counted on his lands producing additional crops. The firm was one of few who actually purchased and held onto their lands; many logging companies leased or purchased lands, letting them revert to prior owners for taxes after the lumber was cut.

At the old site of Pysht the offices of M&R's tree farm still are housed in an original building; the superintendent's home, guest house, and several neat workmen's houses remain. The old cookhouse and a warehouse are crumbling and soon will be taken down. A railroad roundhouse, other camp homes, and buildings all have been dismantled.

Nothing remains of the adjacent, original little town of Pysht, strung out along the river. The railroad tracks were taken up in 1944 and forest roads abandoned. Near the mouth of the Pysht River at Butler's Cove, the Merrill and Ring Recreation Area was opened to the public, including 450 feet of broad beach and tidelands.

(Note: With appreciation, the author acknowledges the use as background the report prepared for the National Park Service, Port Angeles and the Willamette National Forest, Eugene, Oregon, on the Spruce Production Division, prepared by Gail E. H. Evans and Gerald W. Williams in 1984, entitled *Over Here, Over Here*, obtainable in the Clallam County Library.)

Chapter 7
TWIN

Twin (or Twin Rivers) was another small town, more a logging camp, that flared briefly and subsided, as a result of early forest-to-sea logging and the World War I activities of the United States Spruce Division. The settlement lay about twelve miles west of Port Crescent on the Strait of Juan de Fuca betweem the east and west forks of Twin River. Today there is no trace whatever of the town, just a private recreational area near the old townsite along Highway 112 between Port Angeles and Neah Bay. Gone are the steamer blasts, the shrieks of logging locomotives and the crash and bustle of a typical log town.

Available land around Twin Rivers was snapped up soon enough after the newspaper, *Port Crescent Leader,* announced on February 26, 1891, that the Twin Rivers Township had been opened for settlement by the United States Government on November 20, 1890. Almost all claims were gone in two days, filed at the United States Land Register's Office in Seattle.

Because the only shelters for the first claimants were the thick, spreading boughs of the evergreen trees, the settlers cooked over open fires until they could throw up crude cabins.

One settler, James B. Davis, said there was an anthracite coal vein on his land (it probably was bituminous or sub-bituminous, however), while Clallam County Sheriff W.B. Gould filed a claim on lands purportedly showing fifty per cent copper plus some silver. Patrick Dillon of the Monte Cristo Mining Company proved up a claim April 21, 1892, for unidentified minerals in the area. Nothing seemed to come of the mining claims, although later geologists say that the Olympic Peninsula has some of the largest deposits of manganese in the world. Unfortunately, the manganese is spread throughout the peninsula like scattered chicken feed, making it commercially unprofitable to mine. Two mines were promising but failed: the Tubal-Cain Mine above Quilcene and another near the west end of Lake Crescent.

The first post office at Twin was established in 1892, but access to the settlement was either by boat, a winding telegraph maintenance trail through

55

the woods, or beach walking. Steamers did stop long enough to permit small boats to come out to pluck passengers and freight from the deck. Basic supplies came from E.E. Seevers store at Port Crescent.

In July, 1891, twenty settlers stripped bark from hemlock trees to sell to the Pacific Tanning Extract Company in Sekiu, west of Twin. The material was used for all types of leather work. The operation was short-lived.

Crescent Logging Company camp near Piedmont.

Horse logging.

— Both photos Courtesy of Port Angeles Public Library

Some farmers raised beef to sell to logging companies.

One of the first logging companies was Holland and Ackles, which hired a large crew to work in its camp at Twin Rivers in 1893. A.H. Sandy Thompson and Joseph Dillon logged east of Twin from 1892-1902. Since the plateau between the rivers ended in steep cliffs above the harbor, the loggers built a chute to carry the logs down to the Strait.

Twin was strictly a subsistence town until the Chicago, Milwaukee, St. Paul & Pacific Railroad (CMSP&PR), was completed to Twin from Port Angeles in 1916, which enabled companies to ship logs by rail instead of sea. Then came the United States Spruce Division in World War I, a boon to the Twin area, as well as nearby Pysht.

Twin received about 200 soldier-loggers during the Spruce Division efforts, some with dependents, so the town briefly expanded along the plateau between the east and west arms of the Twin River with government-owned or company houses and the usual stores, plus bunkhouses or tents for the single. Michael Earles' Puget Sound Mill and Timber (PSM&T) had been working in the area around Majestic in 1915 and, when the railroad came to Twin, the company established its headquarters there. Men from three company camps worked the area.

Early logger Harry Hall said he went to work rigging high leads for the PSM&T at Twin, moving from Pysht to Twin on the Merrill and Ring (M&R) tug *Crawford*. The logging company houses were built so they could be easily moved by rail to a new location within hours. The biggest attraction at Twin was Harry White's pool hall, and Grange Hall activities drew crowds.

One of the earliest logging superintendents was Jim Flaherty, a Canadian, who later left PSM&T to form Flaherty and Daly Logging Company to work east of Port Crescent. Tom Cannon was foreman of Camp 8 in 1917. Other key residents were Oscar Howard, a locomotive engineer; Ed Brooks, another locomotive engineer, and his wife, the school teacher; Columbus Cogburn and his sons, Austin and Ernest, who were loggers; Henry Taylor, a brakeman for the logging spur railroad; Ernest Thompson, a builder of bridges; and William E. Possinger, a master mechanic for all kinds of logging equipment. Cash Morgan loaded logs, Sam Stamm was the logging engineer at Twin, and "Dad" Hunter and Owen Mulholland lived at Twin with their families to represent the CMSPPR interests.

Residents made their own entertainment, staging picnics, beach parties, sports contests, and dances. One weekend the crews wanted to hold a dance in the messhall, but the floor was too rough. To solve the problem, a man used the oil and graphite mixture used to shine up engines in the maintenance shop. This worked just fine, except the oil soaked into the pastel ball gowns of the ladies after a few turns around the floor. It took steam cleaning to get the stuff out of the floor; no one reported the fate of the ladies' gowns.

The 1918 flu epidemic hit Twin's loggers and families with devastating force. In the Army camps, the doctors recommended that men wear face masks—at least in camp, but many soldiers came down with the flu, anyway. Dozens died and others were weakened. The Armistice of 1919 permitted most soldiers to leave the camps, thus avoiding a wintry repetition of the disease.

Twin's in-town Logging Camp 8 closed in the spring of 1921, even though PSM&T continued to be one of the big three of the North Olympic Peninsula—PSM&T, M&R, and after 1924, Bloedel Donovan Lumber Mills (BDLM) of Bellingham (they were buying property as early as 1921).

In late January, 1921, Twin was directly in the path of a killer wind that leveled thousands of acres of prime timber. Steady winds of 110 MPH were clocked. On January 29, at the North Head weather station at the mouth of the Columbia River (south of the Olympics), Weather Observer Perry R. Hill's anemometer broke at 132 MPH and he estimated gusts beyond that. From west of Lake Crescent to the small camp of Beaver, it was reported that upwards of twenty-five per cent of the timber was down, much of it across the roads. Conditions were no better near Twin. A reliable source estimated that about fifteen million board feet of Merrill & Ring's standing timber was down. That company's foreman MacPherson declared that the noise of trees falling during the storm rivalled claps of thunder. At the mouth of the Strait of Juan de Fuca the aerial span connecting Tatoosh Island to the mainland collapsed, and the lighthouse keeper's pet bull was blown clear off the island into the water. The storm continued to ravage Vancouver Island and, when it was all over, an estimated eight billion feet of good timber was down in an area of about 2,250 square miles. Some settlers were cut off from stores for weeks, surviving on what they had canned or could shoot.

Curiously, about that same time, BDLM was negotiating with the United States Government for the purchase of the Spruce Railroad abandoned after World War I, and also with Clallam Lumber Company to buy timber lands. The day they were to sign the contract with Clallam, the big blow came, destroying acres of timber they had purchased or were purchasing. Aghast BDLM officers appealed to the sellers and managed to get some financial concessions for the losses sustained by BDLM before the ink was even dry on the contract. Another company purchased the Spruce Railroad, but soon BDLM bought it from the interim owner and operated out of Clallam Bay, west of Twin.

Such hurricanes or freak winds have swept the Olympic Peninsula from time to time in recorded history, the worst in latter years occurring in 1962,

58

when tall, tough evergreens in the Olympic National Park were laid down like toothpicks, there to remain because of "leave-it-alone" environmental regulations for parks.

In the 1920s, the Irving-Hartley Logging Company worked the Twin Rivers area as far west as Deep Creek and into the lower foothills of the Olympic Mountains. Logs went to Port Angeles and to the Carlsborg Mill. In 1927, this company reorganized as Crescent Logging Company (CLC) with Petrus Pearson as vice-president. The firm logged area as far south as Joyce, then at Riverside in the lower Calawah and Soleduck areas, also at Piedmont and west of Lake Crescent. The two camps fed logs to the Port Angeles & Western Railroad, which CLC had purchased from the Lyon-Hill Company, extending the rails another 7.4 miles from Lake Pleasant almost to Forks. Twin as a settlement or camp stayed alive until the major harvestable timber had been removed. In 1942, long a customer of the mill, CLC bought the Carlsborg Mill.

Some residents hung on at Twin but when the CMSP&P tore up its tracks from Twin all the way to Disque, just west of Joyce, in the early 1930s, the town died.

There was a small revival at Twin after 1971, when the Ideal Cement Company built a breakwater west of Twin to provide a harbor for shipping clay for cement. It still operates. The material is picked up with a big rubber-tired scraper, taken down to a dock on the West Twin River, and shipped by barge to Seattle. About seventy per cent of the stockpiling of clay is done in summer, because the huge winter rainfall at Twin often makes it impossible to get the large tractors into the pits. A small crew does maintenance during the wet season. Nothing else is left of the town and, except for intermittent tractor operations, today the scream of foraging gulls and the occasional rush of a car down Highway 112 are the only sounds breaking the silence.

JEFFERSON COUNTY

Chapter 8
IRONDALE

— From the collection of The Jefferson County Historical Society,
Port Townsend, Washington

T he site on which Irondale was founded seemed to be jinxed. It died
several deaths. Six miles south of Port Townsend along a lovely bay
with a moderate climate, a village of 400 Chimacum Indians thrived in the
mid-1850s. According to white historians, they were known as warlike and
often attacked canoe-loads of Canadian Indians traveling along the water-
ways. After enduring several such attacks, the Indians of Barclay Sound
(near the mouth of the Strait of Juan de Fuca) collaborated with the

61

Chimacums' mortal enemies, the Snohomish Indians (near today's Everett), to mount an attack on the Chimacums. The two warrior groups approached from opposite sides of the village, stalked their unsuspecting victims, and annihilated every man, woman and child.

In 1859, L.P. Hoff bought 160 acres of land at the mouth of Chimacum Creek from Albert Strand and erected a small gristmill and sawmill. The power system was unique, obtained by the use of a turbine under-shot wheel in a pit, operated by the current in the creek. At high tide the water backed up to create insufficient flow to run the wheel, and the mill had to cease operating during ebb tide. Nevertheless, Hoff processed two shiploads of lumber in his sawmill, rafting them out to the bark *Narramissic* for sale in San Francisco. Hoff ran out of money and his property was sold for debts. Colonel G.O. Haller eventually was the owner and ran the mill briefly, after constructing a small dam for power. Concluding it was a losing proposition, he sold the property to a Dr. W.C. Willison, and Willison to the Puget Sound Iron Company (PSIC).

The PSIC was incorporated July 28, 1879, by James Jones, E.L. Canby, H.L. Blanchard and Samuel Hadlock. Under a thicket of blackberry bushes too dense to walk through, lie the bones of Irondale, a town that hoped to rival Pittsburgh for iron and steel manufacture. The repeated rise and fall of this town, 1500 residents and an impressive, complete steel mill eventually, was a tale of under-financing and shallow marketing research, among other things.

The raw materials were there, a few miles south of Port Townsend. Just under the surface at today's Chimacum was a deposit of bog hematite iron ore, twenty-two inches deep, waiting to be mined; landowners John Lindley, William Bishop, William Eldredge, and Olaff Peterson entered an agreement with the PSIC, permitting them to mine the ore with the provision that they must build a blast furnace and a wharf to accommodate ocean-going vessels. Around the Sound and in the neighboring province of British Columbia, coal and limestone deposits were available. Developing cities on Puget Sound needed iron and steel for new buildings. Except for small operations in Oregon and Colorado marketers found few serious competitors closer than Minnesota or Pennsylvania and believed those distant plants would not be a threat because of freight costs to the west coast.

PSIC's initial blast furnace was "blown in" on January 27, 1881, a small installation that could process only about five tons of ore daily. The owners claimed the resultant product was of the finest quality, and the Chimacum ore yielded 55-56% iron, higher than most ores.

Despite the high hopes the reportedly inexhaustible supply of bog ore at Chimacum was less extensive than first believed. If mixed with other ore—desirable because, of differing composition, ores complemented one another—it might last a few more years, however.

Real hope dawned for a reliable supply of ore, when a big body of magnetite ore was found on Texada Island in Canada's Gulf of Georgia. Irving M. Scott, former head of the Union Iron Works of San Francisco, bought into the Texada mines and the Irondale foundry and added new charcoal kilns and larger furnaces—first a ten-ton furnace and before long, one of fifty tons.

Switching to Texada ore created problems. The furnaces had to run at higher temperatures to smelt the ore, and before long, the fire brick lining actually melted. The problem was remedied but only after a costly shutdown.

Meanwhile, the town of Irondale was platted to serve a work force projected at 250 men. A company store stocked basic supplies. The Chimacum Saloon and the Bay View Hotel opened their doors. By 1883, there were several saloons, two stables, a grist mill, and an assortment of hotels, really boarding houses, for the workers. Homes arose along streets that plunged forthrightly downhill toward the bay—simple homes for married workers, fancier ones for the officials of the company. A real estate company led by Samuel Hadlock touted lot and home sales.

With improved furnaces the company produced 2,317 tons of pig iron in 1883, averaging about that same amount annually for the next five years. Some of the iron went into the construction of the United States battle cruiser *Charleston* and battleship *Oregon*, the latter built between 1887 and 1893 at San Francisco's Union Iron Works.

The plant grew to employ 400 workers, and homes and businesses sprawled across the plateau above the beachside location of the foundry on Port Townsend Bay. Unfortunately, the Chimacum bog iron gave out entirely, and the plant endured costly mechanical problems. The company also experienced several reorganizations and recapitalizations. With an uncertain future and a declining economy and market, aggravated by high labor costs and higher than average manufacturing costs, the PSIC let its employees go and shut down late in 1889. Except for a brief spurt of activity under an unidentified owner, the plant lay dormant for several years thereafter.

In 1901, PSIC was purchased by Homer S. Swaney, an experienced steel man and lawyer from McKeesport, Pennsylvania. With an impressive background Swaney was Irondale's best hope for success. He and others built the Riverton bridge across the Monongahela River, connecting McKeesport and Duquesne. He organized the White Traction Company that eventually became part of the street car service of Pittsburgh. In Seattle after 1901, he attempted to form a company to consolidate all the street car companies of the city and hoped to build a steam railway from Seattle to Port Townsend.

The purchase price of PSIC was only $40,000 and a requirement to buy certain amounts of ore from the Texada Island operation. Before purchase, Swaney hired engineer J.H. Cremer to assess the Irondale property, the local ore and that at Texada. Cremer recommended the Wilkeson Coal Company of Pierce County as a source for coke.

Swaney was very optimistic about Irondale's future and set about lining up financiers to make the Irondale plant into the most important iron and steel producer west of the Rocky Mountains; indeed, he talked of gaining a monopoly. He opened the plant after incorporating it as Pacific Steel Company (PSC). But before any steel production could take place, the long-unused factory had to be renovated and, for a time, the firm continued to produce more pig iron.

To rework the plant facilities Swaney used local craftsmen and forty-five experienced ironworkers from McKeesport. Among the additions at this time was a three and one-half-mile flume to bring water to the plant from Chimacum Creek. With a lack of available coke, PSC reopened with coke made from wood. The maws of the twenty kilns producing coke required 180 cords each day.

To house workers, the company built several homes. Other new employees built dwellings with their own funds. General merchandise stores, a large hotel owned by Canadians, and a post office, telephone and telegraph offices, added an air of permanence to Irondale. More saloons helped to quench the mighty thirst of hard-working men.

Once more the mines at Texada turned out iron ore and to satisfy the need for high temperatures for smelting, the company leased coal claims at Hamilton, Skagit County, to mine top-notch coal for the purpose. Limestone came from the Roche Harbor Lime Company at the north end of San Juan Island.

The Irondale furnace roared again on December 15, 1901, and runs were produced to be tested in Seattle. A most favorable report was received. According to Diane F. Britton in *Irondale, Washington*, there was no other blast furnace on the Pacific Coast at this time. "Consequently, foundries and machine shops from Alaska to Southern California readily bought Irondale's product for 'handsome prices' ... "

Customers for the iron included the Griffin Car Wheel Company, Tacoma, and the Southern Pacific Railroad Company. The iron was used in manufacturing the engines for the battleship *Nebraska*, built in Seattle's Moran Brothers Shipyards (MBS). Port Townsend financiers put together a company to fashion railroad rails from Irondale's iron.

Despite the popularity of the iron, Swaney moved to convert the site for the manufacture of steel. He scurried around to line up significant financing for his ambitious expansion plans, gaining commitments from several Seattle businessmen to organize Seattle Iron & Steel Company, which was to absorb the Irondale facility, an $8 million project. Fate stepped in to quash the venture when Swaney, bound for the "outside" to contact financiers, drowned in the Strait of Juan de Fuca aboard the sinking steamer *Clallam* on June 9, 1904.

Other Northwest business leaders went with him in the tragic sinking, one that caused severe inquiries into safety procedures. The passenger steamer had become disabled the prior afternoon during a gale-force wind and was under tow by the tug *Holyoke*, laboring for eleven hours toward port against gale force winds. Suddenly the leaking *Clallam* sank with fifty-nine passengers and thirty-one crew aboard, of whom only thirty-six were saved. Lifeboats launched successfully were swamped within sight of the ship. Perishing with Swaney were Colonel Charles W. Thompson, president of Montezuma Mining Company and of Washington Cooperative Mining Syndicate, and active partners in five other industrial firms. Peter Larson, said to be the leading contract railroad builder of the West, was fished out of the water eventually but the icy bath damaged his health permanently.

So sank PSC, then, of financial difficulties brought on by Swaney's death. At the time of his death the plant had unfilled orders for 2,500 tons of iron, but the company went into receivership.

The prospect of a successful steel plant on Puget Sound was attractive, though, and in 1906, Seattle developer James A. Moore bought the property out of receivership for $40,000. Moore lost no time in servicing the equipment and reopening the mill in 1907, to the joy of idle workers living hand to mouth. The plant resumed production of iron, and in 1908, Moore had put together adequate capital for expansion, organized the Western Steel Corporation (WSC) and let a contract to MBS to build a steel plant.

The venture was now on solid ground. The officers and investors were well-known. Moore was the President of the MBS, had constructed eighteen business blocks in Seattle and opened choice residential districts. Basically he was a promoter and developer. Herbert E. Law, First Vice President, had opened and operated the Fairmont Hotel in San Francisco and built several skyscrapers there. Jacob Furth, Second Vice President, was the president of both the Puget Sound National Bank and the Seattle Electric Company of Seattle. Robert Dollar, Third Vice President, was the active head of Dollar Steamship Lines, then a major maritime firm. Other directors included W.H. Armstrong, S.G. Faulkner, Robert Kelly, R.P. McLennan and E.H. Heaps, all prominent businessmen of Vancouver, British Columbia.

The assets of the apparent amalgamation that made up the company amounted to $42,300,000, consisting of the iron mines on Texada Island; the Ashford Coal Mines toward Mount Rainier; coal and timber lands (20,500 acres) on Graham Island, B.C., said to contain 100 million tons of coal; standing timber; a limestone quarry; a magnetite deposit near Atlin, B.C.; real estate in Irondale; and the iron plant itself. It would seem the firm had all their raw materials available and under the control of the directorate, since the latter included the heads of Northern Texada Mines, the President of Portland-Superior Cement Company (limestone); and others. Even the transportation of materials would be influenced by the inclusion of the head of Dollar Steamship Lines. The stock prospectus of Western Steel Company was optimistic, according to the following excerpts:

"The iron ore averages from 50 to 68% metallic iron, is low in both silica and aluminum, and is easily accessible . . . easily mined and cheaply transported. [It would come by barge directly to the iron foundry/steel mill.] . . . The advantage of this situation is appreciated when contrasted with the condition now prevailing in the Pittsburg district, where the majority of the ores handled are hauled from 800 to 1,200 miles, by rail and water, with from four to five handlings.

"The freight rate upon structural steel in carload lots from either Pittsburg or St. Paul to Seattle is $16.00 per ton. . . . The lowest rate from any market is upon pig iron, from Chicago to Pacific Coast terminals, at $10 per ton."

The prospectus went on to say that cost of ore delivered from British Columbia to Port Townsend Bay was only $1.35 to $2 per ton, for example. The wide difference in freight costs would form a natural protective tariff favorable to the Irondale plant.

Costs of iron ore, coke, and limestone were quoted at prices below that of eastern markets. The selling price of pig iron to Pacific Coast buyers would average about $25 a ton, less than the eastern suppliers, and still yield $11 per ton gross profit. The market price of steel was estimated at $40 to $60 on the Pacific Coast at that time and, at an estimated production cost of $21.40 per ton, there was a "magnificent margin of profit for the Irondale Steel Company."

The assets of the Irondale Plant at the time of the prospectus (during which the steel mill was under construction) included:

An iron blast furnace plant, redesigned and reconstructed by the Wellman-Seaver-Morgan Company of Cleveland, Ohio, having a capacity of 100 tons of pig iron per day. The blast furnace was 56 feet high, 11 feet "bosh," and 6 feet hearth.

Two hot blast stoves (continuous heating)

Three new Atlas boilers, combined 375 H.P.

Irondale Steel Plant. Rolling Mills on left, blast furnace on right.
– From the collection of the Jefferson County Historical Society,
Port Townsend, Washington

Two Weiner blowing engines capable of supplying blast sufficient for 100 tons of pig iron per day.

20 charcoal ovens.

Charcoal storage Houses, cap. 250,000 bushels.

Wharf and ore bunkers, cap. 15,000 tons ore.

Water system 1-1/2 miles long, supply one million gallons daily.

Chemical Laboratory, office, storerooms.

New, fully equipped machine shop.

Boarding house and thirty employee residences.

Five scows for transporting raw material and iron.

320 acres of ground with 1/4 mile frontage on deep water.

Under option to purchase 1,400 adjoining acres.

The steel plant would add two open hearth furnaces to produce 140 tons of steel ingots daily; a 22-inch rolling mill with continuous furnaces and attendant equipment; one 14-inch rolling mill with equipment; one nine-inch rolling mill, one Butt weld pipe mill equipped for making all sizes of pipes to three inches; and a plant for making galvanized pipe.

With the complete plant operating, the estimated annual profit on steel was $600,000. Operations would be expanded to 500 tons of steel daily within five years, with estimated earnings then of over $2,000,000.

Surely the whole plan appeared excellent and sound. However, the editor of *Pacific Builder and Engineer* was not as confident:

"There are two factors that have militated against James A. Moore, the promoter of the Irondale steel plant. They are his strong real estate proclivities—he has been long recognized as the 'wizard of the real estate field of Seattle'—and the choice of location—without railroad facilities and without an easy labor market.

"There is no doubt that the brass band heralding through the streets the sale of real estate at Irondale attracted much more attention than did the carloads of machinery and supplies accruing demurrage in the railroad yards south of the city. The profits on real estate was a bird in the hand; profits on steel were several birds in the bush."

The editor went on to declare that Moore's lack of experience in steelmaking would not necessarily be a drawback, however, since many business managers were successful in just that—*managing*—and did not have to be technicians. His main puzzlement was how Irondale was to attract workers, when there were no recreational facilities for their free days, out in the boondocks, so to speak. And " . . . no sane manufacturer with experience in interstate and international marketing would select Irondale as the ideal site for any industry depending upon other communities for supplies, labor, transportation, and the common business facilities."

Having made these gloomy pronouncements, the magazine's writers continue in the opposite vein. Irondale "stands unique in 'the romance of steel'; it is where occidental brains and Oriental ores, where American aggressiveness and Chinese passiveness meet to make steel.

"The man who undertakes and accomplishes large things is entitled to the credit for his foresight, although the knockers will say it was luck."

The reference to "Oriental ores" was because the company entered into an agreement with the Han Yeh Ping Company, Hangchow, China, for purchase of iron ore and pig iron to augment supplies at hand. The materials were hauled in Dollar Steamship Lines vessels, since Dollar was a director of Western Steel Company. The furnace was "blown in" on July 10, 1910, and steel began to pour from the hearths to the industries of the West.

The settlement of Irondale was incorporated in 1909 as a fourth-class city and attained a population of 1,500. Lots were going for $1,000 on the hill above the plant and twice that down near the Irondale plant. Lots were purchased and sold for profit within an hour. Oldtimer Judge Wingate said he bought five lots for $100 each one day and sold them the next for $500 each. At the beginning of 1910, the town had graded streets, six store and office blocks, a school, a hospital, the *Irondale News*. An array of businesses, many substantially built of brick, lined Moore Street—a paved street that led from hill to harbor. Halleum and Birmingham's dry goods store, the Luciers jewelry, Lamoreaux drugs, Learned's Port Townsend Mercantile Company (a branch store), Westerfield's Restaurant, two meat markets, and other stores served the early residents. A pink hotel was a conversation piece. Another was the pie-shaped building dubbed the Flatiron Building. Churches were under construction. The daughter of a pioneer family, Mar-

Open Hearth Furnaces–Irondale

– Photo from the collection of The Jefferson County Historical Society, Port Townsend, Washington.

garet Learned said in an interview with a *Tacoma News* reporter in June, 1968, that about 1,300 (probably more like 600 and a 1,500 total population) men worked at the steel mill during its peak. Insufficient housing caused some to live in tents, and weekends were lively in the saloons.

"There were fights almost every night," said Learned. And if a man wearied of the thirteen saloons in Irondale, there was a halfway house saloon between Irondale and Hadlock. One of the saloons, operated by Charles A. Roth, catered to only the higher-paid employees, the foremen and executives.

The steel workers, some earning the handsome wage of $20 a week, were a mixture of local people, Caucasians from the East Coast (especially Hungarian immigrants), native Americans and Chinese. The Chinese workers were housed in segregated barracks in nearby Hadlock "for their own protection," according to one newspaper. Prominent Port Townsend pioneer, James G. McCurdy, praised the Chinese for their honesty and industriousness.

Culture was not forgotten in the city. A playhouse was on the drawing board. A library was to be built. Even a monorail to link Port Townsend and Irondale was suggested. The Idle Hour Theater booked entertainment, and excursion companies offered cruises. Several physicians, including Dr. James A. Webb and Dr. Robert Hill, established practices. Hill owned and managed a three-story, well-equipped brick hospital to which the mill sent employees and their families for treatment. This service, one of the early forms of medical insurance, was available to the workers for one dollar a month dues. Hill once had tuberculosis and accepted other patients with the disease. He put them in open tents and gave them a diet stressing eggs, curing many.

For two years the town of Irondale teemed with activity. Along the 600-foot wharf large ships disgorged iron ore and pig iron from China, barges drew up to unload raw materials, and other ships hauled away the steel and iron manufactures. Coke produced on site for stoking the furnaces began to be replaced by crude oil. *Pacific Builder and Engineer* stated:

"The storage tanks for crude oil occupy the location of the old kilns. The ore and fluxes are taken to the crusher outside of the stockhouse, and reduced to suitable size, elevated and distributed to the bunker system by a bucket conveyor. It is drawn from the bunkers into wheelbarrows and transferred to the tower elevator that takes the materials to the charging floor level. The charging crew dumps the stock into the bell and hopper that close the top of the furnace and the bell is dropped at intervals which admits the material to the furnace. The furnace top is closed in order to prevent the furnace gasses from escaping into the air. . . . These gases are drawn off at the top of the furnace and piped to the boilers and stoves, and com-

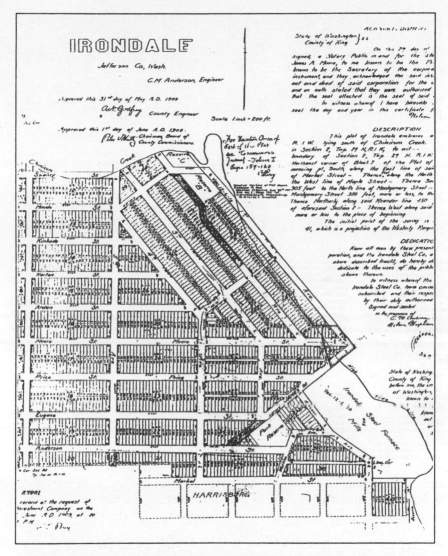

monly produce not only all the heat and power required for the blast furnace, but also furnish a portion of the power used in the rolling mills."

The charge or iron mixture was placed in the hottest part of the furnace, the tuyer zone, and reduced to a fluid. The molten materials then sank to the bottom of the furnace, commonly called the crucible or hearth, where through specific gravity, the materials sorted themselves out. The heavier iron sank to the bottom and the slags stayed on top to be drawn off through tap holes. The iron was then cast into convenient forms and transferred to

71

the steel-making section. There were two furnaces to produce steel by the open hearth process, basically a combination of iron and carbon, with minor amounts of manganese or other elements. After processing, the resultant ingots were rolled into whatever shape was desired, including rounds and squares.

Few anticipated the precipitous end of the operation, as sales were brisk, but financial problems caused the company to fail almost as suddenly as it had soared into success. The mighty Irondale plant closed in the summer of 1911, after only two lively years.

Many rumors flew as to the reason for the failure of WSC. Some quoted an officer of the company as saying that, in the Irondale operation, it cost $18 per ton to produce steel where eastern competitors were selling steel at $18. Others felt James A. Moore was distracted by his extensive real estate developments and not paying sufficient attention to supervising the Irondale plant. Still another rumor was that the United States Steel Corporation put pressure on those who held Western Steel Company's loans. Whatever the reason, the firm was unable to meet its heavy repayment schedule on those loans, and the creditors foreclosed.

Stunned employees and store owners listened to the heavy silence where the constant hum of the mill had signaled financial health for all. Among them was Win Williams, Sr., whose son still lived about two miles from the millsite in 1994. With no unemployment benefits to tide them over, workers swiftly left and store owners almost as soon. In October, 1914, a fire destroyed much of the town's main business district on the south side of Moore Street; another in December completed the job on the north side. Most were empty business buildings. Desperate homeowners turned to arson to reclaim the value of their homes. Some packed up and left furnishings behind to be picked up by the remaining residents. Roth's saloon was removed to the Georgetown district of Seattle. The bubble had burst; by the close of 1915, only about 200 residents remained.

In 1913, Pacific Coast Steel Company (PCSC) purchased the plant, dismantled some of it and hauled parts away. Heaps of raw materials lay unused on the ground and in bunkers. When World War I broke out, the demand for pig iron caused PCSC to restart the plant briefly in 1917. After renovation, about fifty men were employed and the plant turned out about 22,000 tons of pig iron in little more than a year. When the raw materials that had been stockpiled were used up, the plant quit operating on February 27, 1919. After fruitlessly searching for ways to reopen, the company gave up in December, 1919.

The blast furnace was torn down and sold for scrap. Incredibly, the large installation shown in the photos completely disappeared, leaving only foundations, some durable buildings that became homes, and a huge old

72

safe now overgrown with vines. Florence J. Judy said of Irondale in 1920, that despite the destruction from the fires, there were rows of deserted brick hotels, banks, saloons and storefronts on Moore Street. Even they were eventually torn down and the bricks sold.

A few families continued to live in the Irondale area, some working at local mills or in Port Townsend. During the late 1980s an influx of retirees or of vacation homeowners swelled the little community's rosters to join the ghosts of those who had believed that Irondale would become the "Pittsburgh of the West."

Chapter 9
PORT DISCOVERY

In the summer of 1792, Captain George Vancouver entered the quiet refuge of Discovery Bay, a deep southerly penetration of the Olympic Peninsula coastline that creates the Quimper Peninsula over which Port Townsend presides. He anchored near what later residents called Contractors Spit. At a small Indian village that Vancouver called Port Discovery, the ship's crew rested, reprovisioned, and repaired the ships—the *Discovery* captained by Vancouver and the *Chatham* by Hood—before going on to explore Puget Sound. One of Vancouver's sailors died and was buried on Protection Island. Vancouver's original journal describes at great length the flora, fauna, scenery and people of the bay.

Vancouver noted the superb forests, and it is said that he replaced an ailing spar while he was in port, and that John Meares also stopped to replace a broken spar in 1788. In his book, *The Last Wilderness*, Murray Morgan states that William Brotchie, an English captain, sailed into Discovery Bay on a Hudson's Bay Company sidewheeler, the *Beaver*, in the 1840s and noted the wealth of towering, straight evergreen trees. Later Brotchie proposed to British maritime men that they should contract with him to cut spars for the British Navy. In 1850, after he was given the job, Brotchie guided the schooner *Albion*, captained by Richard O. Hinderwell, into Discovery Bay. Brotchie hired Clallam Indians to assist in cutting spars in exchange for merchandise, after first obtaining permission from the Clallam chief known as King George. The Indians enthusiastically went to work under the direction of the ship's carpenter, William Bolton. Bolton later said that the harvesting was no easy task, for the sap "all but drowned the choppers when they got through the bark" and, even after a big tree was downed, it had to be trimmed and dragged through dense forest to the shore by sheer muscle power.

After the ship was loaded with seventeen spars up to ninety feet long, a small boat appeared flying the American flag. Identifying himself as a customs inspector for Oregon Territory, Eben May Dorr informed Brotchie and Hinderwell that they were in violation of customs regulations, rules put into effect only a month earlier. Soldiers from Fort Steilacoom came on board to enforce the command from Dorr that the *Albion* be taken into custody and sailed to Steilacoom. The federal district court in Clark County (today's Vancouver, Washington area) ordered that the ship and cargo be seized and sold. Over the British captain's protest that his ship alone was worth $50,000, it was sold at auction for $1,450. In his book, author Morgan went on to relate that the new owners sailed with a paying cargo to San Francisco and sold the boat there—undoubtedly for far more than $1,450. The incident certainly did not improve Anglo-American relations, when so very recently in 1846 the two countries finally had agreed to a boundary designation.

Across the waters of Discovery Bay John Tukey deserted from his ship that same year, while a crew was put ashore to cut wood. Tukey staked out a claim in 1857 on a picturesque, northwesterly-facing bluff across the bay, and after marrying in the early 1880s, built a rather elegant home. In 1897, the Tukeys converted the house into a resort called Saints' Rest, renamed Chevy Chase and operated from 1913 to 1946 by Mary Chase, Tukey's stepdaughter.

In 1853, the Puget Mill Company (PMC) had considered the site of George Vancouver's original landing for a mill but decided on Port Gamble, instead. The following year, William Webster, an 1853 homesteader and trading post operator, gathered several woodsmen to take up donation claims and hold the timber against PMC or other enterprises. But the Webster group never did build a mill themselves or market the land jointly, so the maneuver was useless.

Port Discovery Mill (PDM) was founded at the site of Vancouver's anchorage by San Franciscan S.B. Mastick and associates in 1858, larger

PORT DISCOVERY MILLS

and better capitalized than many area mills. It was rumored that when the millwrights searched for a foundation on which to undergird the big boilers and engines, they selected a boulder lying just offshore called Vancouver's Rock. The legend is that Vancouver's crewmen had carved their names on the rock while anchored there awaiting Vancouver's return from exploring Puget Sound. Pioneer James G. McCurdy visited there in 1936 or 1937, and found drill holes and fragments but no indication of carved names. The mill was located on Mill Point south of today's Discovery Bay Lodge.

From its excellent location near the entrance to the Strait of Juan de Fuca, the mill thrived. Until the construction of a large mill at Port Angeles, PDM was closest to the burgeoning logging industry developing around Dungeness, Port Angeles, Port Crescent, and Pysht. Coastal loggers along the Strait of Juan de Fuca dumped their logs into the sea for booming, and tugs brought them to Discovery Bay. The company also cut some of its own logs near the port. They used at least twenty teams of oxen to move logs from hill to shore and down a skid road to the mill.

For thirty prosperous years, PDM operated briskly under the Masticks and later Moore & Smith, a California firm. During its heyday in 1885, the mill was turning out large quantities of lumber to be hauled away in a reported fifty-four vessels.

Port Discovery became a boom town of at least 300 people. About fifty buildings meandered along the bluff and beach, as well as a Chinatown separated from the town by a ridge. This conclave often sheltered Chinese who had illegally entered the United States; in fact, over the years, the handy bays and coves of the area were popular with smugglers of Chinese immigrants, rum, Scotch, and whatever contraband was worth the risk.

MOORE & SMITH, PROPRIETORS.
- Photo courtesy of Port Angeles Public Library

The town had one main street running from the hotel to the store which doubled as post office and apothecary. The hotel manager, John Pugh, was so tall that he had to stoop to walk through doors. In its heyday, the general store did about $17,000 of business each month. The 500 Clallam Indians living around the bay certainly contributed to the coffers, a number of them earning wages at the mill. When they came to shop, after pulling their canoes on shore, the Indian women changed into long, western-style dresses and shoes before venturing to the store, re-donning their customary blankets when departing. On rare occasions, north coast Canadian Indians brought their fine weaving to trade.

The closest town of any size was Port Townsend; to get there one took the small launch *Fanny* across Discovery Bay, then a farm wagon "taxi." Occasionally, it was possible to take the steamer *Mastick*, much more efficient transportation.

In 1935, writer H.E. Jamison visited Port Discovery to interview Mrs. William Delanty, an eighty-six-year-old woman who had lived for sixty years in a handsome house on the high bluff overlooking the millsite. She was the daughter of Hall Davis, a Dungeness pioneer.

Like a few other early Port Discovery residents, William Delanty was a captain of large sailing vessels and, in the custom of the day, he often took his wife and children with him on voyages. They brought back treasures from the world to grace their home. Jamison described the home as " . . . a breath of yesterday. They still have the fine old furniture that was shipped from San Francisco when the house was new. The skin of a wildcat is draped over the back of an old-fashioned chair. It was killed just outside their yard. The daughter has a priceless collection of Indian baskets and relics . . . [including] a primitive tool used by the Indians for hollowing out logs for canoes. It was made of an old file, cut in two and sharpened at one end . . . A short handle, made from the crotch of a limb was fastened athwartships to the file with rawhide." Jamison pronounced it the perfect tool. Upon the closure of the PDM, Delanty became the caretaker of the millsite.

During its operation the consulting engineer for the mill was a San Franciscan named Chapman, who doubled as engineer on the steamer *Mastick*. His daughter, Elizabeth Chapman Davidson of Menlo Park, California, later related the romance of Discovery Bay, filled with sailing ships from all parts of the world. She said in a reminiscence: " . . . to sit on the edge of the hill and watch the loading and hear the chanties when the capstan was manned was something not easily, if at all, to be found today. When ships from the Hawaiian Islands came in the sailors would toss cocoanuts overboard and they would drift to the beach where the older children would salvage them and then have a terrible time getting the tough outer covering off. I only hung around in hope." A favorite sailing ship was the *Dashing Wave*, and sometimes Elizabeth and her mother were invited to tea with the captain's wife.

Everyone attended any social event, most held at a community hall. Fourth of July celebrations usually included a flag-raising, speeches, fireworks and trying to catch a greased pig, according to Mrs. Davidson. She remembered seeing a performance of "Uncle Tom's Cabin" at the community hall, in which a contraption hauled the actress playing Little Eva up into the air.

Davidson also saw the ship *War Hawk* drift away from the Discovery wharf after catching fire on April 12, 1883. The company vessel carried lumber between Port Discovery and San Francisco. It was a large ship of 1,067 tons, 182 feet long, with a thirty-five-foot beam. While most of the crew was carousing in a local saloon, a fire suddenly broke out aboard. To avoid setting fire to the wharf and settlement, Captain Commo cut the mooring lines. As it drifted slowly out in the bay and sank, Commo and his remaining crew abandoned ship. Later, under the supervision of Captain T.P. Whitelaw of San Francisco a crew came to attempt salvage by affixing pontoons to the hull. The ship was refloated successfully but, on closer inspection little remained usable of either the cargo or the ship itself, and it was allowed to sink again, virtually a total loss to its owners. For years it was a mecca for scuba divers, as it lay in eight fathoms of water, readily accessible. Not much remains today, although for years its charred masts were visible at low tide.

Meanwhile, smuggling continued unabated. With Canadian waters just across the Strait, a fast sailboat or clever operator of low-lying canoes with muffled paddles or oars could easily elude the smattering of revenue officers. It was said the mill owners themselves encouraged acquisition of mill workers through smugglers. The customs collectors operating out of Port Townsend were well aware that smuggling continued, but were baffled as to how to catch the perpetrators. Routinely they checked steamers coming to Port Discovery from Canadian waters, looking for temporary partitioning or compartments secured to the keel underwater. Smaller boats were harder to check. Customs collector M.J. Carrigan had a running battle with a nefarious smuggler named Jammeson until he quit the customs service in disgust.

The unguarded border also offered refuge to criminals. Author Ruby El Hult in a book, *Lost Mines and Treasures,* tells of a possible buried treasure dating back to 1864, when a British Columbia railroad paymaster embezzled over $60,000 in gold sovereigns. Supposedly he hauled the money in a chest by canoe into Discovery Bay and showed up at Tukey's door to borrow a horse. At Port Townsend the mystery man boarded a ship bound for Olympia but was apprehended and jailed. Although the man never revealed where he had buried the chest, treasure hunters have searched periodically for it along the beaches of Discovery Bay.

Mill owners Moore and Smith apparently prospered in Washington Territory, although they reduced the scale of operations in 1888. Three years later, they went into bankruptcy through failure of California interests—sinking PDM, too, in process. Timber holdings eventually were sold to the Simpson Logging Company.

Nothing whatever remains of the PDM site today, although in a nearby cemetery one might find the names of interesting pioneers and those of sailors who died far from home.

In the late 1920s and early 1930s activity flared briefly after the Port Angeles and Southern Railroad made Port Discovery a stop, actually at the small settlement of Fairmont on the bay). Carlsborg author Harriet U. Fish says that the old roadbed for the railroad was placed neatly, layer upon layer, by Oriental workmen and many portions are still in place along the bay.

In 1930, a mining venture flared briefly—the Discovery Bay 19 Mine, managed by T.B. Purviance. The author examined a stock certificate and wonders if the mine was a total scam, since it required a dollar a month (equivalent to perhaps $20 today) to be paid into the enterprise by each interested person. Cryptic news items from the *Port Townsend Leader* followed progress at the mine:

Feb. 10, 1930:

"INJURED AT WORK AT LOCAL MINE. Discovery Bay 19 mine at the head of Discovery Bay met with the 3rd and most serious accident. William Clipps suffered a smashed wrist working with machinery. Work in progress at the mine at this time includes the structure of the housing for the cage for the down shaft which will be started immediately after the timber work is completed. . . . Work has been hindered in the past months because of frozen pipes. T.B. Purviance states work will go ahead now as fast as possible."

For a time the state contended that some of the mine buildings were located on the road right of way, but the question seems to have been settled.

April 3, 1930:

"DISCOVERY 19 MINE IN OPERATION AGAIN. Credit for resumption of mine operation goes to Mr. Sims. Mr. Purviance says at least $50,000 will be spent this year. The shaft, 8' x 10', is down to 61 feet. It will be put down to 100 and another shaft started from there. The mine is on a pay as you go basis with no encumberances [sic]. As soon as they get low grade ore containing 20% manganese, they have a promise of a 60 Ton smelter."

August 14, 1930.

"WORK RESUMED AT DISCOVERY BAY '19' MINE. Work was

stopped some 6 weeks ago because of water problems in the 115' shaft. A new pump has been purchased which will discharge water at 184 gallons per minute."

Adding fuel to the scam theory are reminiscences from Port Hadlock resident Melvin Kivley. In his book, *Hadlock Hill*, he tells of receiving the manager of the mine, Dan Porter, at his home. Kivley simply was interested in hearing the man's proposition and soon found that Porter was "letting a few people have a chance to invest in Discovery Bay Mine Nineteen." Porter stated that the cookhouse, dining hall and bunkhouse were completed, that machinery was installed and that a tunnel was partially built. But now he needed "a little extra capital for a narrow gauge track for transporting the rich ore out to the jaws of the waiting crusher. The bonds are called grubstakes. They range down as low as ten cents each for children to buy. It will help with their education later in their young happy lives."

Kivley and his wife, operators of a secondhand store, enjoyed the pitch but were extremely dubious. They agreed to have dinner at the mine, however. The two shortly went to the mine site near the hamlet of Fairmont and were shown around the site by Porter, but bought no grubstakes. When other grubstake purchasers began to suspect fraud, however, they called for an investigation, but not before Porter left town abruptly. A geologist hired to examine the mine found no sign of minerals.

In 1935, Andrew Johnson and Charles Gunstone, partners, bought Simpson Logging Company's acres on Discovery Bay, which included two miles of shoreline and the old millsite, and dumped logs into the bay. The partners leased (free) the old Delanty house, part of the property, to house soldiers during World War II. The handsome dwelling burned during the soldiers' occupation. Some time later Johnson and Gunstone discontinued logging and turned to commercial clamming on their extensive beachlands.

Locating a bit south of the PDM properties, the colorful and successful logger, Stillman C. "Stim" Brown, operated the Brown Pole & Piling Company prior to 1940, stripping cedar logs for pilings and power poles. In 1940, he opened a saw mill and sold it to the Bay Veneer Mill in 1960. Brown reassumed the property from Bay Veneer later and went on with the business until 1965, when failing health caused him to quit and sell his equipment. The pilings and dilapidated building visible at the head of the bay are the remains of that operation.

Today no real town exists, either as Port Discovery, Discovery Bay, Fairmont or Maynard. Only a tavern, store, motel, and a few buildings straggle along the curve of the bay. The location's main importance is the junction of Highway 101 with the road to Port Townsend.

81

Chapter 10

PORT HADLOCK

Samuel Hadlock, for whom Port Hadlock is named, was an adventurer, prominent pioneer of the Olympic Peninsula, investor and real estate developer. Born in 1829 in New Hampshire, he came west on a wagon train to The Dalles, Oregon, in September, 1852. He moved south to join the last gasps of the California gold rush but returned to Portland empty-handed the following spring. After working at construction of a sawmill on Shoalwater Bay in 1854, he became footloose again, mining the Oregon beach sands.

Returning to San Francisco, he found his niche as a promoter and dealer in mining stocks, and also sold lumber in San Francisco until 1868, when he and five others built the Tacoma Mill (TM) in Washington, with Hadlock supervising it until 1870.

That fall, after selling his interest in the TM, he purchased the present site of Port Hadlock—362 acres of prime land and a good port—and platted the area. He was associated in the enterprise with Stephen S. Glidden. While records are not very clear, it appears that Glidden then established a small or portable sawmill on the site, probably known as Western Mill and Lumber Company. An oldtimer remembered her father saying there was a saloon and cookhouse at the site around 1870, as well as the mill. A short news item in a Port Townsend newspaper mentioned a ship taking on a cargo from the Glidden mill in 1871.

Apparently Hadlock remained in the vicinity to develop his new town and other properties that included a profitable gravel pit between Hadlock and Port Townsend. He was widowed on June 7, 1873, at the time of or soon after the birth of his son Nathan, whom he raised at Port Hadlock. Port Hadlock oldtimers talk of a later Mrs. Hadlock but Hadlock signed an affidavit on June 13, 1910, stating that he had been a widower since June 7, 1873.

On August 4, 1879, together with several other landowners, Hadlock deeded certain lands to the Puget Sound Iron Company (PSIC) "provided that the said Puget Sound Iron Company shall construct or cause to be constructed upon the land herein after mentioned and described a furnace for smelting iron ore of a capacity of at least 5 tons per day and a suitable wharf." He later sold them further lands along the beach for railroad access. (See chapter on Irondale.)

A real opportunity for Hadlock resulted from a disaster, the burning of the Washington Mill Company's (WMC) property at Seabeck in 1884 or 1885. Without delay, Samuel Hadlock traveled to see W.J. Adams in San Francisco, head office of the WMC, to see if the firm might move operations to Port Hadlock, where he still retained extensive lands south of Irondale. A deal was concluded, and WMC either absorbed Glidden's existing small mill or opened a new one; Glidden's operation disappears from history. Dates for WMC's opening range from 1886 to 1889, more likely the former.

The mill was built on a narrow spit reaching into Port Townsend Bay. The long building fronted on deep water, while the rear projected on pilings over a natural, shallower millpond for storing logs. The lovely harbor and dock could accommodate seven sailing ships at once for loading, and, at the southern end of Port Townsend Bay, only a rare blow could disturb its calm.

Most of the Seabeck mill workers moved to Port Hadlock with their families as soon as facilities were available. WMC erected two rows of

Hadlock Mill.
— Photo from the collection of The Jefferson County Historical Society,
Port Townsend, Washington.

houses on the hill above the beach for its workers in 1890 and 1891. Rodney Kendrick was the first supervisor of the mill, followed by Edward Presbury Blake on February 1, 1890. Blake was sent from San Francisco by President W.J. Adams—who, incidentally, was the father of renowned photographer, Ansel Adams. The Blakes built a fine two-story home overlooking the port. It had to be replaced in 1898; during a chicken-snatching, thieves dropped a match on the adjacent henhouse floor, burning down the henhouse and the Blake's home.

As the mill began operating, teenager Nathan Hadlock was fascinated by the comings and goings of the sailing ships. During the visit of a British ship in the spring of 1889, Nathan became friendly with a nineteen-year-old cabin boy, Alexander Petere. On May 3, the two youths were playing with a gun, opening and closing the lock and playfully pointing it at each other, when in the hands of Hadlock, the gun discharged and killed Petere. The shocked and saddened populace buried the victim at the Irondale Cemetery, now gone (the headstones of Petere and others moved to the Chimacum cemetery). Nathan Hadlock, who must have been the center of life to his widowed father, was nonetheless sent to stay with New England relatives. The banishment and lack of support from his father devastated the boy and he disappeared in 1893, never to be located again. Before he vanished, he signed a quit claim deed in Carroll County, New Hampshire, releasing to his father his future interest in the land around Port Hadlock. Samuel Hadlock thereafter became withdrawn and brusk, a tall, thin figure in a swallowtail coat, wandering around Port Hadlock, absorbed in his real estate and mill interests but smiling seldom and making few friends. He followed up any clue that surfaced as to his son's whereabouts.

Hadlock's business interests prospered, lumber mill, gravel works, and real estate. The mill had its own tugs, two of which were the *Toby* and the *Richard Holyoke*. In the earliest days of sawmilling, each mill maintained a tug near the entrance and aggressively competed for the job of towing it to its destination, while the incoming sailboat hove to, a bad practice since the Strait's waters often were turbulent. In March, 1891, a tugboat pool was formed by several of the larger mills, a sensible move that assured one tug always was on hand at the mouth of the Strait of Juan de Fuca to meet incoming lumber carriers (sailing vessels). WMC assigned its tug *Holyoke* for this task. The cooperative effort resulted in greater efficiency and cost control for all.

The town expanded on the flats adjacent to the mill and straggled up the bluffs. William Eldridge opened a livery stable and James Eldridge a barber shop. The company built bunkhouses and a cookhouse for the millworkers. William Niemeyer opened the Commercial Hotel, and a former Seabeck mill man, Humphrey Oldfield, operated Hadlock House. An uni-

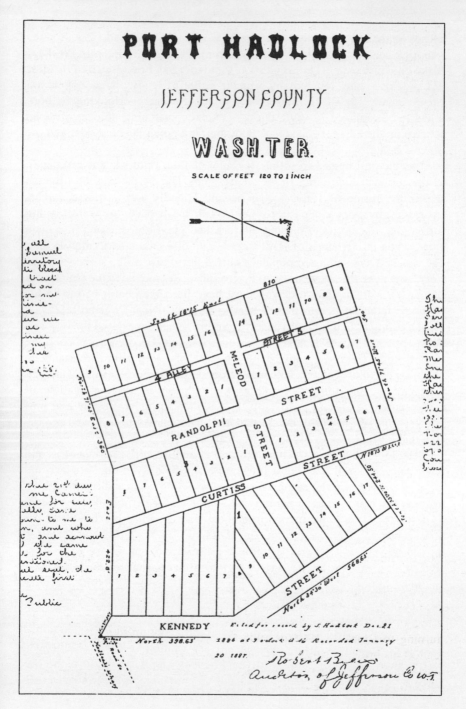

PORT HADLOCK

JEFFERSON COUNTY

WASH. TER.

SCALE OF FEET 120 TO 1 INCH

KENNEDY

Filed for record by S Hadlock Dec 21 1886 at 9 o'clock A M Recorded January 20 1887.

Robert Byers Auditor of Jefferson Co W T

North 398.65'

dentified man started a third hotel known later as the Galster House, in which Samuel Hadlock lived.

Margaret Forwood said in a 1968 article for the *Port Townsend Leader*: "If it is true that Mr. Hadlock had the house [or hotel] built, it is obvious that he hired a forgetful carpenter. The route to the bathroom, which this unsung artisan devised, is not for anyone in a hurry. It involves opening a door, stepping onto an outside balcony and crossing over to a door on the opposite side. Fortunately the Hadlocks were of hardy New England stock. This must have sustained them during many a chilly marathon."

In addition to the neat homes of the general work force, mill owners built camps for about two dozen Japanese workers, a house for Chinese workers, and a settlement largely native American. The various segments of society seem to have gotten along well enough. The most memorable Clallam Indian worker was Young Patsey, who worked diligently until he had enough money saved up to give a magnificent potlatch, then started saving for the next one.

Many workers were of Scandinavian descent; some were sailors who jumped ship at Port Hadlock. As many as forty longshoremen unloaded visiting ships, these single men (mostly) living at the Commercial Hotel. Visiting sailors tended to patronize the Hadlock Hotel and inter-hotel brawls were common on Saturday nights, raging on since the nearest police were at Port Townsend, twelve miles distant. Combatants would swing wildly at each other after falling to their knees, then make up and resume drinking.

The Commercial Hotel's bartender sympathized with the indigent. The hotel was on pilings, and the kitchen sink simply dumped into the bay. At low tide, men waited below the bar with buckets while the bartender left the beer spigot running to drain down to them.

The chief supply store and meat market, also the cookhouse, was run by a popular Chinese, Joe Wah. He first came to Port Hadlock about 1890, returning to China in 1904 or 1905 to collect his bride. According to Chinese custom, Wah kept his wife in total seclusion for the first year, then she be-

Hadlock House.
– *Photo from the collection of The Jefferson County Historical Society, Port Townsend, Washington.*

came "as American as I am," said pioneer Margaret Learned. The Wah family lived well, raised several children, and were well liked in the community.

In 1892, Hadlock leased land to Newman and Tobey for shipbuilding and boat ways. In 1900, William Sehrs opened another shipyard, sending tugs, barges and ferries down the ways. One of his small ferries, the *Nordland*, served nearby Indian Island for years and then hauled supplies to isolated islands in the San Juan Islands well in the 1990s.

The mill was the largest single mill in existence then, according to Guy Clawson, another pioneer, single mill meaning they used only one headsaw. The mill turned out an average of 150,000 board feet of lumber a day. Big customers were the constructors of Fort Worden, Fort Casey and Fort Flagler. Tugs towed rafts to many Sound towns and, as mentioned earlier, lumber ships regularly came to haul the product off to California and beyond. The mill employed several hundred men, and the town numbered perhaps 600-700 in its heyday. But when prices for lumber fell sharply, WMC closed October 10, 1907. Management declared it would reopen again March 1, 1910, and it was leased to the Charles Nelson Company of San Francisco; however, the mill operated for only another year, then closed forever. Samuel Hadlock's investments in real estate were doomed to decline.

For the last three years of his life, Samuel Hadlock followed up rumors from here and there of his son's whereabouts. On one occasion, he went to San Francisco to board a ship for South America, having heard that his son was seen there. However, the sad old man, past eighty years old, became ill and returned to Port Hadlock. He drew up his will on April 15, 1910, leaving everything to his son if he should surface, and otherwise to his relatives. He died September 15, 1912, at Nashua, New Hampshire, at the age of eighty-three.

By June 10, 1913, the Miller Machine Company of Seattle dismantled and removed the machinery of WMC, leaving only hollow, echoing rooms. Soon afterward the structure went up in a spectacular blaze. Nearby residents feared their homes would go, too, but the fire was confined to the mill, which blazed and smoldered for three days. A nearby office and a commissary survived and was used as a store and post office until 1958.

After the mill closed first in 1907, W.J. Adams, San Francisco investor and president of the WMC, turned to a new venture nearby, at the foot of the bay. He secured manufacturing rights for a patent developed by the Classen Chemical Company (CCC), a French firm, for distilling alcohol from sawdust. In 1909, he hired a crew to build the manufacturing plant, also to be named CCC but, before the plant was completed, Adams died in 1910. His son Charles went on with the project, soliciting investment among

Classen Chemical Plant.
– Photo from the collection of The Jefferson County Historical Society,
Port Townsend, Washington.

the local people. Many residents responded, including Joe Wah, who moved his cookhouse or restaurant near the new plant.

The manufacturing plant of concrete, tile and steel included huge vats or boilers for processing the material and yards of pipes and ducts. Immigrant Bruce Matheson from Canada, only nineteen years old but experienced in concrete work, was made construction foreman. His training must have been excellent, for the building is in top condition yet today.

With an endless supply of sawdust available from forest industries nearby, a splendid harbor to house visiting ships, ample water to cool the fermenters and supply the condensers in the steam plant, and a willing labor supply, prospects seemed excellent. The Hadlock plant and one in Oregon became the only western alcohol producers of the time. The *Port Townsend Leader* reported on March 29, 1911, "Two products will comprise the principal output of the works of the Classen Chemical company, alcohol and a new stock food called bastol. The alcohol is by the process of the company rendered free from poison and fully equal to grain alcohol. Two internal revenue inspectors will be stationed at the plant continuously, quarters having been already prepared for these officials."

The Bergius Process used was developed from the work of Louis Pasteur. The French had great experience with yeast cultures and chemistry, and the Classen plant at Port Hadlock was managed by a Frenchman.

The process began with wood waste, which was shredded into chips or already existent as sawdust, then dried in a steam dryer until it contained no more than one per cent moisture. The dried wood was mixed with cold 40% hydrochloric acid. The resultant cellulose was converted to glucose, a process known as saccarification. Then a byproduct called lignin was extracted. A mixture of glucose and acid was moved to an evaporator, where the acid was recovered and reused. Fresh supplies of acid were made from a mixture of salt and sulfuric acid in stone tanks.

The sugar rich solution then was introduced into fermentation tanks. Special yeast was incubated and grown at the plant by a biologist, similar to today's brewmaster. The sugar/wood in the fermenting tanks, known as wort, was inoculated with the yeast strains, producing a liquid of eight per cent alcohol.

At this stage, the product was eminently intoxicating and drinkable. Workmen went to great lengths to smuggle it out in their lunch buckets or other ingenious devices, or to have a drink or two on the job, despite stern precautions.

The liquid was moved to a distillery section. The distillation yielded fusil oils, 190 proof (95%) industrial ethyl alcohol, and more residue.

The residue was combined with molasses to make bastol, a nutritious cattle feed tried out on local herds before marketing it elsewhere. The entire initial output of the plant, both for alcohol and bastol, was contracted for prior to its manufacture. The future looked rosy.

The two and three-story plant bustled as operations began. Conveyor belts transported sawdust from barge to bunker. From the bunkers it was dropped into the vats called digestors to initiate the process described above. The residue went to a second building to be mixed with molasses delivered by C & H Sugar Company of Hawaii.

Barges and ships transferred the cattle feed to warehouses all over the west. Then came the unexpected. While local cattle had eaten the fresh bastol during tests, cattle elsewhere did not like the stored stuff. While the market languished, the bastol piled up and molded quickly, a real mess.

First shipments of the wood alcohol also were unsatisfactory, and all 300 barrels were returned to Classen for refinement. The alcohol was redistilled and accepted by customers.

The Classen plant introduced molasses into the fermenters, a change that they hoped would let them avoid paying patent rights fees to the process patent holders. Competitors noted that the Bergius process could be used to produce refined sugar from wood, a threat to sugar beet and sugar cane growers. The French proceeded to remove their equipment, and—it is rumored—C&HSC saw no reason to deliver molasses or sugar if Classen was going to become a sugar-producing competitor. Since all supplies had to be delivered by water, production costs were said to be higher than for plants situated near a railroad. For all of these reasons and high production costs compared to that of entrenched Eastern and San Francisco manufacturers, the CCC ceased operation in 1913, after less than three years of operation. The unexpected closure of the half million dollar plant left local stockholders (including pioneer Joe Wah) bereft of return on their investments.

Locals were not the only losers. In the 1930s, some distant stock firm sold stock in the alcohol plant to unsuspecting investors. Port Hadlock resident Melvin Kivley encountered one such stockholder in 1934, wandering the streets to locate the CCC. Upon learning the plant had been inactive for many years, he was understandably upset.

A few others tried to set up manufacturing in the fine building, including one company that attempted to produce red dye for automobile tires by grinding up red rocks.

On the spit where WMC stood, the Guilford Clam Cannery Company established a clam farm during the years following World War I that lasted only a few years. The company used the Commercial Hotel as its offices. The next tenant at the spit was the B.O. Kem fertilizer factory, with management quarters at the Commercial Hotel. The WMC, still owner of some property in Port Hadlock, was delighted to sell the Kem Company old employees' houses for about $25 each in these, the Depression years. The Kem Company then loaded the homes on scows and transported them to Alki Point in Seattle to be remodeled into pleasant homes. When the Kem Fertilizer business closed, too, the Commercial Hotel was razed. The Hadlock House was demolished in the 1920s.

Finally the alcohol plant machinery was sold for scrap and the building stood vacantly staring over the bay. In 1979, Ray Hansen purchased the old alcohol plant to convert it to a marina and first-class hotel/resort. The concrete structure lent itself to remodeling in a vaguely Spanish California style. Vestiges of the manufacturing plant were retained for historic interest. The first major event was held in the refurbished building on August 23, 1986. With conference rooms and full facilities, the handsome Port Hadlock Inn operates at this writing in the original CCC plant with the ghosts of past uses cherished.

The population of Port Hadlock declined sharply with the loss of its businesses. In 1934, Win Williams, Sr., and David Bengtson purchased much of "Lower Hadlock," including the defunct Sehrs shipyard and the old Galster House. Over the ensuing years several new small businesses opened along the waterfront; one was a factory producing oakum for ship caulking. For a time Wilson Rutter was the owner of some of the original Port Hadlock, about eight homes and an undetermined number of business buildings along the bluff. These, too, disappeared, one by one. By 1957, the remaining structures near the mill were gone, demolished, sold or moved.

Today the only reminders of the once-thriving town of Port Hadlock or Lower Hadlock, to be exact (as a new business center has recently arisen a few blocks from the beach) are the Ajax Cafe in the former Galster House, former dwelling of Samuel Hadlock, which is well-preserved, the millpond, and the reincarnation of the alcohol plant as a fine hotel. A few ancient stray logs, water-saturated and decaying, remain in the old mill pond to help one remember that Port Hadlock was once the site of a large and prosperous mill and a lively town.

Chapter 11

PORT LUDLOW

On Port Ludlow Bay off Admiralty Strait about sixteen miles south of Port Townsend, one of the Northwest's largest lumber mills operated for almost a century, closing at the end of 1935. The town that grew up around it swelled and declined in relation to the output of the mill.

It is impossible to talk about Port Ludlow without including Port Gamble at the eastern end of today's Hood Canal Bridge, about eight water-miles away, for the two mills (and most of the two towns) were owned by the same company, Pope and Talbot (P&T). Port Gamble is not a ghost town today, as its population has changed little and a large P&T mill still operates there; however, it certainly is historic. Port Ludlow, however, does not exist as a town; in its place is the splendid four-star Resort at Port Ludlow, also owned by P&T.

Port Ludlow Bay was named by Commander Charles Wilkes to honor a sailor killed in battle, Augustus C. Ludlow. In its heyday Port Ludlow had as many as 600 or 700 residents, most of them working for or connected with the mill's operation.

The bay came to the attention of Andrew J. Pope and William C. Talbot of East Machias, Maine, who also had offices in San Francisco, California, in the mid-1800s. Talbot was an experienced ship captain, Pope a businessman. The two men from prominent construction and shipbuilding families had come to San Francisco in 1849 to become involved in business. Intrigued by the tales of giant trees in the Northwest, they decided to open a major mill before ever seeing the country. The two entrepreneurs organized the Puget Mill Company (PMC) for the "purpose of manufacturing Lumber in the Territory of Oregon at Puget Sound," with thirty shares of capital stock at $1,000 a share, or $30,000. Twenty shares went to Pope and Talbot, and ten jointly to Captain J.P. Keller and Charles Foster, all families joined in shipbuilding at East Machias, Maine. These transactions were completed in Maine, while the men were there retrieving families (and in Pope's case, gaining one for he married at the time) and planning for the move to the Northwest. The new associates also inspected with approval the ship *L.P. Foster*, soon off the ways and destined for the new enterprise. Indeed, her value constituted most of Keller and Foster's investment in the company. Keller was assigned to completely outfit the ship, load supplies, and sail around the Horn to Puget Sound.

With the methodical planning that was to mark the management of P&T, Talbot rounded up a skilled mill crew to take along to the West, loaded supplies on the ship *Julius Pringle,* including a few thousand feet of sawn boards to build housing for the men in Puget Sound, and departed June, 1853. On board was a new acquaintance, Cyrus Walker from Maine, an ex-schoolteacher and surveyor.

After a month's stop in San Francisco, Talbot in the *Pringle* arrived in the Strait of Juan de Fuca in July, viewing with amazement the lush stands of giant timber along the shores. He searched for a protected, deep-water harbor close to the Strait, first stopping at Discovery Bay, a promising site, but he wanted to explore the area more thoroughly. While the large ship swung at anchor, Talbot, Cyrus Walker and others set off in a smaller sailboat and a canoe. When they put into Port Ludlow's sunny bay, they found W.P. Sayward, also from Maine, already building a mill at the site. The party looked at other bays and agreed on Port Gamble, then called Teekalet by the Indians. Without delay, Talbot moved the large ship and put the crew to work building shelters at Port Gamble.

It was important to intercept the *L.P. Foster,* to tell Captain Keller where to go, but no one knew when that ship would appear. Talbot went to Seattle, loaded pilings aboard the *Pringle* to sell in San Francisco, and hastened toward the Strait of Juan de Fuca. Incredibly, he encountered the *Foster* just entering Puget Sound and directed her to Teekalet. So began P&T's grand milltown of Port Gamble, soon to be associated with Port Ludlow.

Meantime, Captain William F. Sayward with partner J.E. Thorndyke completed their mill at Port Ludlow, the first in Jefferson County. The output only averaged 3,000 board feet daily, but small sailboats moved the lumber to a ready market around Puget Sound, a place of immense forests but few boards. Occasionally the firm shipped lumber to San Francisco, where the price was attractive—$100 per 1,000 feet skyrocketing to $300 later.

The small Sayward & Thorndyke mill was fraught with mechanical breakdowns that restricted its output. James G. McCurdy in *By Juan de Fuca's Strait* quoted the bookkeeper, James Seavey, October 10, 1854: "This is a record of break-downs. Getting ready to start up early tomorrow by pumping water into the boilers and stuffing them with bread and potatoes. Although a bookkeeper, I have served in all capacities. Engineer worked on pipes till 12 at night, which seem continually breaking. As soon as one is mended another is discovered. Mill idle and dull as the devil—and cold, too."

He went on to report that he heard heavy guns firing in the distance November 22. This proved to be the battleship *Massachusetts*, which came to the rescue of Port Gamble when a party of warlike Canadian Indians from the Stikine River came to assess the strength of the Port Gamble contingent and menaced the residents. Sayward's millworkers were little concerned, because they had formed alliances with the local Indians and thus could call for help, if necessary. McCurdy mentioned that bookkeeper Seavey's small son was a favorite of the Indians—to the extent that he went off with the Indians on one occasion and had to be tracked down by his worried parents.

In 1858, for unexplained reasons, Sayward rented the mill to Arthur Phinney, Zachariah Amos and William Hooke, operating as Amos, Phinney & Co., for $500 a month. Output was increased to 60,000 feet per day and, over a period of time, Phinney bought out his partners. Unfortunately, he died May 28, 1877. The executors of his will found it difficult to get the estate probated quickly, and the mill stood idle. In November, 1878, the mill site and buildings were to be auctioned off. At first, P&T seemed uninterested.

With more than enough business for all, competition among mills around the Sound was quite amiable. P&T had expanded dramatically, with two mills at Port Gamble shipping fifty million feet of lumber in 1877, running one mill at night part of the time. The company had acquired an interest in or ownership of tugs and sailing vessels. In the early 1860s P&T were foresighted in starting to acquire timberlands against the time when the supply of purchased logs might be insufficient to keep mills operating. In March, 1877, the PMC purchased the Cranney and Grannan mill on Camano Island at Utsalady. Therefore, when the Port Gamble property was advertised, Andrew Pope was dubious about further expansion, writing to William Talbot (who was then in New York) that "Ludlow Mill to be sold Nov. 7. If you wish to buy say so. I think we have mills enough."

Talbot sent word to buy, and the PMC bought the Port Ludlow operation for $64,850. Pope died in 1878 and Talbot succeeded him as President. Upon Talbot's death in 1881, C.F.A. Talbot served as president until about 1900 (C.F.A. was Talbot's nephew, son of his brother Frederic).

At the time of Phinney's death, he had been engaged in drastic new expansion. The Port Ludlow mill lay idle for awhile, though, while PMC was busy remodeling the Utsalady operation. The idleness was also due to a glut of logs. A marketing organization of mill owners called Pacific Pine Company, which acted as a sales representative in San Francisco, parceled out orders among member mills. When sales were down, member mills were asked to run shorter times or even shut down for periods, for which they were subsized. This seems to have been the case for the non-operation of PMC at Port Ludlow some of the time between 1878 and 1883; the owners were paid $900 a month not to operate. But eventually PMC (which had become a corporation October 20, 1874) completed work on the Port Ludlow mill, opening it again in October, 1883. It was equipped with fine new machinery and, according to an 1885 manuscript, employed about 120 men and turned out at least 125,000 feet of lumber daily.

The plant must have been one of the first to have arc lights in 1884. Cyrus Walker, then a major stockholder and general manager of the Puget Sound properties, was exceptionally careful about fires, which destroyed so many mills. He required sweeping of cross-beams to free them of sawdust overhead, careful disposal of trash, and soon installed incandescent lighting to replace the customary lighting by teakettle lamps, which had a wick and were fueled by smelly dogfish oil, highly flammable. With arc or incandescent lights, PMC never suffered a serious mill fire.

By 1885, at least 350 people lived at Port Ludlow served by stores, post office, telegraph office, express office, school and the Phoenix Hotel, owned and operated by H. D. Attridge. The settlement was connected to Port Townsend by wagon road through the Chimacum Valley and received daily mail deliveries by steamer.

The wharf extended into such deep water that seagoing vessels could rest a few yards from shore. A unique advantage of the Port Ludlow Bay

Puget Mill Company, Third Street, Port Ludlow, Washington.
– Photo from the collection of The Jefferson County Historical Society,
Port Townsend, Washington.

was that a large fresh water stream emptied in from the west, diluting the salt water enough that teredos or sea worms dropped away, freeing the pilings and stored logs of this pest, common among mill ports. The harbor was a forest of masts—clippers, barkentines, schooners and smaller sailboats. The arrival in port of a new vessel could result in the challenge by the best fighter of the ship to challenge the best fighter of the longshore crew—to the evident entertainment of all residents, especially small boys, such as renowned author Archie Binns. Born and raised at Port Ludlow, Binns told of the excitement of maritime life and of the harbor close-packed with booms and crowded with vessels.

The port not only hosted ships; it created them. Between 1874 and 1880, Hall Brothers (HB) turned out thirty-one ocean vessels at Port Ludlow, most of them under 200 tons. HB moved to Port Blakely in 1880 to continue building ships, but P&T retained the facilities at Port Ludlow to build vessels for its own use.

The 694-ton bark *Kitsap*, the first large vessel built at Port Ludlow, was supervised by a shipwright named Beaton hired by Cyrus Walker of PMC. Walker was not a sailing man but he vicariously loved sailboats and watched the progress of this first Puget Mill-owned lumber carrier like a father supervising a son. In *Time, Tide, and Timber* Walker is quoted as reporting to Talbot about her launching December 21, 1881, "She glided gracefully into her native element amid the cheers of quite a party from Gamble. If her future is as successful as her launching we shall have no occasion to regret her construction. She is the *boss* vessel, and I think you will be proud of her." PMC went on to commission several more vessels; the only other two built at Ludlow, though, were the barkentine *Skagit* and a schooner *Kitsap* to replace the bark *Kitsap* lost at sea.

A big celebration commemorated the launching of the company's first tug, the 140-foot *Tyee*, a coal-burner. Both mills closed for the day, July 22, 1884, so that employees could come to the event. The cookhouse provided dinner, and the company rolled out kegs of beer. A baseball game between Port Ludlow and Port Gamble drew emotional spectators. Employees participated in foot races but no dances were scheduled, because Walker did not want his workmen half asleep the following work day.

Archie Binns wrote of a famous P&T tug that came into the Port Ludlow harbor: The *Polly* "was a lean, grim-looking craft slung low between her powerful paddle wheels, and strangers wondered at the big brass cannon on her foredeck. The *Polly's* real name was *Polikofsky*. She had been built as a Russian Imperial Navy ship and thrown in with Alaska when the United States bought that great country." (From *The Roaring Land*.)

Considering Walker's concern about fire, it is ironic that his own home in Port Gamble burned in 1885. Thereafter he decided to move to Port Ludlow and leave E.G. Ames to manage the Port Gamble mills. At age fifty-eight, he had married Emily Talbot, thirty-seven-year-old daughter of William, and they had a child, Talbot Walker. Forthright Cyrus Walker was ready to enjoy social life. He completed a new home at Port Ludlow in 1887, a mansion really, in a style akin to ship construction. Doors slid open, instead of swung. A grand staircase ascended from the entrance hall, which resembled the interior of a ship, giving rise to the home's name, Admiralty Hall. The two-story building had a square, third-story cupola above the entrance. The finest of furnishings were fashioned for the home, including handmade pieces of black walnut brought from Maine. Walker installed a cannon on the lawn to salute arriving ships and honor holidays like the Fourth of July. When Walker entered business guests, the cuisine equalled that of any fine hotel. He planted exotic trees from abroad and hard maples and cherry trees from Maine, laid out a croquet court, and maintained a small zoo. It included a little black bear and a fawn. The final touches of elegance and protection were two handsome, enormous Great Dane dogs.

The next few years were halcyon times at Port Ludlow. Executives who could afford to do so built other nice homes north of Admiralty Hall, Victorian affairs with bay windows and broad verandas. Several boardwalked streets, trees along the margins, spread from the bayfront. Social events would bring out fashionable dresses for the ladies and elegant suits for men. Some wares came from far places, the ports to which PMC shipped its lumber. Even though the towns of Port Ludlow and Port Gamble were not isolated for the times, with frequent steamer service to Seattle and elsewhere on the Sound (25 cents was the fare to Seattle), daily life centered around one's home. Enlivening the evenings were card parties, parlor games, music recitals, and a Shakespeare Club. Medicine shows promoting miracle cures came by occasionally, and movies were shown once weekly.

The working families did not live in such style, but did have decent homes, emergency assistance and medical help, the fun of company parties, and plenty to eat. Transients lived in company housing. All children attended school, and nothing barred a qualified workman's son from advancing into management.

On one Fourth of July picnic held on the bluff above town, the workmen dragged in a donkey engine from the woods. Residents had built a turntable and benches, the logging operator attached a cable to a drum under the device, and children and not a few adults were treated to a homespun merry-go-round ride.

In 1890, a recessional spiral began that culminated in the depression of 1893, one that sank many companies of the West. P&T's firms, which included subsidiaries for maritime activities, were in a better position to weather the downturn than most. However, the Port Ludlow mill was closed

Port Ludlow showing Cyrus Walker's home, later the Admiralty Hotel.
– Photo from the collection of The Jefferson County Historical Society,
Port Townsend, Washington.

for seven years between 1890 and 1897, bringing hardship to few, because PMC shifted their employees to other enterprises including Port Gamble's mills. After closure of Port Ludlow and Utsalady's mills (the latter never reopened), Port Gamble was busy, indeed.

The fleet of seagoing vessels built up to serve the lumber industry proved particularly useful during the economic downturn of the 1890s. While local demand for lumber flagged, foreign demand remained high. By 1890, P&T had at least fourteen lumber carriers, some suitable for overseas transport, to carry wheat and other products as well as lumber. One of the largest and prettiest vessels of the fleet was the 613-ton, four-masted schooner *Spokane*, launched in 1890 at the HB yards. According to *Time, Tide, and Timber*, all vessels built for the PMC thereafter were schooners. "As a lumber carrier, a schooner had a distinct advantage over a vessel carrying square sails—the ship, bark, and barkentine. A smaller crew was required to operate the craft with fore-and-aft sails on all masts."

Still more economical to operate was a vessel called inelegantly the "bald-headed schooner," the first of which was built on Puget Sound, the *Aida,* completed at Port Ludlow in 1891. This was a schooner without top masts (top masts required an extra man to be sent aloft when sails were furled). Thus, the bald-headed schooner could be operated with just two men on a watch, one as lookout, one at the wheel.

99

Before 1890, most PMC lumber went to Shanghai—fine building lumber, spars, and ship planking. In 1892, heavy timbers for Chinese mines were required at the ports of Taku and Tientsin. And after Cecil Rhodes acquired control of the Kimberley mine in South Africa and formed DeBeers Consolidated Mines, Ltd. in 1889, he ordered vast quantities of mining timbers from PMC to rebuild the underground portions of the mine into safer workplaces, and to build the town of Kimberley for white employees. The first such cargo went out in late 1892. For the long, dangerous voyage around turbulent Cape Horn, William H. Talbot selected the ship *Bonanza* and a veteran skipper, Wilder F. Stetson, who made the round trip (bringing coal as ballast) under nine months time.

Loading a ship at Port Gamble's docks is described in *Time, Tide, and Timber*:

" . . . bow ports were knocked out, and a gangway rigged. The mates took their places in the hold—the chief on the port and the second on the starboard side. Longshoremen moved up and divided into gangs to load the lumber already stacked near the spot where she was moored. As they ran the boards up the gangway into the ports, stick by stick, they sang out `starboard' or `port,' according to the side that was receiving the lumber at the moment. Larger pieces for the deckload were handled by winches powered by the vessel's steam donkey. . . . As she loaded, the mill continued to cut for her cargo, and the additional lumber was hauled from the mill by two-wheeled horse-drawn dollies."

Australia, Hawaii, China, South Africa, and always San Francisco—the lumber ships sailed on. Captain Keller himself, one of the original partners, still actively sailed the seven seas.

Between 1895 and 1897, lumber cargos steadily increased as the depression ended. The rush to Klondike gold sparked a business upturn in the Northwest, with a keen demand for both lumber and maritime transport. Port Gamble mills operated at night again. Walker recommended reopening the idle Port Ludlow mill and, in 1897, after updating some of the equipment, it resumed operations. Orders continued to increase, and between 1898 and 1906, PMC averaged almost 87 million board feet annually. One of the largest increases was in sales to Hawaii, especially for government installations after the American annexation in 1898. Japan also ordered lumber for railroad coaches. British and German shipyards ordered ship decking and other lumber, which had to be of the finest quality. Large amounts were shipped to Australia. Some lumber went to Argentina, Korea, Chile, Ecuador, Peru, India, and Russia—truly Port Gamble and its companion mill, Port Ludlow, were vendors to the world. And then came the San Francisco fire; with offices in that city, P&T's mills had an advantage in post-fire lumber sales.

About 1906, P&T invested further money for updating the Port Ludlow mill. But in 1907, there was a moderate recession and lumber prices declined, while the costs of shipping by railroad rose. Port Gamble and Port Ludlow mills had been located to be convenient to salt water transportation; they did not use rail transportation, and maritime shipping proved an advantage for them.

However, the conservation practices of PMC began to work against them. The company owned about 186,000 acres of untouched timber land in 1907, on which taxes were low. Many other timber companies had only leased land as needed for cutting. In 1907, the taxes on timberland began to increase, placing a squeeze on large landowners like Pope & Talbot. They had paid taxes on their lands since around 1875, the cumulative total far in excess of the burden on later land purchasers. In an appeal for relief of the tax rate, PMC and twenty-one other timberland owners went to court to restrain the county from collecting. W.H. Talbot, then president of P&T, pointed out that a farmer never paid taxes on his grain until it was harvested, whereas the county taxed the same timberlands, uncut assets, over and over in successive years. For this and other reasons, since PMC was operating at a loss for the first time, the Port Ludlow mill was closed from May-November, 1909, until management could decide on the direction to take. The Port Ludlow and Port Gamble mills opened again, but P&T sold a specified number of timber acres each year to assure operational costs and dividends. It also started to cut its own timber, as needed, beginning with lands in Snohomish County between Seattle and Everett around today's Alderwood Manor.

The next two decades were tough ones for the PMC. Both of Port Gamble's mills had been built in mid-century, although Port Ludlow's was a bit more modern. Rail transportation used by competitors, sometimes cheaper than maritime, shaved P&T's profit margins. Many changes took place, where the company sold some of its lumber carriers and substituted barges, or tried towing huge cigar-shaped rafts to San Francisco (they often required three tugs and the offshore weather sank a few).

Operations of P&T were becoming too complex, and in 1914, the company reorganized to recognize fifteen different corporations under its wing. For a decade or more, the company officers agonized over whether or not to sell PMC and its extensive land holdings. The early 1920s were good sales years, but the aged company mills could not produce competitively.

Negotiations began in March, 1924, with Charles R. McCormick of the Portland area for the sale of PMC. It was consummated July 10, 1925, a complex sale that included the retention by P&T of certain shares in the McCormick Company. All during negotiations, the former was dubious about McCormick's cash position, though it consisted of nine corporations with a

Port Ludlow Mill in its heyday.
– Photo from the collection of The Jefferson County Historical Society, Port Townsend, Washington.

total net worth of $4,759,000 as of December 31, 1923. Among the corporations were an active lumber mill, St. Helens Mill Company (Oregon), the St. Helens Shipbuilding Company, and the renowned McCormick Steamship Company. The purchase price for PMC was $15 million, which included over 92,000 acres of timber, mills, and logging camps. The down payment was $1.5 million, with the balance due over a fifteen-year period.

Port Ludlow citizens were all agog over the sale negotiations and another unrelated event. Buried treasure might have spun into the water off the shifting sand beach of Port Ludlow about this time. In the late twenties, according to Ruby el Hult, a flashy man boarded the Ludlow ferry, carrying a black bag. He confided to a crew member that the Chinese were after him, because he had won a fortune gambling in Seattle's Chinatown. "They" expected him to go to Olympia by bus or train; to elude them he headed for the Olympic Peninsula. The night was foggy and, nearing Port Ludlow, the ferry ran aground on Snake Rock. Passengers panicked, and the gambler threw his satchel overboard, starting over the rail after it. The purser pulled him back, protesting mightily, and later the passengers were taken ashore at Mats Mats Bay in lifeboats. However, the satchel was gone in the swirling waters around the rock. Local residents searched feverishly along the shores of the bay to no avail.

Back to more mundane activities . . . from October, 1925, the PMC properties were operated by McCormick. First in the modernization program was the replacement of the obsolete Port Gamble mill, improvement and expansion of the Port Ludlow mill, and establishment of more logging camps. Sidney Hauptman and C.E. Helms were assigned responsibility for the mills and Paul E. Freydig for the logging. Logging procedures were updated to incorporate the latest in technology. By 1926, Port Ludlow was producing 350,000 feet per shift, a new mill at Port Gamble 400,000 feet per day on two shifts, and three logging operations 850,000 feet of logs daily. Both Port Gamble and Port Ludlow's docks were updated with big Colby cranes for loading and handling. A record output of lumber resulted— 512 million feet of lumber for $14 million, second only to the year 1923, but still the operations ran at a loss.

With McCormick still owing ninety per cent of the purchase price of P&T, William H. Talbot scrutinized the financial picture and demanded curtailment of PMC spending. By 1929, P&T still was "holding the bag" for most of the payments and interest due, despite cooperating with McCormick to the fullest in extending special credits to pay off debts incurred in other McCormick enterprises. P&T requested Charles McCormick to step down and elected Sidney M. Hauptman as President, with instructions to slash costs. Even though some improvement resulted, by 1933 in the "Great Depression" the McCormick Company's lumber and steamship interests were essentially under the control of P&T. William Talbot had died in 1930, meanwhile, and George A. Pope, Sr., became President. The PMC operations were still in dire straits, because of heavy interest and other financial requirements. A workers' strike in 1934 did not help matters. Cash flow was critical. One way of saving money, when costs often exceeded sales, was to curtail production, so the Port Ludlow mill was closed forever on December 4, 1935.

During 1936, the mill machinery was sold. Soon all that remained were the concrete boiler room, the steam turbine powerhouse, and some pilings. A stream of employees and families departed. Art Swanson, formerly office manager and later store manager at Port Ludlow, leased out the store in 1940, but by then, population had declined so the place could not survive and was closed. The old mill building, dilapidated but sturdy, was demolished in 1957 by Richard Watts of Bremerton. He found all sorts of relics in the process—old lamps, spool cabinets, lanterns and other antiques that were snapped up by visitors. As buildings and board walks were torn up, children found coins that had sifted down through the cracks.

Port Ludlow had become the ferry terminal for service from Edmonds until the building of the Hood Canal Bridge; travelers continued to provide a small income for remaining residents. Cyrus Walker had moved to San Francisco in 1907, and his home became the Admiralty Hotel in 1914, a fashionable sort of small resort with beautiful gardens, onto which an annex to house 125 people was built later for more utilitarian use. But the building's lumber deteriorated, and the hotel was torn down for scrap in 1940.

A number of abandoned homes were barged away to Silverdale, Washington, for use as emergency housing during World War II. By 1958 only four original buildings remained in old Port Ludlow—three homes and the former hospital. In 1965 the ferry ran no more and only one original home survived. The population was down to perhaps 100 people.

Meanwhile, Port Gamble's mill continued to operate and the town population was fairly stable. In 1953, P&T celebrated its centennial at Port Gamble. Hosts were Cyrus T. Walker of Portland, the first Cyrus's grandson, vice-president; George A. Pope, Jr., president of the company; Hillman Lueddemann, vice-president and general manager of the firm, a consultant who had been brought in to straighten out finances in 1936; Washington's Lt. Gov. Emmett Anderson; and Governor Burton M. Cross of Maine. During the ceremonies a boulder from Maine brought to Port Gamble on a P&T ship was dedicated, a plaque installed on it in memory of Maine men, Andrew J. Pope, William C. Talbot, and Cyrus Walker. A white pine tree from Maine and a Douglas fir from Washington were planted adjacent to the boulder as living memorials. Just as in the old days of major ship launchings, fireworks and partying followed.

In 1967, P&T moved to utilize the Port Ludlow property, drawing plans for a major resort, hotel, golf course, and private homes. The Resort at Port Ludlow, indeed, became one of the Northwest's showplaces. The Beach Club now stands on the site of Cyrus Walker's home, a conference center where a school once stood, and a vacant bank slopes to a protected marina for pleasure boats where once big ships slid resoundingly into the water. Under lawns are the old foundations of the mill. P&T still owns the site, but in 1995 it was managed by Village Resorts, Inc.

(A special thanks for background on Pope & Talbot to P&T and Edwin Coman, author of *Time, Tide and Timber,* Stanford University Press, 1949.)

Chapter 12

TUBAL CAIN MINE

When Washington State's riches were just being discovered, the little-explored Olympic Mountains were believed to hold gold, silver and manganese. Traces had been found in foothill streams, and manganese existed wherever construction machinery dug up the earth (though not in profitable quantities). Mount Constance in the Quilcene District was considered one of the most promising locations, but the Olympic Peninsula has broken the hearts of all mineral prospectors. Nowhere has a profitable mine resulted from combing the lonely valleys and ridges.

U.E. Crane claimed an extensive pumice mine on the ridge between the East Fork of the Dungeness and the Big Quilcene River in 1901. Among others filing claims was C.P. Anbust. During the 1890s, Silas Marple, a young man from Brinnon, explored the ridge known later as Iron Mountain and filed a claim in 1901.

Marple gathered financing from substantial people such as Charles A. Denny of Seattle and Frank Hanford of Lowman and Hanford, to form the Tubal-Cain Copper and Manganese Mining Company (TCCMM) in 1903. (Tubal-Cain comes from the Bible, Genesis 4:22, the smith who forged bronze and iron tools.) A headline in the *Port Townsend Leader* of June 14, 1903, trumpeted: "A MONSTER LEDGE OF IRON HAS BEEN DISCOVERED!" The account went on to say that the ledge was forty to fifty feet wide and was high grade manganese. In addition, on the opposite side of the ridge there appeared to be an equally promising deposit of copper.

Between 1905 and 1909, more than 100 claims were filed on Iron Mountain. An optimistic report was issued to the TCCMM by mining engineer E.M. Knapp in July, 1905. He explained the lay of the land, stating that ". . . the entire mountain is now a succession of perpendicular bands 10 to 150 feet in thickness, running nearly parallel to the direction of the mountain. The vein structure is the result of substitution or replacement. . . . From 200 to 300 feet from the east wall is an immense outcrop of manganese ore, 20 to 96 feet wide, carrying copper in both sulphide and metallic form. This outcrop is traced throughout the entire length of the mountain."

Tubal-Cain Mine about 1912.

— *Courtesy of USDA Forest Service*

Knapp went on to say flatly that this was a copper vein with a manganese capping, explaining that, with this much manganese showing, the copper vein which he expected to find at a much lower depth was surely very substantial. On the western side of the mountain, he took assays from samples that resulted in ribbon ore, 14-1/2% copper, and ore above the small tunnel at 17-1/2% and 5% copper (apparently two samples). Knapp admitted that the ingress to the site was difficult but suggested that, to handle the ore, a wire tram could be built about 3,000 feet from the western tunnel to the Dungeness River without difficulty, and that the river would also furnish power.

On the strength of this bright analysis, TCCMM pushed ahead with the construction of a practical trail to the site. The nearest town was Quilcene, about ten miles away as the crow flies, but for man it was at least twice that. Like the infamous Chilkoot Trail of the Yukon gold rush, the trail to Tubal-Cain was extremely steep. Only burros were considered hardy enough to withstand the slopes, the storms, and the bad footing on slippery clay and rock. The packer, Bert Macumber, and his helper, Earl Sewell, heroically managed a pack string of burros, coaxing them up the rigorous trail with tools and provisions for the builders. As a camp was established for about thirty-five men, the hardware for construction of mining buildings, a complete sawmill, three pelton wheels, and air compressors went up on burro-back. Eva Cook Taylor related in her thorough pamphlet on the subject, *The Lure of Tubal-Cain*: "Items too heavy or awkward for one animal, such as the pelton wheels, iron stoves, mine carts, shafts, and the like were slung on poles between two burros. . . . On switchbacks, or steep uphill pitches, burros had to really work in teams or one would be shoved over the side . . . " Attempts at using horses for such loads failed; one horse simply lay down on the trail rather than accept the load.

Claim holders helped to improve the trail, thus satisfying the requirement for an annual $100 improvement assessment per claim. The mining excitement led to the establishment of two small settlements, Tull City on one side of the mountain and Copper City (TCCMM mine site) on the other, and the Crow's Nest Hotel halfway up the trail, a shelter badly needed during winter storms.

Only when the TCCMM crews had physically accessed the ridge did they fully realize that the claims described by Knapp were near the top of Iron Mountain's sharp ridge roughly 7,000 feet in altitude. It was all but impossible to work on either side of the ridge; thus they chose a site at 4,500 feet altitude at the base of the mountain, basing their selection on Knapp's conclusion that the vein would be found much lower than the manganese outcropping on the peak. Taylor wrote that one person looked at the mine site and said, "It looks like they picked the best camp spot they could find with water, timber, pasture, and beautiful scenery, and then drilled there."

During the summer of 1905, TCCMM installed a log dam on the nearby creek, then built a flume from a high stream to provide water power for the sawmill. Crews finished the camp: a two-story bunkhouse, cookhouse, office, powder house, blacksmith shop, and a covered walkway from bunkhouse to mine, so men could work in winter or during storms. Later the company built a more substantial powerhouse to operate the drilling and ventilating equipment for the mine tunnel. While the tunnel was being drilled, the company acquired other claims, until they had more than forty under their control. TCCM drilled 2,000 feet into the mountain and constructed 1,500 feet of side tunnels.

Their findings must have been poor, because after that year of 1905, TCCMM continued to work the mine but issued no known reports about progress. TCCMM crews worked all year, despite heavy snows. A visitor to the mine during the winter of 1911-12 reported that the snow was ten feet deep. In March, an avalanche destroyed the sawmill, powder house including dynamite, barn and clubhouse. The eight men left in the bunkhouse took forty-two hours to shovel their way to the cookhouse. The buildings were rebuilt in spring, and it was said that a millwright was going to the TCCMM mine to install a stamp mill, but it may have been propaganda for the stockholders' benefit.

Even though drilling on the tunnels continued until 1915, nothing worthwhile was found. TCCMM simply faded away and disappeared from history without explanation, after spending a reported $100,000 in development costs. With its demise, most others discontinued their explorations, too.

Eva Cook Taylor told the author that most geologists believe that any veins of ore were fragmented and no vein ever existed at Tubal-Cain Mine, but TCCMM's president believed the tunnel simply was in the wrong place.

Fifteen claims on 215 acres remain in private hands deep inside the Olympic National Park. It is unlikely that any development of the mine will ever take place. Today the main tunnel is closed about 600 feet inside, the power house deteriorates, and the pelton wheels lie in Copper Creek Canyon. One may see sections of two-inch pipe here and there. . . . And the hike to the site is still rugged.

SAN JUAN COUNTY

Chapter 13
ROCHE HARBOR

One of the Northwest's most popular rendezvous for yachtsmen was once a genuine boom town. Roche Harbor was the thriving company town that grew up around the Tacoma and Roche Harbor Lime Company (TRHLC), established in 1886. TRHLC operated for seventy years as a benign autocracy under John S. McMillin until 1936, then his son Paul to 1956, when the entire town of Roche Harbor, including 4,000 acres and twelve miles of coastline, was sold to Reuben J. Tarte. For more than three decades the Tarte family operated businesses at Roche—a yacht harbor, airport, restaurants, gift shop, store, and the Hotel de Haro, the original company-owned hotel. In 1989, the family sold the resort to V-Mail Corporation and Roche Harbor Lime & Cement Company to Richard Komen.

Roche Harbor enjoys a delightful location at the northwest end of San Juan Island, one of a group of islands sprawled across Puget Sound between Bellingham, Washington, and Victoria, British Columbia. The establishment of a settlement at Roche Harbor predates Washington State. Hudson's Bay Company (HBC) erected a trading post at the lovely, scenic location in 1845, adding a salmon curing facility in 1850. In 1853, HBC placed sheep on the southeastern end of the island to roam the treeless grasslands monitored by Hawaiian sailors turned sheepherders.

A few Americans drifted onto the lovely islands, too. Before long, the British and Americans were vying for ownership of the San Juan Islands (of which San Juan Island was one), since the 1846 boundary designation of the 49th parallel did not specify whether the border ran through Haro or Rosario Strait. A rather mundane event, the shooting of a marauding British pig by an irate American farmer, led to tensions that brought two garrisons of soldiers to San Juan Island—the Americans stationed near the southeastern end, the British Royal Marines near Roche Harbor. It was a normally tranquil twelve-year confrontation with the garrisons giving parties for each other, until Kaiser Wilhelm I was selected to settle the controversy. He established the border through the Haro Strait, and the military posts were decommissioned.

While the British marines were ensconced at nearby Garrison Bay, their commander, Lieutenant Roche, assigned them to mine the limestone outcroppings at Roche Harbor. The materials were shipped to Victoria in empty whiskey or meat barrels for delivery abroad on merchant vessels and gunboats.

After the British soldiers left, Joe Ruff preempted a claim on the limestone properties. His interests, never developed, were purchased by Robert and Richard Scurr in 1881, who established a camp and began to mine the deposits. A couple of years later, Indiana lawyer John S. McMillin came from the East to settle in Tacoma, practicing law for awhile before becoming manager of the Tacoma Lime Company. In 1884, McMillin was assigned to search for additional lime deposits to feed the company's kilns and purchased the Scurr enterprise at Roche Harbor on behalf of Tacoma

Harbor View of Tacoma and Roche Harbor Lime Company.
— Photo courtesy of San Juan Historical Society

Lime. A new corporation was formed as Tacoma and Roche Harbor Lime Company (TRHLC), with McMillin as a stockholder ($1,800 worth) and president. One of the first projects he completed at Roche Harbor was the twenty-two room Hotel de Haro, utilizing portions of the original log HBC post.

Next came a massive construction effort, resulting in a completely modern lime quarrying and production plant. Using fill, TRHLC extended the shoreline about eighty feet to a seawall built of boulders. To replace Scurrs' two small kilns, TRHLC eventually built two batteries of kilns, one of five (two of which were renovated from the British kilns), the other of eight bottle kilns. The firm built warehouses to store up to 20,000 lime barrels awaiting shipment, one thirty feet by 200 feet on land, the other thirty-six feet by 140 feet at the wharf. Added were bunkhouses for the workers, a company store, offices. and a maze of tracks and trestles. TRHLC bought patent rights to an innovative machine where revolving knives carved out barrel halves from lengths of fir or cedar logs. The halves were cemented together, eliminating the necessity for barrel staves. The company built a barrel factory in 1897, using many Japanese immigrants for its crews.

The considerable investment in facilities was worthwhile; the lime deposits were extensive and ready markets awaited production, including the new Irondale furnaces.

The limestones were extremely pure and uniform in composition throughout the deposit, and it was possible for the company to guarantee a content of calcium carbonate in the product exceeding 98%. Analyses by three different companies (one in England, one in Everett, and one in New York City) in 1888-1902 verified the carbonate content to be, respectively, 98.21%, 99.06%, and 98.57%.

The extent of the limestone deposit was not so much a thickness of one strata, but several distinct layers in the quarries caused by the earth's folding. A geologist, Roy McLellan, stated in 1927 that the valley leading to Roche Harbor from the southeast (Rocky Bay) probably follows a natural fault or fracture zone. The Roche Harbor limestone deposit is believed to be truncated by this fault, and the area suffered greatly by slippage and folding in the geological past. According to geologist McLellan, if these theories hold true, the northern extremes of the limestone strata at Roche Harbor should occur at the bottom of Haro Strait somewhere west of Battleship Island.

The lime deposits cropped up here and there along the westerly side of San Juan Island, but were not concentrated and were unprofitable commercially. In 1923, Orcas Lime Company, the operator of a quarry on Orcas Island, started an operation a half mile south of Roche between Westcott Bay and Mosquito Pass. Only one kiln served the small operation. The other limestone operation was at the base of Mount Dallas on the western shore, a significant deposit operated in the 1920s by Henry Cowell & Company, but it was not as pure as that at Roche.

The procedure for quarrying was as follows: The limestone was broken loose by blasting, then broken by hand into clumps of the required size, sorted and classified as to quality. The segregated groups were then loaded onto railway cars pulled by a small locomotive (at first by horse teams) for delivery to hoppers which fed the kilns below by gravity. The kilns were along the seashore.

During the panic of 1893, nervous TRHLC stockholders considered scuttling the company. Just the chance McMillin had been waiting for. He bought out several investors on the time payment plan and gained a firm controlling interest in the company. According to David Richardson in *Pig War Islands*, he promptly voted himself twice his former salary, which made it possible for him to make the payments to stockholders.

Richardson described another financial maneuver that made money for McMillin. The separate corporation, Staveless Barrel Company (SBC), was also owned by stockholders, with McMillin a major one. Now McMillin the individual "negotiated a contract with McMillin of the Lime Company, to provide the latter concern with hogsheads for its product. Next he sold the contract to McMillin of the SBC for some $200,000 and took that corporation's note in payment. This note he then returned to the company [SBC] to pay for the stock he had subscribed for. There remaining in the treasury of the barrel company $200 of actual money, McMillin submitted a bill for that same figure and paid it to himself as a legal fee for organizing the company." Understandably, the minority stockholders were a bit shocked at these shenanigans.

Now that McMillin had control of the operations, he settled down to enjoy life at his island paradise, for the San Juan Islands enjoy a benign climate, splendid marine views, and easy living.

He built a fairly modest home for himself, the building now housing Roche Harbor Restaurant overlooking the harbor, and acquired a fifty-foot yacht *Calcite* for entertaining guests and family. The home he built for his oldest son Fred, to whom he largely turned over management of TRHLC, was more pretentious. Called "Afterglow Manor," the home overlooked Spieden Channel. The Mediterranean-style home with tiled roof was surrounded by well-groomed gardens, had a gazebo, carriage house, and other amenities. One approached the home through stone-pillared gates.

The McMillins lived in baronial style, staging lavish parties. According to Lynette Evans and George Burley in the book, *Roche Harbor*, John S. McMillin might invite 1,100 people for an outdoor salmon barbecue in the banquet court beside the Hotel de Haro. Two stone fireplaces still stand

Home of John S. McMillin is now a restaurant.
Photo courtesy of San Juan Historical Society.

John S. McMillin.
Photo courtesy of San Juan Historical Society.

there from the court, inscribed with the words, "Friendship's fires are always burning." Other entertainments might include a fashion show or lunch aboard barges pulled by the tug *Roche Harbor*, with dancing afterward. McMillin hired his own photographer to record the events.

The gardens McMillin planted, though changed, still decorate the entrance to Hotel de Haro and other buildings. A walkway from hotel to pier was covered with flowering clematis, and the vines also softened the outlines of the hotel. Servants in white uniforms escorted arriving guests from their ship to the hotel. Among the notables staying at the hotel was Theodore Roosevelt.

All of this activity provided employment for several hundred people, and the town's population may have reached 600. No outside business was allowed in the town, only that owned by McMillin. The town lay between the workers' homes at the east end of town and the Japanese conclave at the west, the central district consisting of a church, store, post office, offices, school, a water and power system, the hotel and all of the lime company structures. Bunkhouses stood along the hillside near the church (still standing) for single workers. The autocracy of Roche Harbor was criticized by some, and equal numbers pointed out that McMillin did provide stable incomes to thousands of workers over a period of a half-century or more, and that the company and its officers were kind and assisted their workers in need. Conversely, when a young worker, Micky Doyle, tried to organize a union at TRHLC, asking for an increase in daily wages from $2 to $2.25 and reductions in the costs of board and room, Doyle and forty-nine others were summarily dismissed.

McMillin was a staunch Republican; in fact, he attended every Republican convention from the time Washington was a territory. He lobbied heavily in his company town and the surrounding islands for his candidates and, although his workers' votes could not be coerced, author Richardson said, " . . . under his towering and ever-present influence, it seemed almost un-American to mark one's 'X' for any other party." When Republicans won, McMillin's enthusiasm was expressed by flashy Roche Harbor and Friday Harbor parades. McMillin tried to extend his sphere of influence to Friday Harbor, with mixed results. He battled, on occasion, with the island's newspaper editors and was accused of undue influence during local elections.

His summary handling of situations did not go without retribution. In 1906, McMillin had an opportunity to sell the company for about $800,000. At this time, the minority stockholders came to life. Still seething over the manner in which McMillin had acquired control of the stock, and of the handsome profits he made in the arrangements over the SBC, a group of stockholders charged John S. McMillin with fraud. In a separate accusation, McMillin also was charged with negotiating preferential rates with the steamship and railroad companies that carried his lime barrels, while he was a railroad commissioner of the State Railway Commission. An injunction filed against the company, pending settlement of the suit and accusations, effectively killed the opportunity for a profitable sale.

Everyone on San Juan Island who had some grudge against McMillin came out of the woodwork. The *Islander* newspaper fearlessly outlined the charges, along with other Northwest papers. During the period of the suit, critics claimed that TRHLC's real value was far greater than the amount on which it paid tax. As a result of a fiery indictment by the editor of the *Islander*, TRHLC's assessed values were adjusted.

Despite these editorials, the *Islander* was perceived by locals to be unduly influenced by the Republicans and McMillin. An opposition paper was formed by O.G. Wall and G.A. Ludwig of Minnesota, with the first edition of the *Friday Harbor Journal* appearing September 13, 1906. When William Schulze, endorsed by the *Journal* and its supporters, won the position of representative in the State Legislature over the old guard (and *Islander*'s endorsement), his backers staged a victory parade through Friday Harbor deliberately calculated to outshine McMillin's past affairs.

However, in court, McMillin was absolved of all charges. According to author Richardson, "The Lime Company president's stock purchases were

Harbor View of Tacoma and Roche Harbor Lime Company.
            — Photo courtesy of San Juan Historical Society

legal, the court found, and so were his actions as majority stockholder afterward. As to the staveless barrel affair, the judge found McMillin had urged the Board of Directors to buy the machine, and when they declined, was within his rights in acquiring it for himself."

Now that the transactions were considered neither illegal, immoral nor unfair, according to the judge, both newspapers dropped the matter and turned to attacks on each other, the *Journal* finally winning out.

Fire leveled the SBC in the early 1920s. At first the blaze was blamed on an angry competitor, but later an employee admitted setting it. The barrel company was not rebuilt. A worse fire on July 28, 1923, caused by flames spreading from an untended cooper's forge, involved the entire plant and the warehouse at the dock. The lime company quickly rebuilt, as lime was enjoying a boom market all over the world.

One of the factors contributing to TRHLC's success was the advantage of a good harbor, plus ready access to the open Pacific Ocean through the Haro Strait, which has a minimum width of about six miles and an average depth of around 900 feet (and at one point 1,356 feet)—obviously an ideal shipping channel. Roche Harbor was entirely protected on all sides, about a half mile in diameter with a twenty-four-foot entrance channel at low tide, deep water that leads to the still-existing wharf. The company shipped its lime on merchant vessels that called at the protected harbor or were owned by TRHLC, vessels such as the *Star of Chile, Archer, William G. Irwin*, all ocean-going schooners, and smaller sailing craft, tugs, barges, etc. Lime was shipped to Puget Sound ports on small cargo and passenger vessels like the *J.P. Libby*, one of the craft called the "mosquito fleet." The latter were a story in themselves, rushing to and fro all over the Sound to provide transportation before roads and railroads. Some time in the late 1920s or early 30s TRHLC became known as Roche Harbor Lime & Cement Co.

Consistent with his "empire mentality," McMillin decided in the 1930s to raise an impressive mausoleum to hold his remains and that of his family. His beloved older son Fred had died in 1922 at the age of forty, a terrible blow to the magnate. He turned his business over to the younger son Paul, but it was said he never forgave Paul for not being Fred.

The mausoleum project was not totally to satisfy McMillin's wish for immortality; it also was calculated to keep some of his idled workers employed in those trying Depression times. The striking memorial still stands. In the center of a ten-acre plot soars a seven-pillared structure mindful of Greece or Rome. The architecture was influenced by Masonic and biblical tenets. In the center of the pillars are a round table and six chairs, all built of limestone and cement. The chair bases are crypts for the family members' ashes and, indeed, do hold them as they have died. The chairs were

118

positioned so that the midsummer sun shone on the crypts of McMillin and his wife. The mausoleum was completed in the spring of 1936 at a cost of about $30,000. Claiming that his father had become somewhat senile and that the company did not have the money to spend, Paul cancelled his father's order for an expensive bronze dome decorated with a Maltese cross, thus earning his parent's unswerving condemnation. McMillin barely had completed the mausoleum when he died after a brief illness on November 4, 1936, and became its first occupant.

Paul, it is said, then ran the company with as much verve as his father had, continuing to prosper for another couple of decades. In a declining market and with worsening finances, Paul McMillin sold the entire town to Reuben Tarte on September 19, 1956.

Although the lime operation still had forty employees and orders to fill, the Tarte family (Reuben and two sons, Neil and Lawrence, sons-in-law Byron Halvorson and Bob Tangney) found the equipment obsolete. Neil Tarte and Bob Tangney ran the lime plant and filled the outstanding orders for a few more months, until the power plant and pulverizer failed, effectively terminating the lime operation by October 1.

Under the enthusiastic and imaginative management of the Tarte family members, Roche Harbor, a company town, was converted into Roche Harbor, a resort town. Reuben's wife Clara kept up and even improved the

McMillin's chair at the family mausoleum lists his achievements.
— A JoAnn Roe Photo

gardens. She also requested reconsecration of the church as Our Lady of Good Voyage Chapel, the only privately owned Catholic chapel in the continental United States. Carillon bells toll each day, a memorial to Reuben Tarte, who died July 17, 1968, and Robert Tangney, who was killed in an accident July 4, 1971.

The workers' homes became guest cottages; the old McMillin home a restaurant. A warehouse became the site for a store, and Hotel de Haro was fully restored to a charming small inn. Like McMillin, the Tartes were proud of their enterprise. On Fourth of July holidays, they showed their appreciation to good fortune by staging a spectacular fireworks show. Each day of the summer season, just at sunset, employees of the Roche Harbor Resort lowered the big flags of the United States, England, Canada, Washington State, and a Roche Harbor house flag. McMillin would have appreciated that nicely.

Under current management the Roche Harbor resort continues to attract capacity crowds of tourists and yachtsmen.

SKAGIT COUNTY

Chapter 14

AVON

Today it is hard to "get hold of" old Avon; its remaining buildings are mixed with latter year homes and straggle from the banks of the Skagit River to the highway between Burlington and Anacortes. But Avon's boundaries were sprawling at the turn of the century, too, as one of the earliest river ports.

Thomas McCain was the first homesteader in 1876, and Charles Conrad lived there briefly in 1881, A.H. Skaling and W.H. Miller in 1881 or 1882. Mr. and Mrs. Skaling built a home, store and wharf, immediately used by people coming into the country. Skaling's son, P.E. Skaling, was the first white child born around Avon, September 21, 1883. Other early settlers, Richard Vernons, R.E. Whitneys, Sam Wiles and family soon added their progeny.

In 1884, Skaling hired a surveyor to plat a town and called it Avon after the river in England made famous by Shakespeare. Skaling, a friend of Methodist John Wesley, advertised for settlers, declaring the town to be a "dry" town, no liquor to be sold anywhere within the platted area. Within a surprisingly short time, a substantial settlement grew up around Skaling's store, a stop for the increasing numbers of riverboats serving the home-steaders and goldseekers. At least fifty families lived near Avon, for in Skaling's 1884 advertisement for settlers he wrote that a lodge of Good Templars having fifty members had been established.

At the time, rivers were the only practical means of transportation, for the deltas of the Skagit and other lesser rivers spread out across the land in a maze of swamps, tributaries and mud. What was not watery was tall forest. In a letter to a friend Skaling wrote: "I will not tell you how big the trees were for you would not believe me." He described a trip by horse and buggy west from Avon on an Indian trail: ". . . when the trail left the river and started through the heart of the dense forest, darkness closed in. With Douglas fir, spruce and cedar trees 150 to 200 feet high, it wasn't long until total darkness came. . . . The deepest dungeon could not have been darker. We had not been in the country long enough to learn how necessary it was never to be caught out at night without a lantern."

Early settlers recognized the fertility of such land and embarked on a cooperative project of cutting the trees, diking and controlling the streams—much as the Dutch did with their low-lying lands in Holland. Avon was centrally located for the new homesteading farmers and loggers.

Will Pitts opened a ten-room hotel and a livery stable in 1884. A.M. Flagg started a boat-building business at the same time. H.W. and Fred Graham had a general store, as did Blumberg-Miller & Company. W.A. Farrell provided blacksmith service, T.N. Ovenell a meat market, and J.W. Dicks an implement store to cater to the growing number of farmers. A sawmill opened employing fifty men, and W.I. Duncan supplied a billard hall for recreation, while C.H. Martin & Company set up a bottling works for soft drinks. The *Avon Record*, W.E. Boynton, editor, opened in 1890 and closed in 1891. The town added two millinery stores, a barber shop, a furniture store and a Dr. A.C. Lewis. Industry came to town in the form of a broom handle factory and J.H. Reylea's wagon construction shop. No doubt, boarding houses and rooming houses abounded to serve the heavy numbers of single men entering the area for logging and sawmilling. Area residents organized a I.O.O.F. lodge.

The temperance mood of the town was fostered by the strong membership of the Avon Methodist Church organized in 1884. The parishioners built their church in 1887, a sturdy and not unattractive structure that still stands on the Avon-Allen Road, to which it was moved from its original riverside site. In 1886, Liberty Hall was erected for the Good Templars lodge members. The Avon Cornet Band members sporting handlebar mustaches gave concerts in the hall. A handsome, two-story school building with a bell tower was built in 1892, to serve grades one through eight with eighty-seven students in attendance. Avon was a "comer." The town even made a bid for the county seat in 1884, but lost to Mount Vernon. Within a decade the downtown area outgrew the narrow confines of the river dike and moved a block away from the river.

Avon.

But this was logging country and not everyone was a teetotaler. While the Seattle & Montana Railroad (merged into Great Northern Railroad in 1907) was being built in the early nineties, an entrepreneur set up a tent liquor store, which moved whenever the railroad workers' camp moved on. A mile north, a new settlement called North Avon grew up near the large Avon Lumber Company's sawmill, principals of which were H.W. Graham, Robert Wiley, John Wiley and H.M. Gibson. The mill was adjacent to the railroad tracks for ease of shipping finished lumber, and a depot served the community. H.W. and Fred S. Graham filed the plat for North Avon in 1890. North Avon did include a saloon for the thirsty, the Sample Room or Sample House. Graham Brothers opened a grocery store beside the tracks and eventually a feed store served the developing farm community. As time went on, the two small towns were joined by building a boardwalk that whole distance, made of two by fours on four-foot framing, effectively keeping foot passengers out of the mud. After all, the depot was in North Avon, affording an alternative to riverboat travel.

Founder Skaling had second thoughts about Avon remaining a temperance town. He advertised in the *Avon Record*: "NOTICE . . . TO PROPERTY HOLDERS IN AVON. All persons who are dissatisfied with the Prohibitory Clause in their deeds will be relieved from the same if they will pay the cost of acknowledging and recording the necessary documents. A. H. Skaling."

Avon remained a temperance town for many years, despite Skaling's offer. Nevertheless, liquor was available and led to the area's one known murder, that of William Gorsage by his wife, Jennie, a native woman. Gorsage drank heavily and, when intoxicated, would come home, beat and kick his wife. On December 14, 1900, after such an episode, Jennie shot him as he slept off his binge. Her son, daughter, and sympathetic neighbors testified on her behalf and she was found guilty only of manslaughter, carrying a penalty of one year, six months in jail plus a five dollar fine.

Temperance or not, the town continued to prosper. In 1891, two sawmills operated in the original Avon, one owned by M.E. Jacobs. An early shingle mill operator was Robert Larson, who sold red cedar shingles to Wagner Brothers & Angell of Grand Rapids, Michigan, from his Avon Mill (AM). John W. Hall, who came to Avon in 1890, bought the mill in 1892, operating it for many years thereafter. In 1906, the AM turned out 60,000 shingles a day.

Hall became one of the town's most prominent citizens; indeed, his two-story home still stands near the river. The population of the town reached 800 to 1,000 residents, many of them continuing to travel by riverboat until decent roads appeared. However, on August 16, 1904, a fire raced through the steamer *Elwood* as it was loading at Avon's dock, completely destroying the vessel belonging to Captain H.H. McDonald.

When the Avon Mill became bankrupt in 1905, investors including Lewis Schwager, W.B. Nettleton and J.B. Price picked up the company and renamed it Minnesota Lumber Company. Logs came from the nearby Bay View ridge. A huge forest fire in 1906 caused the new company to falter, and by 1910 it closed the Avon mill and moved on to brighter forests with more available logs.

A curious occurrence in 1906 was related by pioneer Eben Bennett. He and others were skating on the frozen Skagit River when the ice began to crack and roll in a wavelike motion. "You could hear it a long way off. At that time we did not know what it was...[but] it heaved up. There was a crack about a foot wide . . . [a skater] fell right into it. We grabbed him by the hair and pulled him out of there." Later the skaters learned that the San Francisco earthquake had struck at that time of day.

Blamed on beaver and muskrat intrusions, the Skagit River broke through two hundred feet of dike near Avon in 1918, flooding farmlands to LaConner and Mount Vernon. Originally many trees grew on the dikes, falling into the river to create habitat ideal for beaver and muskrats, which tunneled and undermined the dikes until they collapsed under pressure.

The river made strange noises as it rose during floods. According to an Indian tale, an Indian man had a wayward wife and, when the river started rising, he tied her to a rock in the river. As the water rose and began to

John W. Hall, owner of Avon Shingle Mill.

— Photo courtesy of Frances Leander

cover her, she cried out. The legend asserts that a rising river still creates that chilling sound.

The railroad at North Avon, used by many logging firms, came in handy during the liquor prohibition years of the 1920s. To fuel their logging locomotives, the English Logging Company of Conway imported coal from British Columbia through Sumas on the Northern Pacific Railroad and was switched to the GNR and logging spurs near Sedro-Woolley for points west. Hidden in a coal gondola might be sixty to eighty sacks of good bottled liquor. Usually the customs officers were not about to dig through dirty coal to look for suspicious goods. Accommodating engineers later parked that particular gondola on a siding, permitting bootleggers to swarm onto the car and extract the sacks. Sometimes train employees might drop the bags into the brush at a prearranged spot for waiting receivers. If the train crew noticed any police activity, the train simply rolled along in all innocence to its appointed destination.

As the trees were harvested and the land cleared for farming, the logging and lumbering families moved on to new arenas. A factory for making starch from potatoes came and went. The boardwalks between Avon and

North Avon disappeared when the Avon-Allen Road was blacktopped by Henry Kaiser, road contractor.

Avon had no railroad to sustain business and, as automobiles and highways took over transportation from riverboats, Avon's importance as a port disappeared and its businesses had to move to livelier commercial centers. Residents were forced to look elsewhere for employment. In the 1940s a pea cannery thrived for a short time. Later three industries helped to support the community: Darst Bulb Company, Mudville Nine Nursery, and Dow Industrial Service, a subsidiary of Dow Chemical Company for servicing refinery and pulp mill equipment. Besides the original Hall home, a few early century homes are left, plus the remains of the school's gymnasium that once echoed to the cries of 250 school children. Newer homes are being built haphazardly between the old communities of Avon and North Avon, towns with little identity today.

Chapter 15

BLANCHARD

Blanchard is a sunny site facing southwest at the southeastern shore of Bellingham Bay, Puget Sound. The winter northeasters are blocked by the Chuckanut Mountains. Across Puget Sound is a backdrop of the Olympic Mountains with Sound islands decorating the foreground. An ideal place for a town. Blanchard was named for George Blanchard, an early homesteader who took up land for logging in 1885, then opened and ran a post office until 1891.

He was not the first settler. Wesley Whitener and John Gray operated a logging camp as early as 1867 on Blanchard slough, a backwater of Bellingham Bay, joining a handful of other loggers and farmers. An unusual early resident was Lyman Cutler, the man who gained lasting fame by shooting a marauding British pig in his garden on San Juan Island, almost starting a war between the United States and Britain, the "Pig War." He moved to Samish Island, then Blanchard, and started the area's first school in 1873.

Blanchard was a meeting place of sea and forest. The Chuckanut Mountains were heavily forested with prime timber, while the low-lying deltas south of Blanchard were extremely fertile after diking by farmers. Settlers tackled the forests first, dragging out logs to booms in the bay. James H. McElroy installed a crude horse tram railroad at the site in the 1880s, then sold or gave it to George and Dudley Blanchard in 1886. Possibly McElroy had been financially damaged by the disastrous fire that swept the Samish country. Over 1,000 acres of timber burned, driving McElroy and a major logging company, Clothier & English, out of the area until rains came in September. The Blanchards obtained financing from eastern investors, General Russell A. Alger (ret.) and Ravand K. Hawley, and proceeded to tie up vast quantities of timberlands in the vicinity of Blanchard on Chuckanut Mountain. By the winter of 1888, the Blanchards had about ninety men working in the woods, with a payroll of $180 a day. With rights-of-way in place, the Blanchards installed a substantial logging railroad, according to the *Skagit News* of December 10, 1888, one with forty-pound steel rails, standard gauge, although apparently horsepower was four-legged at first.

Rail historian, Dennis Blake Thompson, said in his book, *Logging Railroads in Skagit County*:

"Five Russell log cars were used, each log car carried about 5,000 feet of timber, and the motive power consisted of mule teams. . . . A new steam locomotive was ordered from the Baldwin Locomotive Works and she was shipped from the factory on the East Coast in August of 1888. The shiny new machine arrived in Blanchard on a barge and was unloaded on the long wharf. She was a small pot by railroad standards with 38-inch drivers in a 2-6-0 wheel arrangement and had 14 x 18 inch cylinders."

But it certainly was better than working with mule teams. The mule teams managed by the Barrett family would haul a log train up the incline to the top; after loading, the train was allowed to plummet freely down the slope, slowing down about a quarter mile from the landing on the flats. When the inclines got too steep for even cattle, horses or mules, the men used stationary donkey engines to snake out the logs. The company or its contractor devised a steam-driven skidder utilizing a 20 HP engine. The machine was secured near a dumping site; then a cable was stretched into

Crew of Blanchard Logging Company.
– Courtesy of Skagit County Historical Assn.

the woods, affixed intermittently to sturdy trees. A sort of grappling hook dangled from three metal carriages to lift a downed log clear of the ground and transfer it along toward the engine and storage site.

By 1888, enterprising loggers and merchants had built a floating wharf in Samish Bay near Blanchard, where ships could dock to bring supplies; indeed, until the arrival of the Great Northern Railroad (GNR), everyone and everything traveled by water, usually on the vessel *Salt Chuck.*

The Blanchards used the railroad to log out of Blanchard until 1900. The camp, under Superintendent Dudley Blanchard, employed a large crew at $2 per day per man—a crew that put out 75,000 feet of logs per day in 1888-89. By 1890, output was raised to 20 million feet of logs and employed 100 men. The company owned timber rights to 1,400 acres of land. The Blanchards might have logged longer than 1900, but financier Hawley died, precipitating the sale of the railroad to Lake Whatcom Logging Company in 1901. The latter put the engine to work elsewhere on their facilities and the Blanchard railroad was used very little.

About this time, three noteworthy men and a socialist colony arrived to give new impetus to the town. John Fravel settled near McElroy's slough and reopened the postoffice as Fravel, renamed Blanchard in 1913. Fravel was the former supervisor of a telegraph line through Bellingham toward Siberia (discontinued after a decision to place a cable under the Atlantic Ocean, instead) and was searching for new enterprises. John J. Cryderman, a well-known professional engineer who figured in Bellingham's history, settled on Samish Bay at Oyster Creek around the same time to develop oyster lands, as did Bert Huntoon, an early Bellingham engineer and businessman. The Equality Colony arrived near Blanchard in 1897.

A sober group of settlers, at least at first, were the several hundred residents of the socialist colony, one of a half dozen communal experiments in western Washington. The plan to create utopian communities was part of a master blueprint to socialize an entire state and what better than Washington, just born in 1889. The socialistic or communitarian approach had grown from the immigration of certain politically-minded groups plus the economic disruption that followed the Civil War, prompting dissatisfied people to try a new approach to life. The parent organization, the Brotherhood of the Co-operative Commonwealth, attracted considerable interest for a few years. National leaders of this movement included F.G.R. Gordon of Manchester, New Hampshire, who started with the Socialist Labor Party and eventually changed his political beliefs to become a lobbyist for the conservative National Association of Manufacturers (and denied any socialist ties of the past). Norman Wallace of Warren, Maine, was a founder of the People's party in Maine, along with a dedicated employee, Ed Pelton. In 1887, a keen sympathizer, Edward Bellamy, wrote *Looking Backward,*

Equality Colony.

— Courtesy of Skagit County Historical Assn.

2000-1887, a book that excited many to join socialist clubs. Then there was the well-known Eugene V. Debs, president of the American Railway Union, who accepted the position of organizer for the socialist-minded group, the National Union of the Brotherhood of the Cooperative Commonwealth. He pulled together several like-minded groups to form the Social Democracy of America, which moved along in an uneasy alliance with the Brotherhood. Colonization was a paramount aim of the latter, and Ed Pelton was sent to the Northwest to choose a site. After looking at several, he arranged to buy 280 acres near Blanchard under his own name, to avoid confrontation with local residents. Mr. and Mrs. Carey Lewis had contributed a home plus four and a half acres of planted crops to the effort, to which came the first fifteen colonists November 1, 1897, and called their new home Equality, after Bellamy's novel. Lewis and his wife at first were invaluable to the community, diligently teaching newcomers agricultural methods suitable to the climate. Later Lewis seemed to have lost his way and become excessively ethereal.

The new colonists dug into their work with verve, if not always ability; skilled workers were at a premium. Buildings arose, crops were planted, about 200 people came to join the colony, work hard and dedicate themselves to socialism. Each family was required to pay $160 for the privilege of joining the group, but could work out the sum, if necessary. As the colony grew, not everyone was accepted but calls went out for specific trades needed. Eventually the Colony had its own lumber mill; accounts report that 600 men and boys worked there. The mill equipment included a 35 H.P. donkey engine to remove stumps and help in yarding and loading logs. The colony members used horsedrawn wagons to bring logs to the mill. Other members tried their hands at fishing and built a smokehouse to cure herring catches. Some built small boats and caught salmon along the Sound.

Early in 1898, the Equality colonists were surprised to learn that national leaders intended to move their offices to Edison, about three miles from Blanchard with access to water transportation. After the officers came and managed from their "ivory tower," the hard-working colonists and they constantly wrangled over who was to do what, be paid how much, and so on. Outside jobs paid more and life looked more attractive to young men, so a number of them left.

Colonists engaged in shoemaking, tailoring, dressmaking, wagon repairing and furniture manufacturing. According to Charles LeWarne in *Utopias on Puget Sound*, printing was an important activity, and a press was installed at the Colony headquarters in Edison. The first issue of the group's official newspaper, *Industrial Freedom*, appeared May 7, 1898. The four-page newspaper expounded socialism and reform, plus local news of the colonists.

At first the colonists crowded together in small cottages only fourteen feet by twenty feet, then built two larger, two-story apartments, mainly as sleeping quarters.

After completing buildings and facilities to meet basic needs, colonists were able to relax a little. They opened schools for the children, and colonists held dances and musical events, to which outsiders came, too. Religion was considered an unnecessary practice, but it was not forbidden and Christian services of various kinds were held.

Yet only 100 persons remained in the communal life by 1901, according the newspaper *Reveille*. By 1903, the organization's newspaper had suspended publication, and only thirty-eight people remained at Equality. In 1905, a relatively radical anarchist, Alexander Horr, and his cohorts came to the colony and sought to lead the colonists into greater activism. The colony installed a vegetable and fruit cannery and groups set production goals for their various enterprises. However, Horr's rhetoric was too restrictive for many, to "unite all libertarians in a compact and flexible weapon with which to constructively undermine the basis of monopoly and invasion." Factional quarrels developed and old and new colonists argued about the rights to properties. Old colonists accused the Horr group of practicing free love. Financial chaos developed in the struggle for leadership and direction. Then the large and important barn built in 1898 burned, along with thirty cows and two horses. Factions accused each other of arson. The colony was dissolved in turbulent legal proceedings by June 17, 1907, just ten years after it began so hopefully. Some of the colonists settled in the vicinity; others disappeared.

Back downtown in Blanchard, after the Blanchard family left, milling languished for a time, although perhaps a good dozen logging camps operated in the vicinity of the town. By 1903, the GNR had relocated its line to run along Bellingham Bay through Blanchard, fortunately for the town.

Now that one could ship lumber by rail, George A. Cooper, F.D. Alpine and D.A. McMartin built the Hazel Mill (HM) on McElroy's Slough in 1906, and received logs. Six years later their mill was joined on the slough by the Samish Bay Logging Company (SBLC), formed by employees of a large Eastern logging company—James Norie, Josiah Howard, and Henry Auchu. They sent some logs to the mill; most were boomed and sold to larger mills.

Railroads or not, the timber still had to be brought out of the woods to the railroad with oxen or mule teams, often four yoke of oxen or eight horses to a rig, then loaded onto the flatcars with ox or horse power.

The well-financed SBLC built a second railroad into the Chuckanuts to harvest timber, routed along today's Chuckanut Drive to Oyster Creek, then sharply upgrade into the forest. A powerful 75-ton Climax locomotive pulled the loads handily, replacing a small Shay locomotive that had been used briefly but had insufficient power. The route was short-lived, for in 1915, the State of Washington sought to build a road connecting Bellingham and Mount Vernon along the right-of-way used by the new railroad. The automobile road, Chuckanut Drive, a scenic highway today, was built by convicts, who were stationed at a shoreside camp below Oyster Creek. SBLC was forced to pry up its rails; the company used them to encircle Chuckanut Mountain with small logging railroads. Hiking on the mountain in the 1990s, the author encountered old rails and rail debris from this period. Subsequently, the company utilized the new automobile road and built connecting roads to remove timber by Mack truck.

Trucking was not for the fainthearted, according to driver Rodney E. Gray. His truck was pulled up and down inclines by cable and donkey engine on two rows of planks for the wheels. Some inclines were as steep as 62%! In his memoirs Gray said that one time the cable broke, he jumped out of the truck, and it careened down the slope to crash into a stump.

On a normal workday, when the truck reached the slough, a steam donkey pulled the load off into the water, and the boomstick men pushed the logs to the mill. A set of tide gates controlled the level of the millpond or slough, retaining sufficient water at low tide to float the logs.

The HM struggled along and SBLC bought and expanded its operations in 1919. The firm used another incline railroad on the eastern slope of the mountains facing Alger. The work camp was near Lizard Lake. Thompson says in his book:

"Magnus Anderson recalls that many Italian laborers were employed on the track gang and they preferred to live in their own section of camp. They baked their own bread in brick or rock ovens and the finished loaf was 12 to 18 inches in diameter."

The camp was in the path of a 1925 fire. Women and children were evacuated down the incline railroad where a logging train would remove them to safety, but the train had been overtaken by the fire and the refugees had to flee on foot to Blanchard.

Logging trains were individual at the time. Although SBLC preferred a Climax locomotive for the unusually steep grades, the Shay engine was still popular, built by the Lima Locomotive Works, Lima, Ohio. On the Shay, the boiler was offset to the left to allow three vertical cylinders to be mounted on the right, more equally balancing the weight.

Thompson wrote: "These cylinders propelled a drive shaft geared to all wheels through flexible joints. This arrangement allowed the powerful locomotive to crawl over very poor track and still pull and train without derailing." Poor track, indeed! One worker claimed that it was impossible to keep the rails aligned. Thompson also described an unusual "disconnected truck" type of logging car. "Each 'truck' was a four-wheel carriage fitted with a 'bunk' or beam to support logs and a coupler on each end. Two of these were a 'set.' Going empty to the woods they were all coupled together in a continuous string, having the appearance of a 'long line of wheels.' When loaded they were separated the length of the logs; the weight of the load in place and an occasional chain kept the 'car' together. They had no automatic brakes; a hand brake wheel on one side controlled the individual brakes. Before descending a grade, brakemen would run along the slow-moving log train tightening the brake wheels with sticks. Then at the bottom of the grade the brakemen would again run along the train, this time 'knocking the brakes loose.' To facilitate handling the brakes the railroads tried to keep the trucks so arranged that the brake wheels were all on the same side of the train . . . unfortunately much like trying to keep a class of grade-school children walking in a straight line." (In *Skagit Settlers*, Skagit County Historical Society, 1975.)

The mountains behind Blanchard were dotted with logging camps. Due to poor transportation, most men lived in bunkhouses but married men soon found ways to live in Blanchard. The millworkers settled there, and the plat of Blanchard was recorded by Terry and Fanny Coble on March 7, 1911. The plat of Morrison's Addition to Blanchard was filed the same day by Wendell P. and Lydia E. Morrison. In the early part of the twentieth century the population of Blanchard topped 1,000. There were stores, one owned by Ernie Hinkston, saloons, meat markets, a pool hall, barber shop, Methodist Church, the Blanchard Community Hall, and large boarding houses for some workers.

The town was known as a very tough place on weekends, when the workers tried to spend their money as fast as possible on high living, cards, and booze. After 1912, the remarkably efficient Interurban Electric Railway ran through Blanchard, giving them a choice of carousing in Bellingham, Bow or Mount Vernon.

On the whole, drunken sprees excepted, the woodsmen were totally honest. The freely spent money was a catalyst for criminals, though. The year 1914 was especially bad with at least three robberies in Skagit County with the worst one on February 20. Three men boarded the Great Northern train at Burlington and, near Blanchard, they stepped into the vestibule and donned masks. When they reentered the passenger car, they told startled passengers, "Never mind, it's just a joke. . . ." But one man stationed himself at the front of the car, the second at the rear, and while one held a gun on the passengers, the other went through and asked for valuables. When the gunman turned to lock the door behind him, Thomas F. Wadsworth, a Canadian, jumped on the bandit and wrestled with him. H.R. Adkinson from Vancouver and R.L. Lee from Bremerton leaped to Wadsworth's assistance. When the gunman seemed to be losing the fight, the second bandit strode up and coldly pumped bullets into all three would-be rescuers, killing them, then shot through the car at random to discourage further opposition. The train rumbled through the darkening afternoon toward the Samish station. One robber pulled the emergency cord and the train came to a halt only a hundred feet short of the Samish station. Waiting passengers could see the drama being played out inside. Several men tried to come to the aid of the hostages but were met by the thieves, guns drawn, as they made their escape.

A massive dragnet went out. Rumors flew. A strange gray launch had been cruising in Bellingham Bay just before the robbery. Smoke was seen on Cypress Island. A bloodstained suit was found in Tacoma along with clippings about the holdup. No suspects resulted. A month later an ex-convict, George Ball, was arrested in Alberta and returned to Skagit County to face prosecution for the crime. He and the deputy were met at Mount Vernon by an ugly crowd in a lynching mood, but Ball was protected and later released as innocent. The crime remained unsolved, even though the GNR put up a $30,000 reward for capture of the bandits.

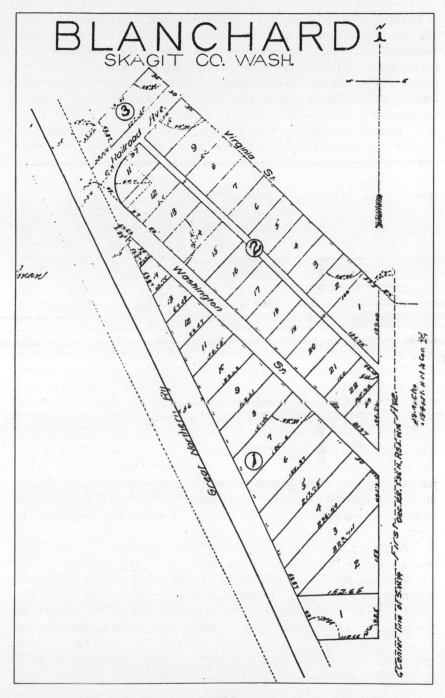

BLANCHARD
SKAGIT CO. WASH.

SBLC under W.B. Hopple, Vice President and General Manager, continued to enjoy brisk business, now that it had ample logs, a mill and good transportation. In 1922, it operated two sides (a side was a complete set of equipment that made logs into boards) with a daily output of 110,000 board feet of lumber. About 100 men worked in the woods. The company maintained a commissary, an electric light plant, and a machine shop. According to Thompson, the railroad had tracks totaling eight and one-half miles. Rolling stock consisted of twenty-six skeleton cars and two flat cars.

When the timber ran out nearby, the company started work on its holdings near Lake Samish, sending the logs on its around-the-hill railroad to

Crew of Blanchard Logging Company.
  – Courtesy of Skagit County Historical Assn.

Blanchard. The company built another incline railroad 4,000 feet long above Blanchard on a 42% grade to access timber. Finally, in 1928, the company closed down for lack of logs and moved its operations to Panama.

Around this time, Blanchard's most famous son probably left home to seek his fortune. Born in 1908 to a Blanchard logging family was Edward R. Murrow, later to become a famous war news commentator, broadcasting eyewitness reports of the sounds of bombing raids in London. He was director of the United States Information Agency from 1961-64, and narrated two television shows, "See It Now" and "Person to Person." When things were hectic, Murrow often said he would trade it all to "sit on the dike at Blanchard with a gun, waiting for a duck to fly by."

May Wray and Ernie Gross, brother and sister still living in Blanchard, remember that the town was really beginning to die as early as 1925. Conversely, a new/old enterprise in the area—the Rock Point Oyster Company—expanded in 1923 and offered jobs to some Blanchard residents.

Natural oyster beds had been worked along Chuckanut shore by Dennis Storrs as early as December, 1888, and stock was moved to the south of Samish Bay by Spero Semento. However, Japanese immigrants were responsible for the establishment of a significant commercial oyster business in 1919. J. Emy Tsukimoto and Joe Miyagi immigrated to Olympia and while attending school, both worked to support themselves—Joe as the houseboy for John C. Barnes and Emy as the young proprietor of Olympia Oysters. Later the two friends assessed the possible sites for an experimental farm where they could try establishing oysters imported from Japan, and settled on Samish Bay. With financial backing and advice from M. Yamagimachi, a partner in Jackson Fish Company, Seattle, and others, the two youths purchased 600 acres of oyster flats from the Pearl Oyster Company (POC) and successfully planted 400 hundred cases of oyster seed from Miyagi Prefecture in Japan. They took hold there in Samish Bay off Blanchard and still thrive today.

Why an imported oyster? Because the Olympia oyster then being raised was much smaller and took four or five years to mature. Those grown on the East Coast and sent to the large cities of the West often suffered spoilage from long days enroute. The Japanese oyster was larger by far than the Olympia, more the size of Eastern oysters, and matured in only three years.

Everything looked rosy for the new venture, but in 1921 the government passed what was known as the "anti-alien" law, forbidding aliens to own land, and the two young men had never been naturalized. Fortunately, John Barnes, for whom Tsukimoto had worked as a houseboy, was a friend of E.N. Steele, a State Senator and dabbler in oyster culture around Olympia. The two purchased the POC from the Japanese on May 18, 1923, and continued to employ Tsukimoto and Miyagi. Operations continued much as before. The company was renamed Rock Point Oyster Company (RPOC).

The Pacific oysters (as they have become known) were becoming marketable but educating the stores and restaurants to use them was a difficult matter. Haines Oyster Company of Seattle was the first to handle the Pacific oyster. The proprietor, Earnest Whitman, and J.M. Steele (E.N.'s father, who was helping out) devised innovative promotions. When some objected to the dark rim around the oyster, Whitman and Steele advertised: "Look for the oyster with the velvet rim. It assures you that it is grown in the pure waters of Puget Sound. . . . the same as the Olympia Oyster." They hired promoters in markets to serve cracker sandwiches containing fried oysters. Don's Seafood and Don's Oyster House, two key seafood restaurants, accepted the oysters and started by touting them as "Specials of the Day." Before long the marketing spread into Oregon and California. The RPOC has continued to this day to market a fine product and provide jobs for Blanchard-area residents. Oysters were brought into the plant for shucking by dredging for them in the mud flats or hand picking them, usually close into shore and along Samish Island. From 1956 to 1990, Blanchard-born Ernie Gross was the captain of the oyster barge, <u>Clara Ann</u>, named after owner E.N. Steele's wife.

Since oysters respond to water pollution quickly, the Steele family was vocal in the efforts to maintain clean water in the state, working through the Pacific Coast Oyster Growers Association. E.N. Steele was a State Sena-

Hinkston's store in 1993.

– A JoAnn Roe photo

tor from Olympia and was able to wield some influence in this direction. The oyster operation stayed in the hands of the Steele family until 1991, when it was sold to Taylor United, Inc. (TUI), of Shelton, Washington.

The decline of Blanchard as a town and trading center continued unabated after the mid-1920s, however, after the dissolution of the Equality Colony and the closure of the mill in 1928. Over a period of time the SBLC lumber mill was dismantled and the scrapped machinery and yarders sold to Japan. Stores closed permanently. The last center of commercial activity was the grocery store and post office owned and operated by Don and Jeanette Coble. That, too, closed in 1970, and the post office moved. The GNR railroad tracks are maintained, because the line is considered part of the coastal defense network. The old depot was relocated slightly to become the community hall. No stores remain today, but about sixty people live in the little town of Blanchard. Mae Wray says that more people with little children are coming in to fix up old homes and enjoy small community life. The Methodist Church, TUI's Samish Bay Shellfish Farm (the RPOC) and the Chuckanut Manor restaurant north of Blanchard are all that remain of a once-bustling little town.

Chapter 16

CLEAR LAKE

Overlooking a small lake that was a storage basin for the giant Clear Lake Lumber Company (CLLC) a century ago, Clear Lake enjoys a pleasant site in a bowl-like valley about three miles south of Sedro-Woolley. Seemingly designed without regard for existing buildings, some mere feet from the road, Highway 9 slices through the town.

Clear Lake is a company town, pure and simple, that outlasted its mentor. At least 1,000 people lived there around 1915, plus another 500 or 600 in camps around the periphery of the town. By 1925, the mill, heart of the town, failed and brought down many Clear Lake businesses with it.

Prior to intense pioneer settlement, one of the traditional winter houses of the Noo-qua-cha-mish Indians was located at the north end of the small lake, a huge structure made of upright cedar boards with a shed roof, all tied together with cedar or spruce fibers. A disease killed almost all of the group between 1830-35. In that general vicinity Robert Pringle settled in 1877, followed by John Isaacson, just eighteen years old from Gotland, Sweden, and in 1878 John Dart. Isaacson cleared land to build the first cabin on the *site* of today's Clear Lake town, planting extensive orchards, vineyards and gardens. In his diary he mentions trading W. Pringle a pair of rubber boots for three days work (or $3), barter being a common medium of exchange in those days. Prior to 1900, he worked at logging, an industry as old as the town, and wrote that the logs were sent by chute from the hills above the lake and pulled to water by ox teams.

Charles Edgar Turner is credited with building the first cabin in the Clear Lake *area* in 1884, then so isolated that he had to hire an Indian and canoe to ferry him across the Nookachamps Creek so he could walk to Mount Vernon for supplies. Formerly of Mount Vernon, Xavier and Mary Bartl took up land north of the lake, too, in 1884, their family members to remain in the area as influential citizens.

But it took another Bartl, Jacob Bartl, to plat fifteen acres of the Pringle land, an area known as Mountain View in 1890. He obtained a post office on May 21, 1891, as Clearlake later written as Clear Lake. Sparking inter-

141

est in the settlement's future was the coming of the Seattle, Lake Shore and Eastern Railroad (SLSE) in the fall of 1890. It was completed from Seattle to Sumas in May, 1891, connecting with the Canadian Pacific Railway, and later taken over by the Northern Pacific Railway.

With transportation and basic facilities available more settlers came. Alexander Smith built a hotel in 1891, believed to be the first one, and sold it to Charles Eagan and Robert Lannigan in 1894. Jacob Bartl opened a store in 1894, shortly selling it to Niles & Reynolds, who resold it to Wallace Beddell in 1899.

Some of the finest timber in the world covered the mountain foothills adjacent to Clear Lake—about 70% fir, 20% cedar, 6% hemlock, and 4% spruce, white pine, larch, and deciduous trees. It did not go unnoticed long. In 1891, brothers John and Michael Day began building a shingle mill on Clear Lake's site to produce shingles from ample cedar trees as old as 400 years. In financial trouble in 1895, the mill was leased to McMaster and Hiatt. McMaster bought out Hiatt and in April, 1898, joined forces with H.B. Waite of Minnesota, apparently a financier, and added a sawmill, moving in equipment from Gig Harbor. McMaster and Waite Lumber Company bought a street car from Seattle, using it as a sort of locomotive. The odd machine was about forty feet long and burned wood in a small steam engine in the center of the car, but apparently the power created made operations more efficient than dragging logs out with oxen.

A news note in the *Skagit County Times* of April, 1899, reports: "In 25 working days in March McMaster and Waite's mill at Clear Lake cut 6,000,000 shingles with 10-block and hand machine, the biggest record ever made in this time. Ed Adams packed 7,000 in 57 minutes, this record beats the world."

All was not smooth going. The locomotive ran brakeless down a steep grade, jumping the track to its demise. Until a new locomotive arrived, it was impossible to transport the heavy bolts from the logging camps and the mill shut down temporarily.

Meanwhile the town of Clear Lake grew rapidly. In December, 1899, the business district consisted of: The Central House with Mrs. J.A. Fredrichs, prop.; The Seattle House, Mrs. J.A. Johnson, prop.; the Lake House, Mrs. Handy, prop.; another unnamed hotel run by C.L. Whiting; Alexander Macdonald's meat market; a telephone company, and the Clear Lake Community Church. A school building purchased for $10 served the children while plans were made for a new facility to cost $1,000 (it cost $1,500 and opened in 1901 with 130 students by 1905).

The early town had its lawless moments. One night the caretaker at the Beddell Store was awakened by the sounds of a prowler. When he shouted out "who's there," the prowlers sent two bullets through the door and fled.

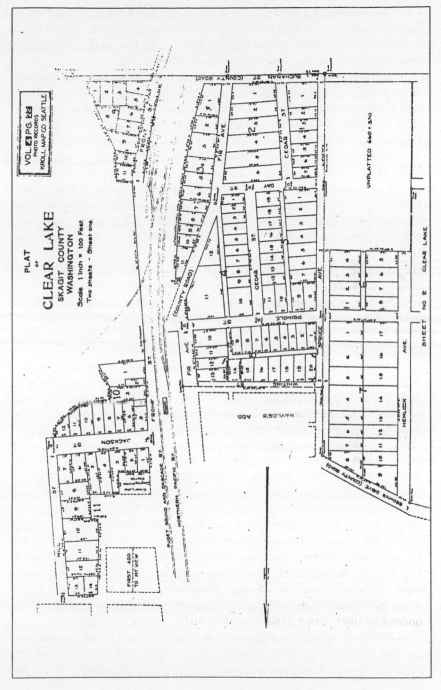

The restructuring of McMaster & Waite continued, merging and shifting participants. By late 1899 or 1900, the mill was called Bratnober Waite Lumber Company, managed by E.M. Warren. J.E. Bratnober soon purchased McMaster's interest and took over as manager of the company from Warren, reorganizing as Clear Lake Lumber Company (CLLC) with F.H. Jackson as president. A Clear Lake Shingle Mill operated at the turn of the century, at least 1898-1904 or beyond, the majority stockholders being S.T. Smith and R.H. Kellogg. It is believed that the shingle mill was subsequently owned by CLLC and leased out to various operators over the years.

CLLC was forced to make considerable investment after its mill burned in November, 1902, to rebuild a larger mill and to set up logging camps near the logging railroads. A March, 1903, news item reported: "The Sound Iron Works has secured a contract for all the transmission machinery and the repairing of that portion of the engines and wood-working machinery not totally destroyed by fire. The new mill will be an Allis double band with a larger capacity than the old one."

Machinery for an electric light plant arrived in March, too, to furnish lighting to Clear Lake, Sedro-Woolley, Hamilton, and Big Lake.

The new mill was capable of processing 50,000 feet daily and had a planing division. The shingle mill continued to cut 25,000 feet daily. In February, 1903, the company had two logging camps and 100 men working in the woods, hauling out the logs on a network of tracks.

In 1906, the *History of Skagit and Snohomish Counties* listed the following businesses: Beddell's store, Clearlake Lumber Company's general store, Starland & Boye's store, Stevens Hotel run by Lafayette S. Stevens (an adventurer noted for discovering minerals in the area, too), Central Hotel operated by J.A. Frederick, Alexander McDonald's meat market, A.J. Grierson's bakery, Thomas McEwen's confectionery and barber shop, and three saloons. J.A. Sisson was station agent for the SLSE. Other records include at this time the Mountain View Grocery Store, which opened in 1903. Wallace Beddell traded a yoke of oxen for a lot and built a two-story building for his enterprises in 1906. As he was the postmaster, he moved post office operations into his store, too. About 350 people lived in town at that time and more in logging camps nearby.

Meanwhile, in 1906, the Day Creek Lumber Company started operations, barging a locomotive up the Skagit River and literally building a railroad under it from shore to woods. Ownership of this company changed frequently. By 1910, the original owners (J.E. Potts, A.E. Freeman, and C.E. Johannsen) sold out to George Miller, who joined with Byron R. Lewis and his Skagit Logging Company only briefly, leaving Lewis the survivor. To access his woods holdings east of Clear Lake, Lewis extended his railroad, Puget Sound and Cascade Railway (PS&C), incorporated in 1911 and

144

W.O. Beddell Building.

— Courtesy of Clear Lake Historical Society

including F.H. Jackson, Thomas Smith, J.C. Wixon, and T.J. Meagher.

This gave Lewis a considerable advantage over other operators and, in April, 1913, CLLC merged with Lewis' enterprises to form a new CLLC, of which PS&C was a subsidiary.

At this point, Clear Lake began its journey as a company town, with most of the residents involved in the large firm's enterprises. According to *West Coast Lumberman*'s 1917 directory of Pacific Coast mills, the president of CLLC was then F. Horton, F.H. Jackson Vice-President, and B.R. Lewis Secretary. By 1923, the president of the company was B.R. Lewis, and, as they became mature, his older son, S.B. Lewis, became general manager and the younger, A.L. Lewis, assistant manager. F.H. Jackson then was secretary. Jackson's cousins Frank and Roscoe Horton of Winona, Minnesota, were always heavy investors and stockholders.

The company expanded PS&C to serve its sprawling logging camps, eventually having an estimated fifty miles of main track criss-crossing the lands south of the Skagit River, plus at least that much more in spurs. The main lines went from Mount Vernon to Clear Lake, then veered east to Finney Creek, Pressentin Creek and other timber sites. At Potts a major branch went south along Day Creek in a virtual maze of spurs. As indicated in the story on Hamilton, the railroad went right by the iron and coal fields; developers could easily have used it to haul iron and coal but apparently the interest in mining had waned. The locomotives were (around 1919) two mainline Baldwin locomotives, 120-ton and 90-ton, plus an assortment of 50-ton to 70-ton Shays.

An incline railroad of 2,680 feet (1922) near Day Creek helped to get logs out of the steep foothills. Water-cooled brake bands like those of a mine-hoist eased the descent of the loaded cars. The cars were lowered two at a time and the system handled fifty cars in an eight-hour day. At the bottom a car ran by gravity to a switch and, upon its release, went to the mainline by gravity for pickup by a locomotive. At Camp #2, well east of Clear Lake, the railroad was fed with logs from another, mile-long (5,375 feet) incline railroad built in 1923 that rose 900 feet in a 35%-40% grade at Pressentin Creek. At the top was a huge steam snubber with about two miles of two-inch cable on the drum.

While building a rail spur along Day Creek, workmen rolled over a large stump and found an abandoned still. The stump proved to be hollow, and operators had entered the top of the stump and lowered themselves to a room dug from the earth below. In the room there were the remains of a sophisticated still and wires evidently used for signaling the approach of strangers identified through peep holes in the stump.

Fifty million feet of logs could be stored in Clear Lake while awaiting mill operations. CLLC's lumber operation included an eleven-foot Allis-

Clear Lake Lumber Company.

– Courtesy of Clear Lake Historical Society

Chalmers band mill, ten-inch edger, and a sixteen inch by thirty-two inch sizer. The shingle mill ran "two sides," big and little, and used Atkins and Simonds' cut-off saws. Shingle bolts were sorted before they came to the saws, providing more consistently fine shingles. Everything was kept as clean as possible and well-swept to minimize the ever-present danger of fire.

Facilities included a lath mill and a planing mill. A mammoth crane handled big timbers and loads of lumber. Under cover were thirteen dry kilns and four immense drying sheds, where twenty cars could be loaded. Mechanics in a car maintenance shop repaired and inspected the 225 logging cars. An employee commented:

"Before we load cars, we go through each one carefully. We sweep them clean, pull all nails, and equip them with 2-inch strips. An exposed nail has been known to do a great deal of damage; in fact, to ruin a good piece of lumber."

By 1910 or so, the CLLC was producing a million board feet of lumber and two million shingles annually on its 200-acre site on the lake, and around 1920, 100 million feet of lumber and 200 million shingles! Much of the time, all the cedar and grade #2 and #3 logs were dumped into the lake for milling. The #1 fir was dumped into the Skagit River at Mt. Vernon for booming and sale abroad, but such arbitrary log allocations were affected by market needs. The nearby timber supply was considered almost inexhaustible, but the company took some steps to reforest for the future. CLLC intended to stay indefinitely and spent money on good facilities.

In the heart of the forest south of Lyman, CLLC fashioned cottages near the PS&C for its married workers, a constructive idea evolved by Lewis, "since it encourages and protects the man of family, enabling him to live at home while doing his work in the woods . . . the dependable man, tying his own welfare into the prosperity of his employers." The settlement called Potts was something of an experiment. Each insulated home was fourteen feet by forty-two feet, providing two large rooms, well-lighted, with ample cupboards and closets. The homes were built on skids so that, when the logging sites became too distant, the town could be hoisted onto flatcars and moved. Quoting a reporter who visited Clear Lake around 1922 to write a pamphlet about the firm:

"There are automobiles in Potts. Ruddy-faced children play in the grounds about the cottages. On some of the neat little residences there are comfy, homey names like 'Idlewild' and 'Bide-a-Wee'; there are window boxes splashed with delicate shades of the nasturtium, and there are other little patches of attractive flowers in the front yards . . ."

The three outlying logging camps averaged from 125 to 160 men each, who lived in railroad cars, all steam heated and electrically lighted, with plumbing and hot and cold water. The car camp included two dining cars, each capable of seating 100 men at one time. A generator in the laundry car had a boiler to supply steam and heat to run a 7 KW turbine for the lights and an ice machine. The car had a sleeping room for the operator, a large drying room for clothes, and four zinc-lined showers for the men. The cook car was efficient with three rooms: a meat house, supply room for dry materials, and the kitchen itself. An office for the timekeeper and foreman, a car with seven rooms for supervisors, and a library car with a card room completed the setup. The sleeping cars for the general worker, about six in each camp, had four compartments of eight bunks each. The pamphlet writer commented:

"Time was when each logger carried his roll of blankets as he traveled from place to place. His quarters were insanitary[sic], and the logger was no better than his surroundings, often filthy and infested with vermin." Not so with CLLC quarters. "There are Tiger double-bunks, felt mattress, two sheets with cotton blanket under bottom sheet, pillow and pillow case, two wool blankets zero gray, and over the top a bed cover of brown canvas."

The cars were designed by the company itself and were fourteen feet wide by sixty-four feet long, painted red with white trim on the outside, light gray inside. Each logging camp also had a house for the superintendent, a blacksmith shop, a house for waitresses, and other necessary structures—all built on skids to be moved as needed.

The married men from Potts had their own speeder to access the current logging sites, accommodating thirty-five men at a time, and could get to work in about a half hour.

At Clear Lake recreation was not overlooked. A ball park rang with the cheers of onlookers. A building was turned over to the employees as a clubhouse, to become known as the Skagit Club, open to employees after a screening process to secure the "right type of man with a good, clean record." The building still stands as a residence. A theater operated next door. Schools were good and churches full on Sunday.

Notices in the *Skagit County Times*, a Sedro-Woolley newspaper (since the Clear Lake newspaper did not open until 1921), give a picture of social life:

February, 1912.

"A big ball is to be given in McDonald's Hall in Clear Lake Feb. 24th by the young ladies of that city. Music will be furnished by the Sedro Woolley High School orchestra."

May, 1912.

"About 150 guests were taken to the Clear Lake Lumber Co.'s new camp on a passenger train composed of flat cars recently, where they were entertained at a supper and dance by the employees."

May, 1913.

"On May 12th Lakeside Rebekah Lodge of Clear Lake will hold its first annual roll call. On that date the lodge will be 2 years old. It started out with 17 charter members and now has 126."

February, 1914.

"Chester Sanders of the Princess Theatre at Sedro Woolley is in Clear Lake this week planning the scenery in the Stoddard Opera House, the building has a seating capacity for over 200, aside from the gallery."

Despite CLLC's precautions about fire, a blaze in May, 1916, originated in a dry kiln, possibly from overheating of the shingles, burning about four million shingles, three dry kilns, a loading shed and three box cars. The facilities were promptly rebuilt; the dry kilns back in operation within a month or so. CLLC did not want to miss the opportunities provided by the government in wartime. The Fir Emergency Bureau ordered sixty million feet of fir in September, 1917. Among the list of mills to which orders were dispersed was CLLC for 366,647 feet of fir.

Among the businesses in Clear Lake town between 1922 and 1926 were: Clear Lake Restaurant, Mrs. Nettie Basin, Prop.; Clear Lake Hotel with home cooked meals for $7 a week; Clear Lake Hospital and dental clinic (it burned in the 1930s); Clear Lake Confectionery in the Clear Lake Hotel, C.D. Moore, prop.; Dr. J.R. Leeper, optometrist; Adams Drug Store; Renstrom and Stephenson's meat and dairy products store; M. Westlund's Clear Lake Auto Company; the First State Bank of Clear Lake (paying 4% on time deposits, not very different from savings accounts rates in 1994); Clear Lake Lumber Yard with H.L. Crandall as manager, and real estate and insurance man, C.J. Cheasty.

An employee of CLLC until 1924, Violet Eldred Dynes reminisced in 1967 about life at Clear Lake. Living toward Sedro-Woolley, her family would walk the railroad tracks from the Skagit River to their home to avoid the muddy roads. However, they never walked after dark, because trudging the tracks were bindle stiffs or hobos enroute to seek employment at CLLC.

Dynes described the silent movies at the Skagit Theater, successor to Stoddard's smaller one; the Adams Drug Store soda fountain where sundaes or floats were a dime; and avoiding Tuffy Boyd's Pool Hall patronized by the mill men. She waxed nostalgic over the smell of cedar smoke like "no scent on earth," and the mill whistles vying with school bells:

"The mill whistles would blow and a steady stream of working men would stem their way either to or from the mills. The big company store was a bee-hive of activity. . . . There was the elite part of town and all other degrees down to the humblest shacks. . . . The big locomotives pulling long trains of flat-cars loaded with huge fir logs were always coming into town and their klonking noise accepted as natural."

*L: Skagit Club.
R: Skagit Theater.
Both maintained by CLLC.
— Photo courtesy of Clear Lake Historical Society*

*Main street of Clear Lake.
— Photo courtesy of Clear Lake Historical Society*

*The Magnolia Saloon.
— Photo courtesy of Clear Lake Historical Society*

Like children everywhere, Clear Lake youths gathered at the train station to watch activity. Dynes said the white-jacketed Negro porters were fascinating, and the children dreamed of traveling abroad to see strange sights. One day the sights were horrible:

". . . the Sedro-Woolley Stage drove in front of an onrushing train. The train shoved the old gray stage down the track a ways, then upended it in the ditch. Long loaves of bread and bodies of people, some severely injured and one or two killed, flew out in mixed confusion on the ground. . . ."

Occasional crime destroyed the usually idyllic life depicted for the small town by its 1920s residents. One of the oddest crimes occurred in January, 1923, when bandits broke into the Nels Trudeau barber shop and stole all the razors and two razor hones, leaving the cash.

In keeping with the benign monopoly of a company town, CLLC maintained a company store. Customers claimed that CLLC had fair prices, competitive with private enterprise. A reporter stated that, when times were tough during World War I, B.R. Lewis cut wages in camps and mills but also slashed prices of necessities at the store. On paydays at the mill the one-armed paymaster first computed how much an employee owed the company store, then plunked down the remainder in silver and gold coins.

Even though CLLC practiced rather fair paternalism, they did not totally escape labor conflicts. The Lewises were adamant about banishing known and active members of the International Woodworkers of the World (I.W.W.) from their employ, who occasionally were physically escorted to the county line. B.R. Lewis was quite active in politics affecting the lumber industry, especially in supporting Full Crew Bill No. 244, which sought to reduce the number of required employees on trains (the position being that modern signal devices made some of them unnecessary). Such reduction would save money, of course, but train crews fought the measure on the grounds of safety.

A flood swept down the Skagit Valley on December 10, 1921, washing away small shingle mills and homes along the river and spreading into Clear Lake. According to the *Clear Lake News,* ". . . at 2 o'clock the Clear Lake Lumber Co. shut down their plant and began to remove their electric motors. A dike was thrown up around the Skagit Club, Skagit theatre and the Silcox Hotel. The purpose of this was to save the maple floor of the Skagit theatre. . . . At 11 o'clock [that same night] the water head reached the fireplace at Clear Lake Lumber Co.'s power plant and the fire was put out and the lights consequently put out. . . ." Townspeople suffered damage to household goods, a few cattle and other stock were lost, and one farmer lost much of his acreage in cabbage because driftwood covered his fields. Trains were detoured around the flood area. After causing much hardship, the river

151

receded the following afternoon. Then came freezing weather and residents ice skated on schoolyard ponds.

A glimmer of foreboding ran through remarks by B. R. Lewis reported in the *American Lumberman* of 1922: " . . . I feel that readjustment of the lumber business in the West has progressed very satisfactorily during the last two years. While we have lost an enormous amount of money during that period, we have at last reached a point where we are making a profit. . . .business has had to adjust itself to a new standard. Higher wages and shorter hours have necessitated the use of more capital in business . . ."

In an article for the local newspaper, February, 1924, a reporter wrote that Clear Lake was growing rapidly. An article indicated that CLLC built new homes, then sold them to employees or others. The same edition reported a huge order of "Jap squares," a lumber dimension that was placed on railroad flatcars bound for ships at Bellingham's harbor, no doubt for Japanese customers. During 1924, CLLC received four carloads of new machinery for its mill, as well as several new donkey engines for the woods.

Even though CLLC was operating at capacity and a profile of the company in 1923 indicated no particular trouble, financial problems were brewing in 1925, totally unanticipated by the rank and file employee. On May 14, 1925, the *Sedro-Woolley Courier-Times* reported that the CLLC had entertained about 2,000 employees and family on its farm fifteen miles from Clear Lake, transporting them to the giant picnic in twenty-three flat cars and box cars, a gala affair. Later that month the company sent big lumber shipments to the east coast by rail and ship (from Everett). In June CLLC bought a new "gas car" for passenger service. And, seemingly unexpected by all, on August 20, 1925, came the stunning announcement:

"Receiver Asked for Clear Lake Lumber Co. . . . Clear Lake Mercantile, Puget Sound & Cascade Railway not affected . . . "

Surprisingly sparse news appeared in the local newspapers until February 9, 1926, when the Mount Vernon newspaper declared that receivers for CLLC had been appointed, and the Sedro-Woolley newspaper that the store also had been placed in the hands of a receiver. Details of citizen reaction and the plight of the CLLC owners were barely aired thereafter in the newspapers.

Dominated by CLLC, Clear Lake just seemed to quietly die with the cessation of work at the mill. The Bank of Clear Lake failed in 1925 along with CLLC and was absorbed by the C.E. Bingham Company of Sedro-Woolley (which, in turn, had troubles during the dark days of the 1932 economy). Clear Lake's First National Bank continued to stay solvent until 1933, when bank examiners closed it; among its "assets" were $133,700 worth of South American bonds, their true worth unknown. However, by the time this bank had been fully liquidated in 1938, depositors did receive 87% of their funds.

CLLC's properties were said to be worth $5 million and were sold at public auction April 23, 1927. When the highest bid was considered inadequate, the property was sold on August 20 to the Bank of California. Restructured as the Skagit Valley Lumber Company (SVLC), the lumber mill and logging operation reopened in February, 1929, with 200 lucky men re-employed. Management said they hoped to have 450 working again before long. Only two months later, in April, 1929, the SVLC or the old CLLC holdings were absorbed into the $12 million corporation, Puget Sound Pulp and Timber Company (PSP&T). PSP&T intended to build a huge pulp mill at Everett and rehabilitate Clear Lake's operation, along with other Northwest mills in trouble, to furnish the logs. The old CLLC operations became PSP&T, Clear Lake Division.

Despite the market crash of 1929, an inauspicious time for a new company to begin operations, PSP&T did build its Everett mill. While it was getting organized and reviewing its future, a forest fire burned thirteen bridges on the PS&C, necessitating rebuilding if the railroad were to operate. PSP&T renewed operations at the CLLC Division in May, 1931, logging six days a week, then closed in August to reopen in late January, 1934. But the Depression deepened, certainly noticed in Clear Lake by workers being laid off steadily. Destitute single men developed a hobo village north of the CLLC log dump called called "Hooverville," because President Hoover was blamed for the poor economy. The men created housing from packing crates, flattened oil tins, scrap sheet metal and cardboard. They made stoves from oil drums and cooking pots out of tin cans. To the CLLC Division's credit, despite their own economic troubles, they intermittently donated money to help the men.

While CLLC Division was struggling along, the PS&C continued to haul freight as a common carrier, connecting with other railroads in Mount Vernon. But it was a losing battle for them, too, and in 1935, PS&C received permission to cease operations.

Markets dried up; consolidation took place, and PSP&T closed the Clear Lake sawmill in 1935 and the shingle mill in 1938. Logging did continue for some time back in the hills. Under a headline of "Growing Demand for Hemlock in Pulp Industry Brings Changes in Logging Operations at Clear Lake," in the November, 1936, *West Coast Lumberman,* an article describes a high lead logging setup in the Mill Creek area along a rail spur seven miles long to tap timber west of Pressentin Creek, and in the Finney Creek watershed via a twelve-mile spur. "In this area the company has a large block of owned and contract timber which will provide many years

153

logging. This side is operated with a Willamette skidder and high lead unit together with a Skagit gas cold decker."

Ongoing logging of the area, farming, and small businesses kept the town going through tough times and war years. Between Clear Lake and Big Lake the Knapp Brick and Tile Factory operated from 1911 to 1934, producing as many as 150,000 bricks daily. Around 1955, the Northwest Talc & Magnesium Company (NT&M) under N.F. Jensen opened a plant to grind and dry seventy-five tons of rock a day. It milled, dried and shipped barite to Alaska for use in oil drilling operations. Talc came from upriver beyond Marblemount, the Skagit Talc Mine, its rock ground for use in making paint and insecticides (the owner was one of the principals of Valumines). Unable to meet pollution standards, NM&T closed in the mid-70s. The talc mine ceased operations, too.

In 1954, C.E. Potter opened the Potter Shake Mill, producing about forty carloads a year of shakes. For three decades the small business employing twenty people produced shakes but, when shakes on homes became regarded as a fire hazard, business lagged and the company closed in 1985. A second shake mill—the Buchanan Shake Mill has persisted.

However, as the century draws toward a close, the town—too close to larger Sedro-Woolley to maintain many shops, and dead to the timber industry—is a ghost of its former lively self. A few stores keep open to serve the locals and the occasional tourist, but most of the town's business buildings burned over a period of years. A bid for incorporation in 1948 failed. The post office in 1995 rented 365 boxes to patrons but many live outside of the town itself, inhabited by perhaps 200 families.

The extensive logging outside of town has left its debris inextricably intertwined and often invisible in new growth forest and brush. Desirous of preserving its history, the town organized a historical society. Had they existed back in 1924, they might have acquired a superb mastodon bone that was found in the nearby forest and donated to the University of Washington. The director of Clear Lake Historical Association, Deanna Ammons, has found during her hikes the remains of trestles over canyons (just rotting pilings and a few surprisingly sound ones), twisted remains of burned bunkcars, boilers, bedframes, and moss-covered skids. Each year the lush growth continues to reclaim and cover the intrusions.

154

Chapter 17
COKEDALE

A lhough located in Skagit County about four miles northeast of Sedro-Woolley, Cokedale had greater ties to Whatcom County and Bellingham because of the involvement of Nelson Bennett and C.X. Larrabee in the Cokedale mines.

Lafayette Stevens, however, one of the initiators of coal prospecting near Hamilton, found the coal seam at Cokedale in 1878. With others, he developed the mines lightly. A reporter for the *Skagit News* wrote on March 8, 1887: "Two hours from Sedro we come to what is the Stevens coal mine and cabin. From the top of the hill we look down 75 or 100 feet to the cabin and entrance where we found George Pierce, the man in charge. He says the coal is equal to the Cumberland coal." But Stevens moved on to new prospects.

Geologists speculated that the Cokedale deposits were the same as that of Hamilton, and later geologists believed that the Hamilton, Cokedale, Blue Canyon, and large Bellingham coal deposits were all part of the same veins that extended northwesterly under the Georgia Strait to Nanaimo on Vancouver Island. The *Northwest Mining Journal* reported that the Skagit coal fields were newer than the carboniferous age but older than the Cascade mountain range. Imprints of fossilized leaves and other materials indicate the creation of the seams in the Eocene Period. However, the turbulent geologic forces that formed the North Cascades fractured the deposits and dashed any hopes for neat, accessible coal seams to mine.

Even so, since the Cokedale deposits appeared to be excellent coking coal, financier Nelson Bennett of Fairhaven (Bellingham) acquired the property in 1889. He began development of the property, then sold it to C.X. Larrabee in 1891. Bennett primarily was known as a railroad man and Larrabee a developer, so the two had various interlocking interests.

Bennett had completed the Fairhaven and Southern Railroad (F&SR) to tap the mineral and timber wealth of the Skagit, connecting Fairhaven and Sedro-Woolley by 1889, and added a spur to the Cokedale Mines in

July, 1890. The F&SR intended to build south from Sedro along Clear Lake, Lake McMurray, etc., but crews from the Seattle, Lakeshore and Eastern arrived in a crucial, narrow pass near Lake McMurray fifteen minutes before the F&SR men arrived, effectively shutting out the rail line from the route. Before long the F&SR became part of the Great Northern Railroad.

Larrabee lost no time in hiring crews and setting up a coal mining enterprise in the hills above Sedro-Woolley. By 1892, four coke ovens were at work; by 1895, thirty operated and ten more followed in 1896. Known superintendents during this early period were Richard Jennings and C.E. Buchanan.

The *Fairhaven Herald* of June 21, 1893, reported that "At present there are thirty men employed in and around the mine, not including a force of men putting in three washers, under the efficient superintendency of C.E. Buchanan, who so successfully constructed the washers for the Blue Canyon Company. The washers will be completed within a week or two, and will greatly increase the quality of coke being burned by the company's ovens by making the coal so much cleaner. The capacity of the washers will be 100 tons per day. Two elevators are also being put in. . . . Two ventilating shafts run into the mines, which insure perfect safety to the miners, the inspector having reported the mine to be the best ventilated of any on the coast."

The reporter went on to declare the mine's future would be strong for years to come, and the coke produced fully equal to the "famous Connellsville, Pa., coke."

The three veins of coal at Cokedale were described as: the north or Klondike vein, with a thickness varying from ten to twenty-five feet; the middle lying 140 feet higher than the north vein with a thickness of four to eight feet; and the south vein, another forty feet above the middle vein, petering out to a thickness of six inches to two and one-half feet. The seams at their outcrops stood almost vertical, but in the lower mine workings (as tunneling progressed) dipped slightly to the southward.

Miners drove the first tunnel into the hill 1,267 feet to cross-cut the formation and intersect seven coal seams, only three of which were economically worthwhile, described above. They reached the Klondike 1,200 feet into the mountain at a depth of 275 feet below the surface and the seam reached thirty feet in width. The middle vein was encountered 1,050 feet from the mouth of the tunnel, and the upper seam at 1,000 feet. According to a state geological bulletin, the upper seam had a solid hanging wall, and a slope of thirty degrees was sunk on this seam for 240 feet to a vertical depth of 120 feet below the water level, and a gangway was driven on the vein with cross-cut tunnels to the Middle and Klondike seams. On this slope level the Middle and Klondike seams were mined. An analysis of Cokedale

Cokedale.

Coal revealed .53% moisture, 8.29% ash, fixed carbon 64.51% and vol. com. M (combustible material) 26.67%. Coke made at Cokedale came out with a 86.38% fixed carbon reading and 8.6% ash.

The deformation of the coal was so pronounced that miners could take out nothing but small pieces at a time. After removal, the coal was washed, the coarser remains diverted for steam plant and domestic heating, the finer taken to the nearby coke ovens. At least forty ovens were of a beehive appearance, each with a five-ton capacity. According to the Washington Geological Survey Report of 1902, the Cokedale mine's 1901 output was 12,643 tons of coal; in 1902, 19,017 tons of coal and 601 tons of coke.

The *Seattle Post-Intelligencer* of May 10, 1902, reported: "The production is, according to smelter men, as good as is manufactured in the country. It is shipped to Everett, Tacoma and Butte. One hundred men work there."

The Cokedale mines (like those at Blue Canyon) were dangerous to work. The walls were poor, and some miners swore the walls had a tendency to press together after the coal was removed. Water was a problem.

However, the Skagit Coal & Transportation Company operated the mine from 1895 to 1904. This corporation was filed on November 29, 1888, with the following trustees: Nelson Bennett, Edward M. Wilson, Edgar Lea Cowgill, Theo Sears, Theodore L. Stiles, Samuel E. Larrabee, and Charles X. Larrabee. The 1895 output was 20,704 short tons. Except for a bad year in 1899, production averaged close to that figure, declining to 10,650 in 1904. The mine closed from 1905 to 1916, resuming operation in 1917 as Cokedale Coke Co. Between 1917 and 1920, annual figures were far lower than the original operations: 1,000 short tons; 5,897; 3,820; and 2,988. The Tieg-Tennent Coal Company took over to produce 1,433 tons in 1921, then the mine ceased operations forever.

A dreary settlement arose around the mine and the 1900 census counted 131 residents. Little personal history of the mining operation or camp can be found. Another settlement straggled around the junction of F&SR Railroad with the Seattle and Northern in the flatlands of the Skagit Valley. At least two shingle mills started business at that point—the Green Shingle Company, doing 125,000 per day, and the Robeson Shingle Company. Much later after the closure of the Cokedale mine, the Skagit Mill Company logged the area. Near Cokedale Junction several railroad cars were abandoned and sat rusting until the late 1930s when they were sold to Japan as scrap.

It is almost impossible to find anything of the mining camp today, except for a water-filled tunnel excavation on private property. Along Highway 20, a considerable distance from the mine, one can see runoff of black slag along a stream. Owners of the property in 1992 said that the two creeks into which the slag was dumped recovered entirely and fortunately suffered no permanent damage.

Chapter 18
HAMILTON

Although Hamilton is much better known for its coal prospects than its iron, it was the latter that caused the most optimism at the turn of the century. J.J. Conner is credited with locating the iron in 1881, but the coal came first.

Two peaks soar abruptly almost from the southern bank of the Skagit River: Iron Mountain on the east, 2,500 feet high, and Coal Mountain on the west, 2,800 feet high. The two are separated by Cumberland Creek. The coal was discovered in 1874 by Amasa Everett, the same prospector who later piqued the curiosity of gold-seekers by mining the upper Skagit River. He was joined in the coal discovery by Lafayette Stevens and Orlando Graham. Stevens interested James O'Loughlin and James J. Conner of LaConner in the prospects. The Skagit Coal Company was incorporated September 18, 1875, for $960,000, offices in

Iron and Coal mountains.

– Photo by JoAnn Roe

LaConner, by the following trustees: James J. Conner, Lafayette S. Stevens, Bedford L. Martin, Amasa Everett, Orlando Graham, James O'Loughlin, Henry L. Yesler, William W. White, and A.W. Piper. Amasa Everett (and likely the other two discoverers) sold his coal claims to "Conner & Loughlin," no doubt the corporate group, in October, 1875. Conner's group filed on 160 acres of coal land and recruited a force of laborers.

These claims—the Skagit, the Cascade and the New Cumberland—were then thoroughly investigated by experts and pronounced to be of the best quality. The Skagit coal vein was on the east face of Coal Mountain above the Hatshadadish Creek only about a mile from the river landing. The *Star* of December 16, 1876, stated:

"The coal vein dipped at an angle of sixty degrees. Three shafts had at that time been sunk, seventy, twenty-five and twenty feet deep, respectively, with an entrance a hundred and twenty feet above the bed of the creek. Seven strata of coal had been uncovered, each running from two to eight feet in thickness. . . . Four veins there had been uncovered, dipping at an angle of twelve degrees. . . . The principal vein here was six feet thick and of pure, solid coal. The New Cumberland claim, divided from the others by Lorette creek, was opened by a tunnel a hundred and fifty feet long, and the coal was found to be of a quality equal to the best for coking, forging and mechanical work."

Amasa Everett, Skagit pioneer.
– Photo courtesy of Skagit County Historical Society

No wonder, then, that the founders were excited. Anticipating an influx of workers, developers platted Hamilton on the north side of the river below the two mountains in 1877. Later a post office, general store. and other businesses opened.

Development of the mines was greatly inhibited by the presence of the two immense log jams on the Skagit River (see Skagit City) that prevented any vessels from going far above Mount Vernon and roads virtually did not exist yet. Conner mined twenty tons of the coal and sent it out to San Francisco by canoe and boat, a complex transportation means involving several transfers of cargo.

By 1879, the river was pretty well navigable but drift continued to plague steamers for another ten years. The United States Government ap-

160

propriated $20,000 to build and operate a snag boat but the sum only covered construction costs with nothing left for operations.

The steamer *Josephine* with many members of the press ventured upstream in September, 1879, to assess the news of coal and gold. At the present site of Hamilton, passenger James H. Armstrong fell from the upper deck of the steamer into the river and was drowned, even though rescuers made valiant attempts to locate him. That same steamer *Josephine*, four years later, incurred greater tragedy when the boiler exploded, killing about fifteen passengers who were calmly eating dinner. The vessel was totally destroyed and sank, except for part of the cabin and hull. An investigation laid the blame on the vessel's engineer, who had not kept sufficient water in the boiler.

Not satisfied just with coal, Conner still probed the mountains near Hamilton and found iron around 1884. He shipped a limited quantity of ore from the Tacoma Ledge to the Irondale smelter, but the trail of disposition of his claims becomes confusing after that. Since production of iron requires considerable investment, the author conjectures that he sold at least part of them, for the *Skagit News* of December 30, 1884, states: "The Tacoma Steel and Iron Company who own the Skagit iron works have become incorporated for $3 million dollars." The directors were: Arthur Davis, F.T. Olds, Peter Odegard, W.F. Daniels, C.S. Torkelson. The sale or lease of claims to that company failed to result in significant development.

Conner continued to seek new prospects. L.K. Hodges in his 1897 book, *Mining in the Pacific Northwest*, summarized his activities, saying Conner had "found magnetic iron on the surface of the Mable claim and brought it to Seattle to be tested. He obtained a button so thickly coated with copper that he at first thought it was entirely composed of that metal." However, the assays showed only 4.8% copper but 35% magnetic iron ore. Conner completely ignored indications, albeit faint, of gold and silver in the ores and concentrated on the iron.

Others probed for metals or coal, too. A.E. Barthwick opened the Crystal Mine near Sterling, about ten miles east of Hamilton. The assays were roughly equivalent to those of the Hamilton area. In September, 1887, the Oregon Improvement Company bought about 1,600 acres of coal land for $860,000 and sold it within the year to Nelson Bennett, Edward Wilson and two others. Bennett planned to enter the deposit with the machinery used to bore the Cascade Tunnel in Stevens Pass but nothing seems to have come of this venture.

The Skagit Cumberland Coal Company (SCCC), its offices listed as San Francisco, California, was incorporated March 28, 1889, with Patrick M. Mackay of Seattle appointed as agent. It, too, spent considerable money developing its holdings. Accounts conflict, but *Sebring's Skagit County Il-*

lustrated indicated that SCCC bonded the Conner claims in 1890; apparently the Conner group leased some of its claims and did not work them, but it is difficult to piece together what exactly happened to Conner.

In 1889, the mining area was assessed by Muir Picken, a mining engineer. Picken said, in addition to the known coal, there was also a good measure of brown hematite (Hodges said magnetic ore, a better quality) iron ore, carrying from 45% to 50% of metallic iron in the region. Iron ore claimants filed the Tyee, Mabel, Last Chance, and Tacoma claims with the state. Picken said the coal and iron deposits covered an area eighty miles by twenty-four miles and were part of the same deposit that runs through Nanaimo, British Columbia.

SCCC began serious work on May 1, 1890, constructing a flume 600 feet long with a 75-foot head to carry water to the compressor. The compressor would run three 3-1/2-inch Rix & Furth drills. This machinery was delivered by the river steamer *Bailey*. Work in the mine's tunnel was hazardous. The tunneling intercepted underground springs, a small subterranean lake, and worse. In 1889, the men were at work when they heard a terrible roaring and fled for the tunnel's mouth, none too soon, for water came with such force that it carried stones weighing two tons out through the mouth of the tunnel and tore ore cars to pieces, breaking the castings with awesome force. The pocket of water was finite, however, and with some change in the direction of excavation, further catastrophes were averted.

The activities at Hamilton brought excursion boats with sightseers from the lower Skagit settlements. In 1890, 150 vacationers boarded a Skagit River steamer, complete with a cornet band. According to the local newspaper, the group picnicked at Lyman in a "beautiful grove fixed up for such occasions," and reached Hamilton about 4:00 P.M. Many scrambled up the steep slope to view the mine workings, and a few entered the tunnel to bring out souvenirs of coal. The excursion returned to Avon, from which it had left, sponsored as a fund-raiser by the Avon I.O.O.F. Lodge.

With the possibility of a future iron or steel mill in the area, a town to be called Cumberland was platted in 1889 for the south side of the river, but it never developed. The town of Bessemer was located in 1890, about six miles above Hamilton, to tap the iron ore trade, but it died at birth, also.

W.D. O'Toole, Washington, and L.F. Menage of Minneapolis, Minnesota, patented seven claims in the same area near Hamilton, 900 acres over all, and formed the Puget Sound Iron Company to exploit the minerals (not the same company as that at Irondale, apparently, for Irondale PSIC was organized by different investors in 1879). Dr. Willis E. Everette, a mining geologist and assayer, took 600 pounds of ore back to Tacoma in November, 1890. He was reticent about his impressions but said to a news reporter that, if the assays were favorable, the O'Toole-Menage syndicate would immediately proceed to erect a blast furnace at a cost of not less than $200,000. During 1890-93, the company did considerable prospecting and development but failed during the Depression of 1893.

Hodges stated that E.C. Strong, an experienced Colorado miner who moved to Hamilton, examined the iron claims in 1896 and theorized that the iron capping was merely that, a capping overlying copper deposits. He confirmed his beliefs by sinking a shaft through the magnetic iron and found, not too deep, significant copper. Hodges said the highest assays ran 20% copper plus some gold and silver, then valued at $44 a ton.

This situation set off a new frenzy of claim-locating, as miners followed the copper belt toward the North Cascades. Hamilton as a town boomed more than ever.

Hodges said that the Everette claim, on which Strong had drilled, had a ten-foot ledge on which the shaft was just beginning to show the change from iron to copper. At the time of Hodges' writings, the claim was owned by W.M. Mackintosh and Dr. G.B. McCulloch. Six men of the Hamilton Copper and Gold Mining Company sank a shaft that showed about the same array of metals as Strong's experimental drilling. Strong joined with J.J. Conner as the Last Chance and Star to work a ledge parallel with the Everette claim; and J.J. Conner, H.C. Conner, and Judge Henry McBride (everyone was getting into the fray) worked the Tacoma and Scottish Chief on still another nearby ledge. A promising ledge containing three claims was worked by W.H. Hainsworth and Samuel Thompson as the Little Pittsburg group; and O'Toole, the former partner in Puget Sound Iron Company, still owned iron claims along Marietta Creek, two and one-half miles from Hamilton, on which he now prospected for copper.

Historical records and writings thereafter largely ignore the copper prospects of Hamilton, so one must assume that none of the prospects were commercially promising.

Alleviating the problem of shipping costs, the Seattle & Northern (S&N) railroad built a line from Anacortes to Hamilton in 1891, with connections to Seattle, Lake Shore & Eastern at Sedro-Woolley, ten miles west of Hamilton.

Hamilton was touted to be the coming "Pittsburgh of the West," and its population boomed. The town of Hamilton was officially incorporated March 13, 1891, but the official plats go back to 1889 and locals said that 1,500 people lived and worked there in 1890. The original plat included a whopping 555 acres, chopped back to only sixty acres in 1925. Hamilton was referred to in the Skagit News of July 22, 1889, as "quite a town," with a heavy male population. Early problems facing the new town government

163

included whether to confine brothels to one location or permit them to operate wherever their owners wished.

At least twenty-five businesses opened, including general stores owned by William Hamilton and A. von Pressentin, hardware store, clothing and furniture stores, two livery stables, a Chinese laundry, the Bank of Hamilton, the short-lived *Hamilton Herald* newspaper (soon sold to the *Concrete Herald* and operated for a time as the *Hamilton Recorder*), and the even shorter-lived *Logger*, three hotels (The Cumberland belonging to Hamilton, another owned by G.W. Noble), a school, public hall, blacksmith shop, drug store operated by J.H. Smith in 1890, dry goods store, even an opera house, a brick factory, and several small lumber mills—all before the turn of the century. Hamilton and McCall started a sawmill in 1889 to serve the community's need for finished lumber. A daily steamboat called to provide passenger and freight service. Furnishing the town's entertainment were the saloons, about sixteen of them, and an uncounted number of ladies of the night and their establishments.

. . . Perhaps Hamilton was a bit too lively. Crime followed prosperity.

In August, 1890, a desperado held up Captain W.A. Jones, who was returning to Hamilton from Seattle with the payroll funds for Skagit Cumberland's coal miners. As Jones walked to his office near the river, a transient, Joe Frey, confronted him with a revolver, blindfolded and tied him to a tree, and fled with the money. Unfortunately for Frey, he rushed right into the arms of some tough miners, who had heard Jones' cries. When Frey waved his gun around, one miner seized him, another hit him over the head with an oar. He was totally subdued when the deputy sheriff arrived.

A senseless murder shocked the residents in 1892. At Hamilton, steam power for the electric light plant was furnished by the nearby Campbell & Edwards shingle mill. When the lights began to fade, J.L. Warner, owner of the utility, went to the mill to berate David C. Moody, the night watchman and stoker. Moody's excuse was that he had no wood and, when Warner pointed to wood lying across the street, that it was not his job to carry wood. Warner angrily went to get Edwards, the man's boss, and upon returning, Warner and Moody renewed their verbal battle in Edwards' presence. An exasperated Warner grabbed Moody by the neck, whereupon Moody drew a revolver and shot Warner dead. Moody was convicted and sentenced to nineteen years in the penitentiary.

Despite access and power problems, the coal development progressed, especially after the railroad came. In 1893, a coal and iron exhibit was forwarded to the Columbian Exhibition in Chicago, and again in 1894 to St. Louis. Although little coal was shipped, Hamilton remained the eastern rail terminus of the Seattle & Northern, supplanted eventually by the GNR, which extended the line to Rockport in 1901.

164

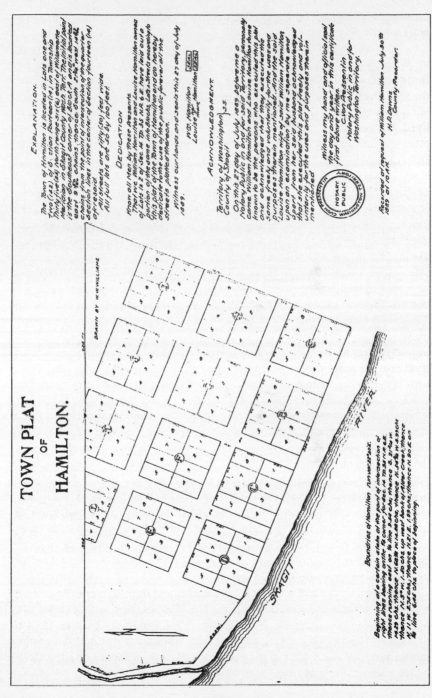

The town suffered immense damage from floods in the 1890s. The Skagit River was a mean adversary. Again and again the waters came relentlessly. About the middle of November, 1892, heavy rains fell and on the night of 18th a warm chinook wind blew and melted snow in the mountains. By the next morning the Skagit was bank-full and rising. Millions of feet of logs and drift swirled dangerously in the river, preventing steamer traffic. At Mount Vernon a big drift jam lodged against a pier for the new bridge; onlookers tried unsuccessfully to break it loose but the pressure snapped the pier. The river overflowed into the town of Hamilton. Nearby homesteaders lost stock and hop crops. Another flood in 1894 caused a Skagit valley farmer to lose twenty-eight of his thirty cattle. In 1896, the Skagit experienced identical chinook conditions to those of 1892, with floods claiming one building in Hamilton. Without respite, the next year, November 17, 1897, again during unnaturally warm weather the river rampaged. It inundated buildings up to eight feet deep and caused most merchants to permanently abandon the original business center adjacent to the river. A curious problem was how to match up wooden sidewalks after they floated away in the swirling waters.

But the town survived and mining prospects continued to fuel development. In 1901, the Pacific Asbestos Company went to work on property south of Hamilton rich in talc and asbestos. Silica, a basis of asbestos, was mentioned in a later engineering report by A.O. Ingalls, Mining Engineer, in the *Northwest Mining Journal*: "The iron ores of this county are of a mineral character, consisting of magnetite, hematite, a mixture of magnetite and hematite, manganiferous iron and chromite. These ores occur in a body of slate iron shale between the sandstone and limestone. There are five parallel veins, extending from the river level—98 feet plus sea to an altitude of 3,000 feet, culminating in Iron Mountain." Ingalls commented that a portion of the deposits were very high in manganese and should be considered manganiferous iron ores, also that they were high in silica.

Pacific Steel Company leased coal claims at Hamilton in 1901, presumably from Conner, to fuel their plant at Irondale. J.J. Conner continued to develop his own coal property, apparently without lasting prosperity. State archives indicate that the Skagit Coal Company was purged from the records July, 1923, as a defunct corporation.

Henry Landes, Washington State geologist, gave an updated review of the Hamilton coal field in his annual geological report of 1902:

"On the property of the Skagit Cumberland Coal Company and on the lands of Mr. J.J. Conner, near the mouth of Cumberland creek, there are a number of outcropping coal veins. The first of these is located on the bank of Cumberland creek, not far from the contact of the coal measures with the underlying mica schist. This vein of coal has a strike of south 43 degrees east, and a southwest pitch of 55 degrees. It lies between sandstone walls, and has a thickness of about 7 feet of clean coal. About a hundred feet stratigraphically above the vein just mentioned, is a second coal seam having approximately the same dip and strike, with a thickness of over 5 feet."

He went on to say there were other veins varying from a few inches to four feet in width, and southward toward Day Lake, outcrops of veins varying from eight to twelve feet.

The *Seattle Post-Intelligencer* of May 10, 1902, stated that not just coal, but the mining of iron near Hamilton was making progress and shipments being made to the Irondale furnaces.

"The ore is used as a flux in refining the other ores which that plant handles. It is sent by railroad to Anacortes and thence is shipped by water to Irondale." (See chapter on Irondale.)

The *"P.I."* also commented that the general area was prospering because of its stills, that "men at Hamilton state that they have often tasted the product of these stills and these say that what it may lack in mellowness it makes up in strength."

It is true that the Skagit Valley drew out-of-work Carolinians to its developing mines and logging enterprises. The hard-working, thrifty people brought much of their Appalachian mountain culture with them, and the *"P.I."* noted, "Near Hamilton is located a genuine mountaineer settlement. Its people come from Tennessee and North Carolina. Some have been there for years. Others are recent arrivals. These men cling to their old habits and clear off small patches of land on the thick timbered hillsides, building shake cabins in the middle of each clearing. They stay very much to themselves."

The ups and downs of mining directly affected Hamilton's growth. The census of 1900 gave Hamilton a population of only 392, a sharp decline from its 1890 boom-town surge, but then it started to grow again. The next recorded population was 900 in 1909, believed to be considerably understated. Citizens led by the Mayor, A.W. Schafer of the Bank of Hamilton, campaigned for more settlers. The town had good schools, a church and two fraternal societies, the Improved Order of Red Men and Modern Woodman of America.

Floods generally could not reach the new location of Hamilton farther from the river, and merchants prospered for awhile. Businesses in 1906 included: Bank of Hamilton owned by J. Yungbluth & Company, J.H. Smith's drug store, Morris Hamilton's confectionery, the *Hamilton Herald* then published by Hans J. Bratlie, the Yellowstone restaurant and saloon with P. Jacobin, prop; J.R. Baldridge's saloon, Thomas Conboy's groceries, Frank Wyman dry goods, another hardware, general merchandise store, etc. Also thriving were: Eagle Shingle Company, Seattle saloon and hotel operated by E.R. Whitney, Mrs. M. Ferbrache's Washington Hotel, Fred Shannon's meat market, P. Gable selling harness, paints and such, and W.W. Raymore's livery stable. Later, the Castrilli's Cheese Factory gained such a reputation that it had customers as far away as Spokane. The Rasmussen Hotel thrived. Bill Soren and his brothers opened a pool hall, grocery store, and cabin rental business. Four miles east was J.T. Hightower Lumber Company's plant and an unnamed logging camp nearby. Dr. R.G. Kellner set up a practice as doctor and surgeon. The Methodist Episcopal Church under pastorate of Rev. Henry Harpst tamed some of the rowdy Hamilton flock, and although the Catholics did not have a church, they maintained a resident priest. Full school facilities, including a high school and gymnasium, served the community.

Conner continued to be the central figure in the mining field, although activities lessened in the new century. The *Skagit County Times* of June 25, 1908, carried an article about J.J. Conner, stating:

"For years past, and through apparently endless hindrance, persecution, and litigation, that which is known as the 'Conner property' consisting of thousands of acres of coal and iron lands, has remained undeveloped. . . . The areas embraced in the Conners coal land holdings consists of 2,182 acres lying south of the Skagit River opposite Hamilton and constitutes the largest portion of what is known as the 'Hamilton coal fields.' The center of the Conner's property is about four miles west of Hamilton, and its bound-

— Photo courtesy of Skagit County Historical Society

aries extend from Cumberland Creek to the east of Day Creek on the west, and from the Skagit River on the north to a mountain range on the south. . . . Twice Mr. Conner had virtually disposed of this property—once to parties in Tacoma and again to the Central Pacific railroad. Rivalry between Seattle and Tacoma spoiled the first chance for development, while contentions for regional supremacy undone the other. Litigation with other claimants has always been a factor . . . " It was unfortunate that, despite all the favorable geological reports, no significant mine ever developed. By 1906, the mining boom had essentially died on all fronts, but the logging industry had grown to eclipse mining efforts, anyway.

Responding to the need for lumber for mine timbering, houses, commercial buildings, and railroad ties in the burgeoning economy of the Northwest, logging companies had moved into the lush forests of the Skagit, Nookachamps and Nooksack drainages about the same time as the mineral boom. So awesome was the timber that a newspaper reported in May, 1884, that two trees were felled near Hamilton—one sixteen feet in diameter at the butt, the other 312 feet long and five feet in diameter at the stump. The entire Skagit Valley and adjacent ridges to the south and north teemed with camps, seventeen of them above Mount Vernon, ranging from six employees to twenty-one. During the main mining-logging boom of the late 1800s, the population of Hamilton soared to about 2,000. Although there were several smaller outfits, two logging companies dominated the Skagit Valley scene—the companies managed by E.G. "Ed" English and the Dempsey Lumber Company (DLC), brothers John J. and L.T. The town of Hamilton was sandwiched between the two friendly competitors, with DLC mainly operating farther east around Birdsview, and English a bit west at Lyman. Lyman-Hamilton came to be considered one location, as far as logging was concerned, although Lyman was also incorporated.

In the very earliest days, logs were dumped into the river, branded and sent downriver to be boomed at a suitable point. Others were rafted and controlled by riverboats; one of the most famous was the *Black Prince.* To surmount snagging on a sandbar near Hamilton operators put big logs in the back and the little ones in front of the booms. The lighter ones floated up over the shallows and dragged the heavier ones along.

The boats also towed rafts of logs to the mills at Seattle or Bellingham, after the logs reached salt water. Among veteran tugboat operators were the Gilkey Brothers; their fleet of tugs operated as far north as Vancouver, British Columbia.

Ed English and Harrison Clothier had founded Mount Vernon in 1877, but English maintained the headquarters of his logging and lumber enterprises at Conway. His realm included huge chunks of the Skagit Valley and parts south. Well-established with many camps at places like Tyee and

169

A Puget Sound and Baker River locomotive.
– Photo courtesy of Skagit County Historical Society

McMurray, English incorporated the Lyman Lumber Company (LLC) in May, 1899, reorganized eight months later as Lyman Lumber and Shingle Company (but retaining some properties as LLC), with financial backing by W.C. Butler of Everett.

Fires decimated some of English's original holdings, and a small mill was sold in 1903. By 1908, the internal changes resulted in the emergence of Hamilton Logging Company (HLC), replacing LLC and perhaps LLSC, a strong and long-lasting firm managed by English.

In 1905, angered by what they viewed to be piratic rates for log-hauling by the GNR, English and DLC joined forces to form their own logging railroad, Puget Sound and Baker River Railway (PS&BRR) on August 30, 1906. Construction moved forward swiftly to complete a railroad parallel to the GNR from Sterling (east of Sedro-Woolley) to Hamilton by 1908.

Since the GNR had extended its line to Rockport, the new railroad took over the former GNR turntable at Hamilton to manage and repair its locomotives. Still another logging railroad, Puget Sound and Cascade Railway, came up the south side of the Skagit River near Hamilton in 1912, but was intended primarily to serve the vast holdings of the Clear Lake Lumber Company.

These railroads were not all that safe. In one accident, a brakeman hanging off a car by one hand was crushed when the train passed another on a siding. The GNR had two derailments within twenty-four hours in April, 1907, both near today's Concrete. No one was injured in the first incident, but in the second the "smoker" plunged over a 25-foot embankment and came to rest on its roof. Of the twenty-three men inside, surprisingly only two died, one was seriously injured, and the rest escaped with cuts and bruises. But the most spectacular wreck that year claimed no lives. During loading, a flat car with four large logs aboard was cast loose accidentally and took off down the tracks on a considerable grade toward a freight train stopped on the tracks ahead. The conductor in the caboose saw the car coming and leaped to safety just in time. The *Skagit County Times* reported:

"In the impact the logs raised and shot forward with a force that sent the largest and longest of them clear through the caboose, tearing out the entire front end, while the other three penetrated the rear and about half the length of the car forward. The trucks under the caboose were driven so closely together that the flanges on the wheels lapped . . ."

Unaware of any oncoming missile, the two engineers up front understandably wondered, as the report put it, "wot t'hell."

During the first ten years of operation of the PS&BRR, the line hauled the output of English and DLC's camps, plus that of Skagit Mill Company and the David Tozier Company, smaller outfits, a whopping 606,000,000 feet.

In 1917, HLC changed its name back to Lyman Timber Company (LTC), with the principals being William C. Butler, Eleanor E. Butler, L.L. Crosby, E.G. English, Alice K. English and N.A. English, capitalized for $1 million.

Mechanized equipment began to replace horse and oxen teams in skidding out logs. A huge skidder soon dubbed "The White Elephant" was installed north of Hamilton. It was mounted on a railroad car, much as a big crane rests on a movable platform and, through a complex rail switching method, could swivel around as needed to give straight pulls from the woods. A crew of eighteen operating the beast could stretch out over 4,000 feet of cable to snake out the logs. According to rail historian, Dennis Blake Thompson, "In 1922, statistics for the 'new' Lyman Timber Company were as follows: ". . .three sides operating, ten donkey engines, five high leads, commissary, machine shop, electric light plant, fifteen miles of railroad using 56-pound rail, three geared locomotives, one hundred skeleton cars, ten flat cars, one hundred and seventy five men employed with a daily output of 200,000 feet."

DLC finished logging around Birdsview in the spring of 1927, removed its logging rails and moved offices to Lyman. However, unable to negotiate

171

for sufficient additional timberlands, DLC only lasted another four years in Skagit County and moved on to fresh lands around Mount Rainier. The company sold its interest in the PS&BRR to the LTC, which continued to take out logs by rail until about 1960, when trucks took over entirely.

Mining never revived, despite occasional flares of interest. The SCCC did not develop further, and archives indicate that it was stricken from corporate records July 1, 1923. At some time between 1900 and 1923, the Cumberland Creek properties went into the hands of the Hamilton Coal and Development Company (principals are unknown).

Geologist Olaf Jenkins, traveling to the site in the 1920s, reported that a group of buildings had been constructed about 500 feet from the PS&BRR, offices and bunkhouses. Fifteen hundred feet upstream on the creek the company had built a dam for water power, flumed down to the site. Below the dam there were at least two tunnels about thirty-five feet long. Above the dam were more significant tunnels entering the mountain as much as 400 or 500 feet; some said one tunnel went 900 feet into the mountain. Apparently it was the intention of the company to tunnel in such a way that all six known seams would be exposed or contacted. The coal was considered a medium grade of coking coal, with a report showing the material to be from 68% to 79% fixed carbon. In a Washington geological bulletin of 1924, Jenkins said that most of the old tunnels and holes were in such bad condition that it was not possible to get very far back into them."

Later rumors of building a huge conveyor across the river to the north shore railroad (GNR) excited the local people, but nothing ever came of them.

Donald L. Corson, writing in *Pacific Search*, December-January, 1975-76, declared none of the coal seams in Washington were very thick, the thickest, in Skagit County, only ranged to thirty-six feet of which only one half was coal. In Whatcom, Pierce, King and elsewhere, seams were only three to five and one-half feet. He said:

"All seams have undergone folding and faulting varying from 30 to 60 degrees. Seams are also often broken and movement of some parts common. In addition sometimes volcanic and glacial material up to thousands of feet deep are over the top of seams."

He said that strip-mining was entirely impractical, and that coal-cutters and conveyors used in the East were not feasible. Thus, the inability to use mechanical means of mining made the coal a poor investment. Between 1900 and 1930, Washington's coal was 30% more expensive than Rocky Mountain Coal and 80% more than the national average. The fractured nature of the North Cascades Mountains, then, ruined any investor's chances of making a profit.

Loggers continued to keep the town alive, though—the logging companies, lumber mills, and the service businesses, even as floods continued to plague the town. What water didn't take, fire did. A fire in September, 1924, destroyed several homes. On April 15, 1925, a huge fire took out most of the business district. Nineteen buildings, some multi-storied, went up in smoke over a three-block area. The fire had smoldered for some time in a wall between the Hardy hardware store and Slipper's general mercantile store. A neighbor, Mrs. A. Belfry, discovered it after smoke turned to flames within the hardware store. By the time storeowners and residents gathered, the fire, fanned by a brisk northeast wind, had gathered too much headway to stop. The Slipper store erupted into flames. The fire jumped to the D.C. Henry residence and an oil house next door on Maple Street, then burned another home.

The fire crew centered their efforts at the Belfry property, managing to divert the fire from house to barns and sheds. Had the Belfry blaze gone out of control, the fire probably would have completely destroyed the business district. As it was, it continued its destructive rage, consuming the J.L. Wall poolroom, a barber shop of W.Z. Harrison, the imposing Washington Hotel, the Jacobin apartments, Shannon Garage and the Shannon home. Jumping the street, the blaze moved on to burn the Jacobin poolroom, Swettenam's storage garage in which there were several cars, the movie theater, and two more homes. The fire finally was contained at the home of John Slipper.

The town remained an entity but never recovered from that blow. Gaps like missing teeth mark the progress of that fire, for few buildings were reconstructed.

The shrunken town remained alive, though. Many of the married loggers lived in Hamilton and came home on weekends. Weekends were for letting off steam; the single men, especially, flocked to Hamilton and Sedro-Woolley to spend their money drinking, fighting, or whoring, and the streets of both towns were raucous. The one marshal in town had a dangerous task. Like an earlier marshal, Jake Woodring, who was beaten to death in 1904, Ed Luton was killed in December, 1929, by a blow to the head from an unknown assailant. His widow Bessie, penniless and pregnant, asked for his job, because it paid five dollars every Saturday night for policing the weekly dance. With the occasional help of sympathetic townspeople, she managed the job but resigned after three months because of her advanced pregnancy.

When the deep Depression of the 1930s reached Hamilton, there was little market for lumber—or anything else. With wild game available and gardens, the people survived without much cash. Destitute young men, ages seventeen to twenty-three, from all over the nation joined the Civilian Conservation Corps (CCC). At Lyman a CCC camp consisted of young New

173

Yorkers. Hamilton drew CCC men from the southern states, most appropriate since the upriver country was settled by many Carolinians. During Depression years the GNR was credited with compassion for local people, hiring as many men as they could afford to repair track, replace ties, fill gravel beds. The company rotated the crews to give more jobless men a chance to avoid starvation.

On toward mid-century the Hamilton Farm & Timber Company employed Hamilton residents, then it ceased operations, too. It was owned by J.H. Smith and five members of the Russell family: James R., Fred C., Lawrence D., Josh W. and Carl H. The Eagle Shingle Mill was an active establishment, owned by John Hadden Slipper, who also owned the Eagle Shingle grocery and hardware firm. The *Skagit Post* was a Fred Slipper enterprise but was moved to Sedro-Woolley, still an active newspaper in the 1990s. Yet one by one the mills and logging businesses either failed or changed locations when the log supply ran out.

In 1994 Hamilton businesses included an olivine crushing business, two taverns, a restaurant and small store. The mainstay of the community for many years continued to be the LTC, which was sold to Soundview Pulp and Paper Company (SPPC) and absorbed several smaller logging companies. In turn, SPPC merged its timberlands with Scott Paper Company in November, 1951, which chiefly harvested and hauled logs to its Everett plant. Scott sold to Crown-Pacific Corporation (CPC) in July, 1979, seeking to reduce the area of its far-flung holdings that ranged from the Canadian border to Mount Rainier. CPC's operations are largely confined to Skagit County, and the firm today is mostly a tree farm enterprise engaged in developing a lumber source for tomorrow's harvest. As Crown Pacific Corporation Ltd. the company employed forty-four persons in 1995, including foresters and engineers, and hired contract loggers as needed. In decades past Scott and its predecessors employed hundreds.

Of course, the severe reduction of this remaining logging operation made further inroads into Hamilton's population. Today there are about 200 permanent residents, but the rich history of the town is not forgotten. The Tim and Jim Bates families and other volunteers have restored the Fred Slipper home and are gathering artifacts for a Hamilton museum. Meantime, the Skagit River continues unabated in its determination to destroy Hamilton. In the 1991 flood, six or seven additional homes were damaged and torn down.

Chapter 19
SKAGIT CITY

When people and materials moved by water through the heavily-forested Northwest, Skagit City was an important small port on the south fork of the Skagit River.

Absolutely nothing remains to identify the town today; only a dike, much repaired over a century, is there to hold back the river. In fact, on the river side of the dike, silt has settled out so that a small treed delta provides a fishing park. The Skagit City school was moved a half mile away and continued to serve as a school until 1940, after which it was abandoned after consolidation of school districts. It was not forgotten, though. Former pupils, friends and spouses founded the Skagit City School Pioneer Association in 1954, spruced up the building, and have regular reunions.

Skagit City originally faced the water and had docks and landings to serve river traffic. As early as 1863, there was an Indian trading post on the South Fork and a dozen families settled along the river nearby. Formed by the arms of the North and South Skagit River and Puget Sound, Fir Island (the land adjacent to Skagit City) was and is a fertile mecca especially favored by the settlers. John Campbell opened a trading post in 1868, John Barker another, on the site of Skagit City.

Crime and swift, if inaccurate punishment, was no stranger to this Northwest frontier. During the winter of 1869, trader Barker was found one morning with his throat cut and his store ransacked. Irate neighbors jumped to conclusions and hung two innocent native Americans, before more sober investigation indicated that a transient, Quimby Clark, was the likely culprit. Smugglers plied the maze of Skagit sloughs and channels, moving on through the San Juan Islands to deal with Canadian accomplices in Scotch whiskey, illegal immigrants, and other goods.

By 1872 Skagit City had a post office, and soon the town was a regular stop and head of navigation for sternwheelers on the river. A smaller hamlet grew up downriver, Mann's Landing or Fir, in 1876, the two towns only about three miles apart.

Skagit City about 1876.

      – Photo courtesy of Skagit County Historical Society

  Immigration into Skagit County was speeded by the belief that upriver gold or other minerals awaited the finder. Only two years after the trading posts emerged, a complete town was in place: a school, churches, several stores, hotels, saloons, a grange with forty members, a Good Templars Lodge with forty-five members and a union hall. A very welcome addition to Skagit City in 1883 was a physician, Dr. William Thompson, who traveled by canoe or horse and buggy to serve the community. Surprisingly soon, the settlers threw up regular board-construction homes, not log dwellings, and social life developed. The *Skagit News* of January 5, 1886, describes a ball:

  " . . . the ball at Skagit City on New Year's night was a grand success. Quite a number went from here [Mount Vernon, organized in 1877] to help celebrate. Music for the occasion was furnished by the Mount Vernon string band. The supper was elegant and well served."

  Steamer service between Skagit City and Seattle was instituted in 1874, Captain John S. Hill piloting the ship *Fanny Lake*. By 1877, John Gates provided weekly upriver mail service.

  That was the date that the lower log jam in the Skagit was opened to navigation. Two log jams had barricaded today's site of Mount Vernon. The older one below the town possibly dated to the 1700s, a tangle of logs and drift that had lodged securely, the river muttering darkly below it. Large trees had grown on the jam, and clearing it for navigation seemed impossible. The second jam above Mount Vernon was growing to resemble the older one. During high water one could work around the channel by using

176

the maze of sloughs or backwaters, marshy paths created by the river as it sought to escape the restraints of the jams, but that was practical only for small boats.

In 1874, settlers petitioned Congress for $25,000 to remove the jams, but an investigator sent to assess the situation estimated that removal would cost four times that much. Tiring of governmental delays, the settlers decided to do the job themselves. By December, 1874, almost half the lower jam had been removed, the men cutting through eight tiers of jammed logs, some three feet in diameter. As work progressed, floods and pressure from the swiftly flowing river caused the jam to move, dislodging a section estimated at five acres in size in 1877. Later that year, workers opened a channel 250 feet wide in the lower jam, but the water was so turbulent that travelers usually portaged around. Two more years of work cleared the river, although drift intermittently closed the 120-foot gap.

With the path to Sound transportation clear, Harrison Clothier and Ed English, the lumber baron, established Mount Vernon in 1877, a fateful event that would soon cause the eclipse of Skagit City and Fir. Bolstering Skagit City for awhile was its ferry service across the Skagit, a valuable link run first by Grant Knight and later by Otto Larson; service continued until 1929, long after any real settlement lingered at Skagit City. Fir also had a ferry.

As the fertile land was cleared of trees to become farms, Mount Vernon and Sedro-Woolley, Burlington and Hamilton became more important transportation centers—more in the center of productive areas. Skagit City was upstaged and faded away, as Mount Vernon became the chief river port on the Skagit. Intermittent fires and the intense floods of the 1890s destroyed buildings and undermined the dikes on which the business district rested.

In time, nothing was left of the once-thriving town of as many as 300 or 400 residents, the most important early south fork river port. The site was doomed, anyway; Fir Island was often flooded; indeed, during the winter of 1990-91, it was completely inundated despite modern diking methods.

177

Chapter 20
SKAGIT QUEEN MINES

Lying in the same general mineral belt as the Ruby and Slate Creek mines of Whatcom County, but farther south, the Skagit Queen Creek mines in eastern Skagit County appeared as promising as those to the north. From the canyons of the Skagit River up Thunder Creek to Skagit Creek, a mere three-mile tributary that drains the mighty Boston Glacier, prospectors found little gold but promising deposits of silver and lead. On Skagit Queen Creek, prospects were especially bright.

Investors O.P. Mason, E.H. Kohlhase, and Robert A. Tripple incorporated the Skagit Queen Mining Company (SQM) for $1 million on July 1, 1905, with offices listed in Seattle. With the investment funds, management constructed a substantial camp—bunkhouse, messhall, storehouse, powder house, and a barn. An assay laboratory was installed at the site.

Assessing the "Great Silver-Lead District of the Cascade Range in Washington" in June, 1907, editor Adair of the *Northwest Mining Journal* said that the "ore is mostly Argentiferous galena. Most of the veins carry the four metals—lead, silver, copper and gold, named in order according to value."

He went on to discuss the claims and veins being probed by companies in the Thunder Creek Basin, including SQM, Thunder Creek Mining Company (TCM), and Standard Reduction & Development Co. (SR&D).

Thunder Creek Basin, including Skagit Queen Creek, was a part of that Cascade Mining District, a high-altitude area at the west end of Chelan County and the east of Skagit County. The Sawtooth Range bisected the district, separating Thunder Creek Basin from Horseshoe Basin. Spectacular, glacier-covered peaks of 6,000 to 8,000 feet punctuated the area. Despite the formidable terrain, optimistic prospectors found mineral signs and heavily staked the area.

It is unclear from the records whether the mine was supplied at first from Cascade Pass, an exceedingly rugged route, if so, or always from the Skagit River/Thunder Creek approach. Regardless, the company set up a

179

supply base and corral for animals at Marblemount, junction of the Skagit and Cascade rivers, and worked from there—a long and arduous supply route, partly choked with snow for at least six months of the year. The Skagit River/Thunder Creek approach involved traversing the narrow passage through the Skagit Gorge, a route so stingy with level ground that, early in the gold rush, miners were forced to pass through on ladders in parts of the gorge. Later pack trails were not much better, although a bridge over the Skagit improved access via the south side of the river toward the Thunder Creek Basin. Still the area could scarcely be any more remote from practical transportation, then or now. When the SQM needed a heavy block for its compressor, the packer selected his biggest mule and put the block on its back. Because the mule could not tolerate such weight for long, the packer provided a tripod and hoist; every few hundred feet he stopped and elevated the load with the tripod to give the mule temporary relief. On another occasion, to send a large coil of cable to the mine, the packer placed one coil on the lead horse, continued it unbroken to the second, and so on. Had any animal faltered or fallen over a cliff, one can only visualize the terrible tangle.

Still the companies pursued their development work vigorously. After absorbing another small company, the Protective Mining Company, a new corporation replacing SQM (Decree of Disincorporation dated February 25, 1908), filed articles August 9, 1907, for $2 million as Skagit Queen Consolidated Mining Company (SQCM).

A United States geological surveyor reported in 1908 that the company had installed a thirty-inch Pelton wheel, operating under a 150-foot head of water, to run a 15 H.P. electric generator. This furnished power for machine drills at the mines almost a mile away, and also electric lights for the mine and the camp. By 1908 the company installed a 10 H.P. induction motor to run an eight-inch by four and one-half-inch air compressor. At the mine two small machine drills were used to push a tunnel into the mountain. The surveyor observed that the equipment was too light for the job.

SQCM owned much of a most promising vein, the Willis E. Everette, which lay mostly in nearby Chelan County. It had been discovered by a doctor-prospector around 1890, and a smelter test at the Tacoma smelter indicated $113 of silver per ton. C.D. Grove, mining engineer, said there were tons of the ore in sight, where the vein ran through the Sawtooth Range in a vein from eight to forty feet wide. At one point it widened to 220 feet. Yet the author found no record indicating that the vein was ever worked substantially.

SQCM planned to install a forty-eight-inch Pelton wheel with a 550-foot head of water, to produce 250 H.P. but it is not known whether or not the plan was completed.

Skagit Queen Mine.

— Photo courtesy of Skagit County Historical Society

At the time of reincorporation, SQCM had one tunnel bored to a depth of 113 feet in the "Dude Ledge." Assays were good, showing $200 silver, $9 gold per ton, but the veins pinched off or were narrow. Probably the main problem was the difficulty of transportation and operation in this rugged North Cascades chasm. Before long, the firm ran out of money and investors were chary of providing new funds.

A nearby operator was the British Mining Company (BCM) with 654 acres of property, including thirty-one claims and four millsites on Thunder Creek, apparently a part of the North Coast group. BMC had built a dam and laid over 1,400 feet of twenty-inch pipe to operate a thirty-six-inch Pelton wheel with a 500-foot head, considerably more power than the SQCM's wheel. Miners had drilled a 660-foot tunnel but did not take out any significant wealth. When SQCM began to fail, the BMC took it over in 1913, continuing to work the claims, but also ran out of money.

Now the TCM acquired the BMC properties and power plant. It had been working conservatively across Skagit Queen Creek from the SQCM. It only had two bunkhouses, a small blacksmith shop, a few workmen, but its crew had drilled into the mountain and taken out ore with an ore car, running assays at Tacoma Smelter. However, after taking over the SQCM, it failed, as well. According to a United States Forest Service historian, a ranger reported in 1920 that remaining at the SQCM site were two cabins, one of which had collapsed, and the power plant on Thunder Creek. Records show that SQCM claims were again in the hands of BMC in 1952.

Meanwhile SR&D extended its operations, seemingly more well financed than the other companies. It was incorporated in 1905 for $1 million and had properties in Butte, Montana, as well as Thunder Basin. Its properties were known as the Lakeside group and the company also shared a portion of the Willis E. Everette vein with SQCM. Its directorate was imposing, including such men as Charles G. Thrasher, a mining expert; J.D. Frost, Tax Commissioner of Washington State; J. Fred Braid of the Seattle Times; editors of the Roslyn and Ellensburg newspapers, bankers and investors. On the hillside above the SQCM, workers completed a concentrating plant and a power plant for the company's own purposes during the winter of 1907-08. By then a permanent camp consisted of a mill house sixteen by forty feet, a cook house of the same size, a substantial machinery building including a blacksmith shop, ninety-mule barn, assay office, and a two-story bunkhouse fourteen by sixteen feet. The latter and the cookhouse were built to withstand snow and avalanche conditions, studded buildings with double floors and roofs having three thicknesses of timber in the walls. The company kept a force of about thirty men on site during that winter, and the supply trains lugging supplies to the site that autumn numbered as high as fifty-six horses.

By the following year or so SR&D had completed its own sawmill to provide lumber for construction, had built a tramway and installed a telephone system. The company worked nine different fissure veins and was ready to send out ore.

Because working the mines was almost impossible without practical transportation to smelter, miners agitated for the installation of a cross-Cascade railroad, or at least one to the Tacoma smelter from the Ruby and Skagit mining areas. If not a railroad, then a practical wagon road. Starting before 1900, mine-to-market road promoters had attempted to gain money to build what was known first as the Cascade Wagon Road, then the North Cross-State Highway, finally the North Cascades Highway (completed as late as 1972). Railroad surveys simultaneously went forward to the extent that one newspaperman in the Methow Valley said dryly that, if all the railroads were built, there would be so many tracks that settlers would be forced to move to the foothills. The other factor lacking in the Cascades, despite rushing streams, was adequate power equipment to run mining machinery. Two companies moved to acquire rights, should it be possible to provide the transportation and power needs. The Thunder Creek Transportation and Smelting Company incorporated August 12, 1908, to acquire water rights in the Cascade Mining District through which a railroad might be built, hoping to provide power for heavy mining industries. This firm, together with the North Coast Mining and Milling Company (officers Dr. W.W. Shenk, George Senior, and A.M. Richards), combined as Puget Sound, Cascade and Chelan Railway Company to build a railroad. North Coast had been working the Colonial claim, originally worked by Jack Durand in the original 1880s rush to the Skagit, near the junction of Thunder Creek with the Skagit River. The rugged mountains defeated their idea of rail transportation, as they had all other hopefuls. By 1919, the North Coast firm was defunct. Yet in 1909, the editor of the *Northwest Mining Journal* said: "A new era is before our commonwealth as a mining area. . ."

Geologist Marshall T. Huntling of the Division of Mines and Geology of Washington State, inventoried the claims in Thunder Basin in 1956, noting that at SQCM's old site, thirty-two claims and four millsites were still patented and three claims unpatented. The ruins of a 670-foot adit or tunnel were visible. His report indicates that, at that time, the Willis E. Everette claim was in the hands of BMC.

Some time after 1915—it must have been after 1956, the TCM claims were transferred to J.S. and Carolyn M. Dovenny. Subsequently on January 18, 1971, Gregg C. MacDonald, Natural Resources Development Corporation, purchased the claims, whereupon MacDonald donated them to Seattle University December 17, retaining the option to repurchase them. He did so on December 18, 1972.

With MacDonald present, the National Park Service mining engineers did a field examination of minerals, declaring that, while traces of metal were found, it was of insufficient quantity and quality to show a commercial value for the ownership. The claims were patented, though, and MacDonald sold the property to Glenn A. Widing of Portland, Oregon, reportedly for the sum of $165,000. Widing waited to see what the outcome would be of the formation of the North Cascades National Park.

No known claims were being worked in Thunder Basin at the time the North Cascades National Park was created in 1968, its borders encompassing Thunder Basin, as well as several areas of Mt. Baker, Slate Creek, and Cascade Pass. However, nearby Valumines was in the process of installing facilities to work claims near Boston Glacier along Cascade Pass. Park Service authorities set out to assess the value of the many claims, patented and unpatented, within the North Cascades National Park lands, reclaiming those deficient in the amount of work required to retain them, purchasing others. Others yet remain active as a result of current work on them and some owners of unpatented claims have vociferously defended their right to continue ownership. Patented claims or privately owned lands predating the park had to be honored, but getting permission to remove ore was another problem.

In 1965 hearings before the United States Senate, Ken St. Clair, representing the Silver Queen Mining Company said that his company held 205 claims in the Cascade and Thunder district. An article in the *Daily Olympian* in 1968 mentioned that one Lowell Warner and others had formed Thunder Mountain Mines in 1966 and owned eighty-eight unpatented claims along Thunder Creek. Geologist Marshall T. Huntting stated that at least 102 valid mining claims existed within the new park's boundaries. Among them were the thirty-six claims on 655 acres in the Skagit Queen Creek purchased in 1972 by Widing, who suggested in October, 1975, that he planned to log and mine the area, possibly building a eighteen-inch narrow gauge railway into the area to bring out ore.

Glenn A. Widing filed a Forest Practice Application on September 30, 1975, for clearance to do "Clear Cut," "Logging, Road Const.," and "Bridge Construction." The clear cut would be high lead and helicopter; the logging would involve a D-9-Cat and loader or crane. He agreed to hand plant two-year-old Douglas Fir seedlings within three years.

NPS required within ten days thereafter an Environmental Evaluation Matrix, which was to be accepted, denied or modified within thirty days of the government's receipt of the matrix. Input from other agencies such as the Department of Fisheries was requested. If road access were required, then an Environmental Impact Statement would be necessary.

The prospect of mining and logging left environmentalists aghast. In a *Bellingham Herald* article of October 12, 1975, Dr. Patrick Goldsworthy of the North Cascades Conservation Council was quoted: "It would be devastation of the worst sort. If anyone were to go in and log in the Thunder Creek valley at the Skagit Queen site . . . this would be a most devastating and disastrous thing." Michelle Whitmore, secretary to Park Superintendent W. Lowell White, was quoted in the *Seattle Times*: "I can tell you that North Cascades National Park does not favor this proposal at all." The Park's spokesman also expressed concern about avalanches in the narrow canyon, if logging were to take place. "Red Alert Memos" flew back and forth between offices.

There were sharp differences between the evaluations of worth provided by the NPS engineers and Widing's consultant. Steven W. Koehler, Koehler Assay and Mining Company and former field geologist for AMAX Coal Company, prepared his own assessment of the mineral potential of the Skagit Queen claims on December 16, 1975. An interesting fact contained in the report is that the Boston Glacier had advanced rapidly between 1950 and 1955, increasing 17%, continuing to advance to the time of report. Koehler said that a mineral appraisal for the NPS by Knowles and Neel in 1973 was "astounding. . . . For example the NPS report claims 11 days of field work, however, only 14 samples were collected for assay." He suggested that the two NPS men failed to understand the nature of the mineral occurrences on these claims, and did not go to certain "gulches" where good ore bodies existed.

Koehler first was flown over the properties on July 23, 1975, while a surveying party set up camp near the old SQCM. During fifteen days the party collected numerous samples, concluding assays over a wide range with the highest in excess of $2,000 per ton. The richest ore occurred in the Willis Everette #1 and the Dude Gulch ore body—which would not have been news to the old prospectors working at the SQM. Koehler's summary and conclusion was that within the ore body are veins that contain high grade silver ore up to 450 ounces per ton and base metals up to 20% total. "This conclusion is in direct conflict with that of Knowles and Neel, 1973."

Based on the results, Widing elected to proceed with plans for a road, advising the Department of Interior (NPS) through his attorney that he wanted to cooperate fully with them (February 10, 1976). On February 23, 1976, Polly Dyer, secretary and board member of the North Cascades Conservation Council, spoke to the 94th Congress, House Interior and Insular Affairs Committee, appealing for money to purchase eighty-nine mining claims and 167 private tracts within the North Cascades National Park and the Lake Chelan National Recreation Area. Included most particularly were the Skagit Queen claims due to the threat of timber removal and mining (complete with ten miles of road, logging, mills). "Operation of the Skagit Queen mine would have a devastating immediate and permanent effect upon the Park's Wilderness."

During the ensuing months lawyers for the NPS and for Widing presented their opposing positions on the questions of right-of-way for a road, in particular. On May 6, 1977, Widing's attorney stated that he had an offer from a Canadian firm for a one-half interest in the Skagit Queen claims (subject to access by road) for $1.5 million; therefore the offer of the NPS (originally $168,700 when made to Gregg MacDonald) was refused.

The hearings went on for the next three years (*United States* v. *Glenn Widing*, Contest Nos. OR MC 4665 and 4666), culminating in a decision "which dismissed Contestee's claims to the Queen and Skagit Millsites in North Cascades National Park." The basis of part of the contest was the question of whether or not two "millsites" on the property had ever been active millsites, a key factor in the disposition of the applications for rights-of-way.

On August 31, 1982, a Notification of Closing was given by Keith M. Watkins, Land Acquisition Officer, to the superintendent of the North Cascades National Park that the United States had acquired Widing's parcels consisting of 644.58 acres for $277,000.

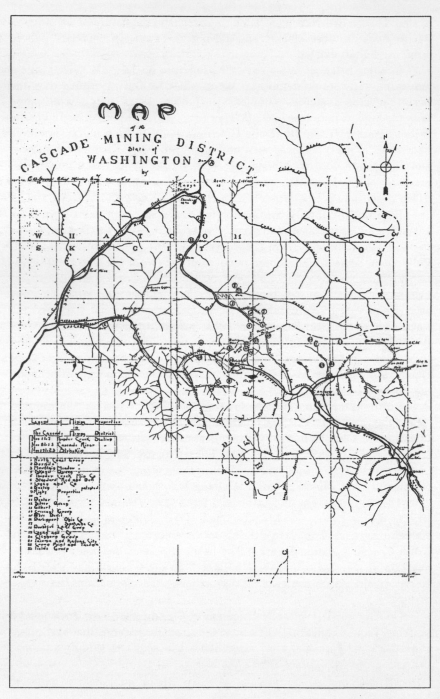

MAP
of the
CASCADE MINING DISTRICT
State of
WASHINGTON
by

Chapter 21
VALUMINES

One of the latest mining ventures in Skagit County, developing some of the oldest claims in the North Cascades, was Valumines, Incorporated, organized August 3, 1960, by William R. Soren and Robert A. Rukke, principals. The claims, which include the famed Boston Lode, were located at the north side of Cascade Pass. The company's misfortune was to be surrounded by the North Cascades National Park in 1968.

Soren, Rukke and their ancestors were no strangers to the Cascades, even though Valumines was a recent amalgamation of Valumines, Inc., and Soren Mining and Milling Co. in 1960. Both men had acquired their claims in Cascade Pass over several decades. Rukke's great-uncle, John Stinson, was in the gold rush of 1880, staking a number of claims in Horseshoe Basin, Chelan County, which came into Rukke's possession. Soren bought several claims during the Depression years at a tax sale, including some holdings formerly belonging to the Silver Queen Mining Company, and added others over a period of time. Rukke's and Soren's claims were back to back on either side of a ridge and, thus, in 1960, the two joined forces and set out to develop the claims.

Prior to intensive work in Cascade Pass, Soren operated a grocery store, service station and tavern in the town of Hamilton. He also developed and worked mining claims, having been a prospector in Montana and Idaho in his youth. He was the principal of the Skagit Talc Company, Incorporated. From incorporation in 1929 to dissolution in 1943, the mine employed ten men and shipped as many as eight sixty-ton carloads a week of talc via the old Seattle City Light access railroad. (Talc is used for carvings and the powder in insecticides.)

For decades prior to 1960, both men worked their claims off and on in their spare time, only becoming seriously involved after the amalgamation of the two holdings. The resulting concern then owned twenty-seven claims, nineteen in Horseshoe Basin, and eight in Boston Basin, also acquiring a partial interest in several other claims and leasing some, including the rich

Boston Lode, Bremerton, Tacoma, Aberdeen, Dakota, Midas 1 and 2, Diamond No. 1, Horseshoe, Cliff Lode, etc.

The Boston was discovered by G.L. and J.C. Rouse and George Sheckler during the original 1879-1880 rush to the Cascades, and obtained by John Stinson. The claims lay above Horseshoe Basin and were supplied from Stehekin at the head of Lake Chelan on the eastern side of the Cascades, about a twenty-five mile hike. Rukke said in 1992 that his uncle John was a stalwart fellow, that he and eight others would stay on the claim all winter, packing in groceries from Stehekin. On one occasion, Stinson fell and broke his ankle about five miles from the claim, then slid on a shovel down a slope to a little cabin, where he was able to splint the ankle and make it home.

L.K. Hodges said in 1897, in *Mining in the Pacific Northwest*: "The Boston . . . has the greatest showing in the district. The ledge crops on the west side of the Boston glacier, which in places has worn away one of the walls, leaving a great body of galena exposed in a cliff to a height of forty feet. The ledge which is divided in the middle by a three foot horse of black porphyry, crops at this point to a width of 50 feet. A cross-cut of eighteen feet from the side of the glacier showed ore for ten feet and a tunnel sixty

Concrete and steel mill for processing ore.
— *Photo courtesy of Robert A. Rukke*

feet along the wall showed galena and sulphides almost solid for the whole width. . . . Assays run as high as 110 ounces silver, 60 per cent lead and a little gold." Two tons of ore were shipped to smelter in the 1890s.

The Diamond vein, part of the Midas group of five patented claims, where Valumines' work was concentrated after 1960, occurs in a precipitous zone and dips steeply to the southeast. It is exposed in the Midas tunnel and outcrops in a creek bed for a distance of 400 feet along the center of the claims as it extends over the mountainside. It is covered with overburden. The vein ranged from sixteen inches to twelve feet, averaging about four feet in width.

Rukke's original Valumines company had driven about 3,000 feet of tunnel over a sixty-year period on its nineteen Horseshoe Basin claims. Rukke and predecessors hoped to get underneath the outcrops and access the principal ore bed. Because of the advance of the Boston Glacier, some of the claims actually lay under glacial ice.

Because there was no road to the Valumines property, all supplies still came by muleback as late as the 1950s and thereafter partly by a short aerial tram. Extremely heavy snows over a long season in Horseshoe Basin, which is affected by the eastern Washington weather pattern, not the warmer western slope conditions, caused a short working year.

Thus, when Soren and Rukke combined, just after the mine-to-market road up Cascade River from Marblemount was completed in 1959 near Soren's property, it was obviously more practical to access the properties from the west, where a natural cleft joined the two sets of claims. It appeared that the Horseshoe claims could be accessed by drilling eastward from the Diamond claim on the west slope. Optimism arrived with the road.

At the time of the merger, the total spent by the two separate concerns probably had not exceeded $40,000 (plus countless hours of physical labor). With capitalization obtained by issuing 345,126 shares, the company was on sound footing.

Soren and Rukke obtained a 200-ton mill in California, moved it to Sedro-Woolley and started construction of a mill building, working essentially full-time. Up to thirty-five men worked at the mine over the next ten years. The mill building was substantially built of reinforced concrete with steel walls and roof to withstand severe weather conditions, and was forty-six feet wide and 110 feet long. Workers moved machinery to the building that includes a jig and classifier to complete a simple tabling mill. Simultaneously the company completed a sturdy, electrically heated building twenty-six feet by ninety feet to house and feed thirty workmen. They built tool sheds and miscellaneous buildings, installed an big ore crusher, a five by six rod mill, and Emco loaders for trucks. After about fifteen years of steady work, the company was ready to ship ore. In April, 1974, assets of the corporation were $325,286 and liabilities $22,719.

The mine was up and running and, with about 2,000 feet of tunneling, achieved by use of electrically operated machinery, the operators took out about four truck loads of ore to Tacoma. The material assayed well and was worth mining. Soren told the author, "Gold was there but it was fine, about a fraction of an ounce to the ton, but it had very good lead, zinc, copper and silver. The silver was the best moneymaker. The vein was fractured in some places and in others there was a good solid vein." Things looked rosy.

Then the company ran into difficulties with the National Park Service, which allegedly refused them access by truck through park lands to their mine; only cars were allowed, according to Soren. Without truck access, the company could not ship ore—unless it would be by helicopter.

Several court suits followed, lasting into the 1980s, all of which Valumines lost. The original contest centered around the Cliff Lode claim, and several other lesser ones, the *United States of America* vs. *Jess Sapp and Robert A. Rukke*, Registered Agent, *Valumines Inc.*, the hearing September 22, 1976.

Under interrogation, Rukke asserted his claims being contested by the government were valid, that "we kept the work up on them under the laws." In addition to mining for precious metals, Valumines, Inc., had tried to market a mineral compound derived from the mine tailings as a fertilizer. The main questioning surrounded the Diamond 1 claim, on which the company had been doing the most development. John S. McMunn, attorney for the U.S., said he had visited Diamond No. 1 several times, as late as September 18, 1974, talking with Soren. At that time he observed workings at the site, including a trestle and a dump, an adit extending through Diamond No. 1 and into the Diamond patented lode claim, and a mill recently completed.

After much complex testimony (which may be read in the offices of the National Park Service, Sedro-Woolley), involving—among other things—whether certain claims were patented or non-patented, and whether the company was going through non-patented claims to access patented claims, the matter was decided in the favor of the United States. Condemnation proceedings were instituted and Valumines was paid a nominal amount for claims and workings, sufficient to repay stockholders but little else.

WHATCOM COUNTY

Chapter 22
AZURITE MINE

Lying almost astraddle the Whatcom-Okanogan County line east of the North Cascades summits, the Azurite Mine was a late-comer in the mining fever. Most prospectors churned through these mountains between 1878 and 1914; the Azurite find came two years later. Although there is an Azurite Peak, Azurite Mountain (skirted by the Pacific Crest Trail), and an Azurite Pass, the mines were somewhat west of the ridge. The name Azurite came from the color of outcroppings containing carbonate of copper.

Two mines succeeded on either side of Majestic Mountain, one quite respectably—the Azurite Mine on the east side of the sharp ridge, the Gold Hill on the west. The Azurite still has possibilities; Gold Hill is dormant.

Founders Charles and Hazard Ballard were prospecting pioneers who came over the mountains from Ellensburg in 1886, worked around Conconully and then various Slate Creek mines. Charles could be called the father of Slate Creek, for he was involved in the two major mills, the Mammoth and the Eureka.

It was 1916 before the brothers discovered the Azurite Mine, assumed by Charles, and 1917 the Gold Hill, acquired for Hazard. The Azurite was a true working mine for several years; the Gold Hill Mining Company sent only one shipment of ore to the Bunker Hill and Sullivan smelter, Kellogg, Idaho. The ore sample did assay at .07 ounces of gold, 93.25 ounces of silver, and 28.15% lead. At 1936 prices, the 3,680 pounds of ore was valued at $84.42, considered an encouraging but unspectacular figure.

Wayne Moen said in his *Mines and Minerals of Whatcom County* that the veins of Azurite and Gold Hill occupied fissures in sheared and faulted quartzite and argillite of the Pasayten Formation. "Inasmuch as several of the veins crop out on steep rocky slopes on which there is little overburden, they are easier to follow than the veins of the Bonita Creek area [Eureka and Mammoth]. . . . Unlike the veins of the Bonita Creek area, which are essentially free-milling gold veins, the veins of Majestic Mountain are base metal sulfite veins." He said the Azurite vein indicated depths of more than 1,200 feet in some cases, and the predominant strikes of the veins dipped as much as forty-five to seventy-five degrees.

Apparently Charles did not get rich from his holdings at Slate Creek or his prospecting in Alaska (1911-15), for he was unable to work his claim seriously until he accumulated some working capital. He told a newspaper reporter in 1926 that, ever since he filed the claim, he had been assaying ore casually from the Azurite, with the best showing at $136 a ton. He said all of the Azurite veins were heavy in iron, rich in sulphur, as well as gold, silver, and some copper, an ideal condition. Oddly enough, he did not patent the claim.

Ballard formed the Azurite Copper Co. of Delaware in 1918, obtaining financial backing somewhere in the East, and began limited mining. In 1918, Ballard hired a packer to bring supplies, a small crusher and concentrator to the site. Using hand tools, he hacked out a short entry into the mountain at 5,080 feet elevation, which he called Discovery Tunnel. He exposed a vein of promising content, mined a small amount, and brought a bar of gold with him when snow drove him from the mountains that fall. The mining remained on a small scale until 1925, when the company was reorganized as Azurite Gold Co. (AGC),

Charles Ballard (right), founder of the Azurite Mine, with friends.

— Photo courtesy of the Okanogan County Historical Society

with Charles Ballard as president, brother Arthur Ballard as secretary. The company issued stock to raise the needed capital to mine the very promising two or three tunnels he and his crew had excavated.

Even after reorganization, Ballard was slow in attacking the prospects. It was October, 1929, before he started development in earnest and on a working scale. Transportation continued to be a huge problem. Before building his permanent camp, Ballard helped to build a road twenty-six miles long from Lost River to the mine, part of which followed the Hart's Pass Road with the balance all new road eleven miles over Cady Pass north of Mt. Ballard to the mine. The building of the road reduced freight costs from $100 per ton using horses to $20 a ton using special tracked trucks narrower than normal. To facilitate hauling, Ballard had worked with a mechanic to develop such a peculiar tracked truck adapted from an International Harvester design.

Ballard built a bunkhouse partly into the mountain for protection against avalanches; in winter often all that one could see was the smoke issuing from the chimney. He added a smithy and mining building.

It was impossible to transport mining machinery from the Whatcom side, so Ballard hauled everything from the Methow Valley. Before his wagon or truck road was finished, the compressor came in by packhorse. Too large to be carried by a single animal, the flywheels for two diesel compressors, nine feet in diameter, were cast in three sections for transport, then bolted together at the Azurite. Ballard planned to run one compressor each week and shut down the other for servicing, but during the first week of operation one compressor threw a rod. It was winter and a courageous repairman from the Chicago Pneumatic Company of Pennsylvania traveled to the mine on snowshoes from Mazama (a camp at the foot of Hart's Pass Road). His tools and personal gear were transported by dog sled.

Despite all this extra work, by midsummer, 1930, Ballard and his crew had dug 100 feet in the Burnham Tunnel, 100 feet elevation lower than the original Discovery Tunnel. The Tinson Tunnel, another 100 feet lower, was pressed forward several hundred feet. The vein of ore was forty feet thick in places.

Ballard told his stockholders in 1930 that he had just started to run a cross-cut entry, the Wenatchee Tunnel, designed to intercept the Azurite vein below the Tinson Tunnel and into the mountain about 1,650 feet. Ballard still used a primitive, homemade rock crusher and reduction system. In a large wooden tank lined with rocks at the bottom, ore-bearing rock was smashed by a weighted, revolving wooden wheel powered by water pressure. After the rock was crushed, Ballard added a cyanide solution to cause the base metals to dissolve. When zinc shavings were then added, the gold alone settled to the bottom of the tank for removal.

During 1931-32, Ballard installed a thirty-ton, $20,000 reduction plant manufactured by the Mace Smelter Company of Denver. By 1933, fifteen tons of matte worth $2,344 in gold, $8 in silver and $29 in copper went to the Tacoma smelter.

At this time, H.A. Guess, vice-president of American Smelting and Refining Company (ASARCO), part of the Guggenheim Syndicate, reconsidered an earlier opinion about the infeasibility of mining the Azurite. The unfavorable report had been tendered fifteen years earlier by a mining engineer sent to assess Ballard's property.

In January, 1934, Charles Ballard announced that ASARCO was interested in leasing the Azurite for twenty-five years on an even share basis and would invest significant capital. Ballard died that same year, but his wife Anne continued to be active in the management of AGC; indeed, Anne became president of AGC. Within the year, Hazard Ballard sold his Gold Hill Mine and joined the Azurite operation.

ASARCO appointed Ray E. Walters superintendent of the Azurite and, under his direction, gasoline-powered compressors and fuel storage tanks, a machine shop, blacksmith building, and sawmill were installed at the Azurite site. After probing the three tunnels already started by Ballard, management decided to start production after installing a mill and extensive mining equipment.

ASARCO built the mill opposite the Wenatchee tunnel where snowslides were less frequent, leaving the bunkhouses with snowsheds where they were. With a construction crew of about 125 men, the mill was completed in five months, two aerial tramways were constructed to handle the ore and tailings, and the mill went into production on November 1, 1936, after ASARCO reportedly had spent $400,000 in development and facilities.

Like Ballard, ASARCO supplied the camp by narrow-gauge truck, engaging Stonebreaker Brothers of Orofino, Idaho, to do the job. In winter the Azurite mining camp was supplied by dogsled on a trail that came through Azurite Pass, not Hart's Pass.

Mountain man Ed Kikendall of Winthrop operated the belled teams, mostly cross-breds laced with husky blood. Kikendall's best lead dog was a lovely, pure white Siberian husky with pale, milky-blue eyes, giving the dog an eerie appearance that frightened people. On the contrary, the dog loved attention but was too dignified to fawn over people and would just sit and wait, staring hopefully with those odd eyes.

With sufficient capital and a good work force, the Azurite operated efficiently. Two employees took the first batch of gold bricks worth $40,000 each out of the mountains without special guards, in a deliberately casual manner. At Pateros, they delivered them into the hands of Wells Fargo guards.

194

Later, the company sent the bricks out of the mountains to the Farmers State Bank of Winthrop—in winter on Kikendall's dog sled. Because of the remote location and the difficulty of escape, no armed robber or bank robber disturbed the system.

The winter of 1936-37 was fraught with exasperation and danger. On December 22, 1936, an avalanche roared down to carry the ore bin downhill and damage the aerial tram carrying ore to the mill. Cable was too heavy for the dogs to bring in, so ASARCO engaged Johnson's Flying Service of Cascade, Idaho, to air-drop the cable from their Ford Tri-Motor plane. It took two trips to carry the cable, as the plane could only carry one reel at a time. The first drop was without incident, the second almost wiped out a suspension bridge across the valley.

In January, 1937, the news came over a short wave radio from the mine that Fred White, son of the ASARCO smelter manager, Tacoma, had acute appendicitis. Ed Kikendall had just left the mine and, when he got part way to Winthrop, met a second dog team and sled carrying elderly Dr. Murdock bound for the mine. Kikendall took over, turned the dogs around and headed back through a howling blizzard to the mine. When they arrived the doctor decided against operating there, partly because of the high altitude. Ed Kikendall, the doctor, the patient, and a small group of supporters left again for Winthrop by dog sled. They were met by a nationally known dog-team driver, Earl Kimball, and his racing team which spirited the patient and Murdock eight more miles to a waiting State Patrol car. It was a 100-mile trip to the nearest hospital, because snow had blocked a

Chuck and Ed Kikendall supplied the Azurite Mine by dogsled in winter.
— Taken from the Okanogan County Heritage, Winter 1974-75

shorter road. The patient was too far gone and died on the operating table. The doctor himself and some of the support crew needed attention.

Incredibly, there were two more appendicitis incidents within nine weeks. When Howard James was stricken, the men did not wait for Kikendall but several volunteered as "dogs" and pulled the sled to which James was bound, others following. Along a steep slope, the sled got away from them and plunged over a precipice. The quick-thinking "dogs" sat down in the snow to stop the sled's momentum, while the poor patient, bound to the sled, swung in midair. James lived to return to the Azurite. The last man, Chris Weppler, was taken out by dog sled and also survived, although doctors said he was perhaps an hour from death. The spent dogs had raced out so fast with Weppler aboard that they were too tired to eat for several hours, and Kikendall slept for two straight days and nights.

Azurite Mine mill.
— Photo courtesy of the Okanogan County Historical Society

Life was not always so harrowing at the mine. Pool tables in the recreation hall, a weekly movie (brought in by Kikendall), card games, and dog-eared magazines eased the boredom of being marooned at the Azurite in winter. Even in summer, the men seldom left camp because it was so far to anywhere.

By 1938, about seventy-five men worked at the Azurite to produce bullion valued at $2500 per day. The operation included thirty-four lode claims and six millsites, two with exclusive rights to the nearest water power sites. The equipment, some described earlier, included a blacksmith shop, compressor house, powder storage house, two electric storage battery engines operating with ore cars in the Wenatchee Tunnel, two storage tanks of 10,000 gallons each for diesel oil, a main bunkhouse with recreation space, and a cookhouse. The mill building, 150 feet by 150 feet, had five levels and a 700-foot aerial tram connecting it with the mine. Four tram buckets carried the ore, each with a capacity of eighty tons. The ore traveled from a bunker on a large endless belt with a magnetic separator to an ore crusher thirteen inches by twenty-four inches, from which it went to a Plat-O-Vibrating screen of half inch mesh, the fine going into the ball mill, the coarse to a fine ore crusher and then returned to the screen. The entire operation was highly professional and profitable.

By 1938, though, the gold supply was petering out from the vein above the Wenatchee Tunnel. New tunnels uncovered gold, but sparse amounts. Work was suspended in 1939, pending the results of an examination of the property by James Orr and a crew from Northwest Testing Laboratories, Inc., of Seattle. The report suggested certain new adits and drifting.

At this point AGC obtained an option from ASARCO on the mill and equipment and arranged for Orr's suggestions to be implemented. Gold was found but not in a profitable amount, so AGC dropped its option. ASARCO removed its equipment in 1942.

According to Keith A. Whiting, who wrote a comprehensive review of the Azurite mining operations in the *Okanogan County Heritage*, Winter 1974-75:

"During the 28-month period of the ASARCO operation, from November 1936 through February 1939, 72,996 tons of ore were mined. This ore averaged 0.426 oz. gold and 0.045 oz. silver per ton. The direct operating costs averaged $8.25 per ton of ore mined. The net proceeds from the ore were $972,000. ASARCO failed to recover its investment by about $120,000."

Meanwhile, the Azurite's sister mine, the Gold Hill was located on Easy Creek, a tributary of Granite Creek. According to Diana Hottell in the *Okanogan County Heritage* of Winter, 1984-85, there were forty unpatented claims and two mill sites across about 750 acres, and numerous shareholders held 3,850,790 shares of stock purchased at ten cents each, after a prospectus was issued in October, 1935.

Of six veins studied and worked, a mining engineer, C.E. Phoenix, asserted that at least one—the Genevieve vein—would produce profitably. Others praised the mine's prospects, comparing it to the Homestake Mine of South Dakota. Indeed, it did appear that the same veins on the western slope, being worked profitably by the Azurite Copper Company ran on through the mountain to Gold Hill's property on the east.

In 1939, under the corporate name of Northern Cascades Mines (Hazard Ballard sold out his interests to Alaskan investors around January 1,

1935), the Gold Hill management indicated that the operations were greatly hindered by lack of a road westward in Whatcom County. Underfinancing was a worse problem, and the mine operators limped along without income. Bob Crandall, a worker at the mine, declared wryly, "The mine enthusiasts had just enough money to keep them broke." Only sporadic work ever was done on the mine after the one shipment of 1936, and that often was handwork performed by stockholders more as a lark than a serious effort.

Many of the investors were local Methow Valley people who found it hard to resist buying mining stock; after all, maybe one might strike it rich. Most took the loss of their investments with a shrug, one sold his for a string of horses, another grumbled that he had hoped his profits would pay for his son's college education.

In accordance with its policies of cleaning away the debris of obsolete mining camps, the United States Forest Service personnel burned the Azurite buildings. However, heavy machinery carcasses still littered the site, a huge tailings heap looming over all. The current owner, Joe Gray, repaired the road to the site in 1992. First he cleaned up the mess left at the Azurite. He invited the Winthrop Museum to examine any of the abandoned equipment and take any pieces that were of museum quality. After that, working with the U.S. Forest Service representatives, Gray voluntarily hauled out most of the debris scattered about. He planned to mine the tailings, as early reduction methods were known to leave about as much metal in the tailings as were retained. As soon as he has completed mining, he told the author that he intends to terrace the large tailings pile, then replant the entire site with grass and other vegetation so it will, in effect, be returned to the forest.

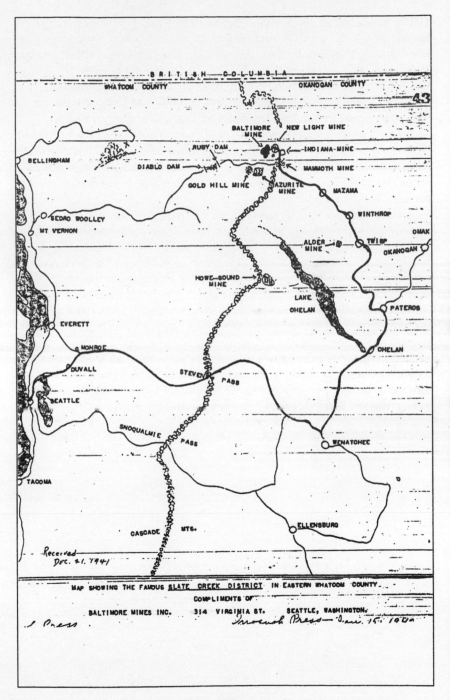

MAP SHOWING THE FAMOUS SLATE CREEK DISTRICT IN EASTERN WHATCOM COUNTY

COMPLIMENTS OF

BALTIMORE MINES INC.   314 VIRGINIA ST.   SEATTLE, WASHINGTON.

Chapter 23
BARRON

Barron was the only real town founded in the Slate Creek or Ruby Creek Mining Districts, but gold fever caused prospectors to straggle into the mountains and form camps as early as the 1870s. Their destination was roughly bounded by the international boundary, Ross Lake, the North Cascades Highway, and the Okanogan County line. Clusters of small camps housed the multitudes in 1880 but the town of Barron would not be born until the second phase of the gold rush in 1892.

Eastern Whatcom County, location of the two mining districts, more properly should have belonged to Skagit or Okanogan County, as it was and is virtually impossible to directly access it from Bellingham. Bisecting the county is the formidable range of North Cascades that includes Mount Baker, Mount Shuksan, Mount Challenger and the north-south portion of the Skagit River that became Ross Lake after the river was dammed. Nonetheless, it was from the west that persistent prospectors followed the elusive trail of powder or placer gold upriver on the Skagit and into the creeks draining the deepest and most remote valleys of the North Cascades. The Skagit River ran wild and free from beyond the international border southward to veer westerly deep in the mountains near Ruby.

According to Mount Baker-Snoqualmie Forest archives, John Rowley, John Sutter, and George Sanger pushed up the Skagit River to Ruby Creek in 1872. Sutter found a ruby in the stream, thus its name. Five years later, John Rowley, Otto Klement, Charles von Pressentin, John Duncan, and Frank Scott canoed east on the Skagit River, until the Skagit gorge closed in and confronted them with impassable rapids. They encamped and panned for gold somewhere near today's Newhalem and found placer or flour gold to an extent. Searching for richer diggings, they packed their tools and supplies and trudged high over a steep mountain, which they named Sourdough Mountain because John Rowley fell down while climbing it and spilled a can of sourdough. The group descended to the junction of Ruby Creek with the Skagit River (the south end of Ross Lake), where they found more free gold but winter weather forced the group back into the balmier Skagit Valley. Elated by their findings, they found it hard to keep the secret.

As soon as snows subsided, they returned to the Cascades on February 1, 1878, without von Pressentin but with two other men. Cold and always a bit hungry, they worked throughout the summer, trying for the big strike. Klement wearied of the search but the others remained until fall. In 1879, they resumed their prospecting early in the spring but now found two other crews working Ruby Creek. Albert Bacon and friends had installed a wing dam about eight miles above the creek's mouth and named their claim "Nip and Tuck." By April, they already had taken out $1,500 of gold dust and Rowley's party accumulated about $1,000. When the parties returned to Mount Vernon for supplies, the news could be contained no longer and a gold rush was on.

As interest in the gold finds spread, merchants from Bellingham, LaConner and Mount Vernon vied with each other for the supply business— that was where the real gold was. Whoever could provide the best supply road would be the winner. In Bellingham, entrepreneurs P.B. Cornwall and E.L. Steinweg investigated in cursory fashion the opening of a trail across the mountains past Mount Baker but decided to wait and see how rich the finds would be. In December 1879 at Seattle, a group of businessmen met at Squire's Opera House and proposed to build a trail through the Skagit Gorge, collecting $1,500 on the spot to get started. The Seattleites gave a contract to Day Brothers & Cockrane of Mount Vernon to build such a trail, but Day later reneged—probably after he surveyed the scope of the job! Even Port Townsend, then the gateway to Puget Sound, hoped to get a piece of the business by intercepting prospectors entering the area by ship and offered Bellingham's Henry Roeder financial assistance to improve the passable trail leading from Canada toward the district.

This, the Dewdney Trail, a rough horse trail, went southeast from near today's town of Hope to connect with a trail along the upper Skagit River. Until the Hart's Pass Road was built later, the trail was the only practical pack trail into the two mining districts from Whatcom. Even so, when Roeder sent a party in early February 1880 to assess the practicability of the supply trail, the men found hungry miners in Ruby coping with twelve to fifteen feet of snow.

Springtime was little better. The Skagit River and the small, gold-bearing creeks became torrents. Avalanches and mudslides were common. The terrain was reluctant to cooperate with the miners, and the merchants wanted to help but could scarcely do so.

John R. Ryan in a letter to the *Bellingham Bay Mail* denounced the efforts of merchants as cowardly. He told of miners lugging forty-pound packs of mining tools plus their grubstake. He tantalized the merchants by saying that, when any courageous supplier brought in supplies, the miners were waiting to buy every item at high prices: flour at $5 per sack; bacon at 30 cents a pound; gum boats $10 a pair. Ryan angrily urged them on:

"In this age of progress and enterprise it is to be regretted that your lordly merchants below will not forward provisions to the Skagit gold mines or at least to the head of canoe navigation. . . . Merchants, what say you to this? If you wish to see the gold veins of the Skagit valley tapped and developed, forward the provisions and we will send you the shining dust."

In 1880, the miners formed the Ruby Creek Mining District, electing George Sawyer as the recorder. The district adjoined the later Slate Creek Mining District. Ruby City was platted but never was more than a collection of shacks, Ruby Creek Inn and restaurant; the site is now beneath Ross Lake. In addition, claims were filed all over the upper Skagit River and its tributaries—Granite Creek with ninety-six claims and Thunder Creek with thirty. However, the gold bubble of the 1880s burst quickly; gold panning or sluicing did not produce enough income. Most of the miners left the area then, but a few stayed and others came in a decade or two later to try hard rock mining. This new episode lasted longer and the mines were more substantial, a few even profitable.

The real boom came in 1892 due to itinerant miner and adventurer Alex Barron's intelligent analysis that all this placer or free gold in the streams must come from a mother lode farther upstream. Methodically he worked his way ever uphill and easterly until he came to a promising area, high in the Cascades, where the gold was coarser and of a different color. He sank exploratory holes in a nearby ledge and "Eureka" he struck gold near the surface above the settlement that became Barron. More an explorer than a businessman, Barron sold his claim to the Eureka Mining Company of Anacortes, Washington for a reported $50,000 to $80,000 and spent the money in riotous living. He may have returned to the mountains later.

Barron's finds touched off a full-fledged boom. Within a few miles of the Eureka and the new town of Barron were active and promising mines—the Tacoma, Goat, Indiana, Illinois, and claims in Allen Basin. Between 1894 and 1937, gold prospectors combed the area thoroughly, their activities spreading broadly from Ruby Creek to Canyon, Slate, Mill and Panther Creeks. During that time 2,812 claims were staked: Slate Creek, 1,628; Canyon Creek, 405; Ruby Creek, 455; Mill Creek, 245; Granite Creek, 68; and Panther Creek, 11. Frank C. Teck, Bellingham Chamber of Commerce Secretary, said in 1905 that, through the year 1904, miners had realized a total of $417,000. However, mine statistics are notoriously unreliable. Several claims could belong to one "property" or owner. Names of companies changed frequently, sometimes to avoid paying dividends to stockholders.

Claims and properties were bought and sold with dizzying speed. The above figures afford some idea of the scope of activities, however.

Eureka began work on surveys in 1894. That same year the Mammoth, Mountain Goat, Gold Ridge Group, and Anacortes claims were discovered. In the spring of 1895, Colonel W. Thomas Hart obtained an option on all those claims for Daly & Clark of Montana. He contracted to build a twenty-two mile wagon road from Winthrop to Robinson Creek. From there a horse trail would access Barron, a growing collection of shacks. Hart commenced development work on the Eureka by shaft and by tunnel on the Mammoth. In July, 1895, Daly sent mining experts in and the reports were not favorable, so he stopped work after spending $60,000.

Another well-respected geologist had a different view. In an 1897 report, L.K. Hodges first described the location of the claims. He said the Eureka group of six quartz and two placer claims was situated on the eastern slope of Slate Hill that formed the divide between Slate Creek and the headwaters of the Similkameen River. (Modern forest rangers do not regard this ridge as the "headwaters."). Hodges said that the spur of land was composed mainly of slate, with porphyry overlying or capping the summit in places. Nowhere did it show any outcropping but was below the earth from four to eight feet. At the Eureka then, the miners stripped off the surface dirt to expose a ledge about forty feet long and thirty feet wide and ran the dirt through a primitive cradle to yield respectable returns before attacking the ledge.

Hodges' 1897 survey reported that the Beck group of five claims was situated on the west slope of Benson Mountain, a part of the same Slate Hill spur, about three miles from the Eureka. These were owned by Melville Curtis, Alexander Barron, and H.H. Soule. The Mammoth Mine was also on Benson Mountain near the Beck group and was then owned by Risley and Woodin (closer to the second Barron). North of the Eureka on the Canyon Creek side of the hill was the Excelsior of Benson and Templar; indeed, the Eureka gulch was forested with claim stakes. Four miles northwest of the Eureka was the Anacortes group of about thirty claims, said to contain some of the richest ore. In 1895, ten pounds of ore had yielded $76.40 in gold. Nuggets valued at $20 were found at several locations in the area. Hodges gave the area a promising future and suggested that the best way to mine the placer gold was by hydraulicking.

As indicated earlier, access to the mining center was chancy. Packers provided the miners with basic needs and even managed to haul heavy equipment into the precipitous locations by horse.

An imaginative Seattle supplier suggested dropping supplies to the miners by hot-air balloon, but the supreme inaccuracy of balloon control squelched that idea. A more practical man, Col. Hart worked to improve

*Above: The cookhouse/
bunkhouse at Mammoth Mine.*

*Left: Alex Barron and Guy
Waring.*

Below: Town of Barron.

*– Photos courtesy of
The Okanogan County
Historical Society*

the Methow Valley wagon road and trail into the Slate Creek Mining District. An engineer and surveyor, he laid out a plan for widening the horse trail to accommodate narrow-gauge wagons, then turned the project over to Charles Ballard, a pioneer prospector and engineer, to complete. With assistance from Melville Curtis, a surveyor, Ballard made the Hart's Pass road operational by 1903.

The road was only about three feet wide, requiring mechanics at Winthrop to devise special narrow-gauge wagons that were pulled by horses hitched single-file or "tandem."

In 1897, Charles Ballard took an option on the Mammoth, got it on a paying basis, and installed a stamp mill paying from $5,000 to $6,000 a month. In 1898, Charles D. Lane, a mine operator from San Francisco, bought the Eureka. He built a sawmill, a ten-stamp mill, developed the mines to over 100 feet and found very rich sylvanite ore. Some ore taken out was 60% gold. The mill was on the west side of Bonita Creek and ore came down from the Eureka *mine* above to the mill. (The original Barron straggled along Bonita Creek, too.) Another adit was virtually adjacent to the mill. Wreckage of that structure or the successor to it, last in the hands of Western Gold Mines, is still at that site on private property.

The mine began to produce $17,000 to $18,000 a month. An article in the *Seattle Evening Times* of September, 1899, indicates that 100 men were employed at the Eureka under the supervision of C.W. Tozier, utilizing about $100,000 in equipment. The *Wenatchee World* of October 23, 1959, states that a verified $120,000 in gold was taken by Lane in two years.

Ballard's Mammoth Mine realized $397,000 between 1898 and 1901. Others were just as lucky with the free-milling gold ore, near the surface and swift to process. A visitor to the Slate Creek district in 1901, D.B. Schaller, said there were about seventy men working in the upper Canyon-Slate creek area, thirty-five of them at the Eureka, at an average wage of $80-$100 per month.

Around 1902, three Scandinavian sailors joined the rush, positive they would be rich men. Of practical minds, they first built a handsome two-room cabin of outstanding workmanship and even a board floor. Only then did they prospect. Finding nothing but barren rock, they left for Seattle to return to the sea. According to C.C. McGuire, an early forest guard, later a ranger, big trees grew up to smother the abandoned cabin, creating eerie scrapings overhead for any traveler seeking shelter, and grew to be known as a haunted "Ghost Cabin."

With lack of transportation or significant support services, Slate Creek miners had to be resourceful. When a miner named Langer shot himself in the leg, his fellow miners brought him, strapped to a board, to the town of Winthrop. There Guy Waring, the storekeeper, sent a messenger to fetch the area's only doctor from Lake Chelan—nearly 100 miles distant. When the doctor arrived, recovering from a drunken spree, he said he must amputate the fellow's leg. Understandably distrusting the decision, Langer refused treatment and asked Waring to do what he could. Waring picked out the loose pieces of bone and bandaged Langer's leg; miraculously, it did not become infected and healed nicely.

When crews had harvested the easy gold, they found the underlying base ore of low grade and, with the Alaska gold beckoning, Slate Creek's bubble burst. Not entirely, though. More well-financed companies pursued the gold through more sophisticated processes, bringing in heavy mining equipment—some of it over the narrow-gauge wagon road. Among the stubborn miners was Charles Ballard.

The *Methow Valley News* of April 1, 1904, quotes Ballard as saying on March 18, "A few days ago we struck in the mine about eight feet in the foot wall a parallel ore body four feet wide and carrying high grade values. We have drifted about twenty feet on it, and it is holding its own." In 1905, Eureka Consolidated Gold Mining Company was incorporated with capital stock of $1.5 million by Charles and Anna A. Ballard and James Cady, with principal business address at Barron, Washington. It is the author's best opinion, after consultations with local historians, that the Mammoth and Eureka came under the same ownership at this time. The Eureka operation was renamed the Bonita and John A. Stewart hired as superintendent.

Ballard said in a newspaper report in 1926 that about 60% of the gold in the Mammoth Mine was free gold and was collected by amalgamation. He said he had purchased the first $100 worth of goods sold by the Methow Trading Company (Guy Waring), Winthrop, to supply three men going into the Mammoth. During the next twenty years he had spent $20,000 with the Methow Trading Company. Ballard complained that the supply costs destroyed the profit to be made, that he once sent out ten tons of concentrates to the Tacoma Smelter and received a check for $660; at $66 a ton, this just about paid half of the cost of packing out the concentrates. The properties came into the hands of William Brown, Everett, in 1915.

Barron's original finds and the rush to Slate Creek caused the establishment of a soon-defunct mining camp called Vera Cruz, somewhere near the mouth of Robinson Creek, where a freight depot and hotel stood until around 1910. A big temporary camp was situated two miles east of Robinson Creek (or at the mouth of Lost River, depending on the source) with about 1,000 miners living in tents for a short time.

The town of Barron along Bonita Creek below the Eureka mine and mill, also attracted as many as 1,000 residents in more permanent cabins. Serving the miners were saloons, a dance hall, at least one restaurant (in a tent, at first), a post office, hotel, and mining buildings such as assay offices. Debris of buildings and outlines of foundations occur regularly along the creek.

Apparently two locations for Barron existed. A long-standing controversy may be solved by Wayne S. Moen's assertion in Bulletin No. 57, Department of Natural Resources (Division of Mines & Geology), 1969, that ". . . a few years later the townsite was relocated a short distance east of Bonita Creek near its junction with Slate Creek. The settlement consisted of a store and a tavern that supplied the basic needs of several hundred prospectors, whose tents dotted the landscape. . . . It was near here that the second Mammoth mill was built in 1905."

At this second location of Barron rows of cabins marched up parallel "streets" on the hill that can be traced quite easily today. Copious numbers of rusting tin cans are mute testimony to the existence of a community, as well as rotting button-style overshoes, outlines of cabin foundations, and wreckage. As good now as ninety years ago are portions of a long, massive pipe from settlement to creekside, no doubt serving the Mammoth mill. Remains of adits in many places between the two "Barrons" are mute testimony to ancient prospects.

In addition to the furor around the Eureka claims, mines being worked industriously included the Chancellor a bit west of Barron, those on Mill Creek and and in Baltimore Basin, over the hill from the Eureka.

Nicholai Aall, later an engineer for Seattle City Light, supervised construction of a sawmill, powerhouse and flume two miles long to serve a 240-horsepower generator that supplied power for the Chancellor Mine. The generator, four feet in diameter, had been cast in two semicircular sections that could be hauled over the road for joining at the site. The generator supplied power to the Chancellor and Bonita (a new name for the Eureka) mines over a 5.6 mile transmission line. Despite the considerable investment, Chancellor only operated for a year. It was simply abandoned by its owners, but as late as mid-century many of the sturdily-built mine buildings were still in good shape. Today most have fallen into the forest or have been destroyed as public hazards.

Another important mine, the North American Mining and Milling Company, operated near the junction of Mill and Canyon Creeks after 1903. Fred Damman of Winthrop said that this is where Alexander Barron had found a "glory hole" of gold worth $20,000 on his way to the big Eureka ledge. The North American, managed by John Siegfried, had forty claims, a tunnel 175 feet long into one of them, and a large amount of ore on the ground awaiting transportation; in 1905 Siegfried had filed labor on fifty-one claims, of which the most promising were the Betty, Borrow & Maybell, Alfredo, Columbia and Maka. A ten-stamp mill was hauled in over the Hart's Pass road, the stamps weighing 1,350 pounds each. The company installed four concentrators. A 5,000-foot tram was built to bring down ore from the Columbia claim.

When the mines of the Slate Creek district failed to create millionaires, the tide of interest slackened and prospectors moved on. Mines closed. Businessmen at Barron fled the townsite in a seemingly precipitous manner, abandoning their equipment, supply stocks, and even personal bedding and clothing. "Tools, equipment for complete blacksmith shops, implements, wagons, bedding, cooking utensils and clothing were scattered everywhere, without semblance of order, just as they were thrown down by their last users. . . . Even the stock in the general store [founded in 1901] was not taken . . . ," said a later visitor to Barron. By the end of 1907, it truly was a ghost town, the facilities there intact but inhabited only by pack rats. In the late 1920s Methow valley resident, Bill Lester, went into Barron and found liquor bottles still sitting on the bar of a saloon, machinery and mining equipment, narrow gauge wagons waiting for ore, and ruffled dresses of the dancing girls still packed in boxes. Over the decades the flotsam of Barron was carried away or cleaned out by the U. S. Forest Service personnel. Unfortunately, some narrow-gauge wagons taken to a store in Winthrop for eventual display at a museum disappeared during the disastrous 1948 flood of the Methow River.

In 1932, a religious group, squatters, attempted to establish a colony near the old Mammoth mine and constructed several substantial log buildings. They hoped to open and operate the Mammoth mine and others, but were forced to leave in 1934 by the legal claim owners and the U.S. Forest Service.

Relatively accessible off the Hart's Pass Road, Barron had two or three short-lived reincarnations, when later prospectors believed that the mines could be operated profitably. Western Gold Mining, Inc., acquired the Eureka properties in 1940, and ran some tests. A caretaker Richard "Slug" Davis, lived at the site and still managed it in the 1990s. Davis' father once carried mail to the mining area weekly, washed dishes until it was time to trek out again, and repeated the process.

A somewhat mysterious and colorful man, Harry Kramer, came to the original Barron and leased the mine (Eureka/Mammoth) around 1945. The story was that he landed in New York at age twelve, could not speak English, and visited every restaurant until he could find a countryman who spoke Greek. He made his fortune thereafter, presumably in the restaurant business. How he happened to hear about Barron and acquire the mining claims is not clear but, starting around the end of World War II, each summer Kramer came to develop his claims and return East in winter to raise money from stockholders. He never was able to pay them dividends, but Davis believes he was honest and *tried* to make money—but did not. Kramer

209

maintained an office in the Vance Building, Seattle, and between 1946-48. his crew was hauling ore to the Tacoma Smelter, apparently insufficient to cover expenses. In the 1950s he ran the mine again with electrical power (generator) to make concentrates, easier to haul. He operated off and on into the 1970s and before he died in 1975, he asked that his ashes be scattered over the "glory hole," but his niece did not grant his wish.

After Kramer's death, the mine was worked briefly by a Canadian firm, whose engineer, unfamiliar with the Western mountains, cut down all the trees above the mill to build an ore tram, a pathway just waiting for a snow accumulation. After preparing for production, the company lost interest and left.

Western Gold Mining Company opened again in 1980, leasing operations to Lyon Mines. At least two large residence buildings served a crew of men. Running two ten-hour shifts, the New Light Mine (the newest name of the old Eureka mine) processed eighty tons of ore daily. With its own power plant, the mill was all electrically operated. A conveyor belt brought the ore down from Barron's old "glory hole" to the ball mill. The mill reduced the ore by chemical action into concentrates, which were shipped in fifty-gallon drums to the refinery. However, in the winter of 1983, Nature accepted the invitation to an avalanche prepared by the former owner, when a massive snowslide destroyed . . . crushed . . . decimated the mill and equipment. The only objects left are heavy, rusting machines here and there; the rest is rubble. The mine site is at 6,000 feet elevation, and copious snowfall on the mine's residence building caused the roof to collapse later. Only one residence remains intact. All of the property is private, behind a locked gate.

Not far below the Eureka, the Golden Arrow mine opened on the old Tacoma claim; shipments of gold and silver-bearing ore were forwarded to the Tacoma Smelter in 1951-53, but work was discontinued. Their excellent buildings still remain, used privately.

Unquestionably, though, there was and is gold in the area from Ruby to Barron; it simply was very fragmented and not arrayed in neat veins like those of the Rocky Mountains. Early milling procedures were very ineffective, often leaving tailings richer than the milled product. Extreme distance from smelters, heavy snows at the high elevations with rigorous living conditions, and difficulty of transportation—even in this modern age—are the real culprits in the failure of mining there.

A Washington geological survey bulletin listed the recovery of gold in Whatcom County ranging from $26 in 1909 to $137,281 in 1917, and of silver $14,371 in 1904 declining to $1 in 1910. The successful Azurite operation came later somewhat south of Barron, a town where gold was present but profits elusive.

Chapter 24
BLUE CANYON & PARK

Hardly a trace remains today of the thriving settlement of Blue Canyon and only a few buildings at nearby Park, important centers during early mining and logging days. They were located less than a mile apart at the southeast end of Lake Whatcom, a broad finger of water thrusting fifteen miles into the North Cascades foothills.

Before settlement by white immigrants, the southeastern end of the lake was a popular transient fishing campsite for Nooksack Indians and occasionally the Samish Indian people, who kept a longhouse and drying platforms for fish there.

The first settlement by immigrants near the site was the post office of Edmunds. On July 1, 1884, Edmunds became Park under postmaster Michael Anderson, who named it after his friend, Charles M. Park, a homesteader in the area formerly a government surveyor with Oliver B. Iverson. Today the lake is surrounded by homes and a good road, but then it was an arduous, five-hour journey from New Whatcom or Fairhaven (towns that later made up Bellingham) to Park, and Blue Canyon did not yet exist. The first travelers rowed from Geneva at the west end of the lake to Park; those who had no boat sometimes came by raft. Noah V. Wickersham in 1884 said that it had taken him two days and one night to make the trip. Anderson rose to the need and started the first sternwheeler service on the lake, using the boat *Edith*. To get the boat from Bellingham Bay to the lake he and others *rolled* it on some kind of conveyance from Bellingham Bay, up and over the formidable Alabama Street Hill of Bellingham to the northwest end of Lake Whatcom—a fifty-day job.

Fred Zobrist purchased a preemption at Park in 1886 from Clarence W. and Anna P. Carter, of which 166.35 acres later became the Blue Canyon townsite, and brought his bride from Ohio to live there. The Zobrist home was large enough that the loft soon became a "hotel" for travelers between New Whatcom and a settlement on the South Fork of the Nooksack River. The Zobrists obtained permission by the county to maintain a wharf ex-

211

tending into Lake Whatcom for a period of five years, beginning in September 2, 1891, for boat unloading purposes. Martha "Mattie," Zobrist said in Jeffcott's *Nooksack Tales and Trails*:

"While we were running the store at Park, pack trains regularly ran between there and the valley [today's Acme Valley], carrying supplies and mail for the many outlying settlers on the South Fork, and the upper Samish, and the business became quite profitable, both to the store and the packers. Trains of as many as ten horses often left the lake heavily loaded with supplies. Sometimes settlers would send their children on horseback, and I would help them arrange their packs for the return trip. In this way I became quite proficient in tying the diamond hitch."

No one knows what happened to Anderson's *Edith* but by 1889, a steamer *Geneva*, owned by Will and George Jenkins, operated on the lake from Silver Beach to Park. That same year Zobrist bought a relinquishment at Acme eight miles distant but lived there only long enough to prove up the claim, maintaining the store at Park for another five years before moving. One of Park's more famous residents of a later date was Russell Hegg, Whatcom County photographer featured in the book *One Man's Gold Rush* about the Yukon gold rush.

In 1883, the government surveyor, Oliver B. Iverson, had recorded the existence of coal above the lake to the northwest of Park. This was not news to the locals, as someone—probably Carter—had built a shelter there and dug a bit of coal. Geologist Wayne S. Moen, Washington Division of Mines and Geology, asserts that the coal seam was discovered in 1887.

A real estate developer from Sheboygan, Wisconsin, Julius H. Bloedel joined forces with James F. Wardner, whom he met in Fairhaven, in 1890 to form the Samish Lake Logging Company, which later began to log near Park. Bloedel also became a major stockholder of the new Fairhaven National Bank in 1890 and its president in 1893. Wardner organized the Fairhaven Water-Works Co., the Fairhaven Electric Light Company, the Cascade Club and two Fairhaven banks. He had numerous other interests in northeastern Washington and Montana, as well, among them mining ventures. Promoter Wardner took an option on the Blue Canyon coal mines, declaring that the vein ran thirteen feet thick and the coal was of the best quality. The newspaper, *Bellingham Bay Express* of November 15, 1890, indicates that some work began that early: "Mr. J.F. Wardner and associates [probably J.F. McNaught and C.W. Carter] have commenced work on their coal mine on Lake Whatcom. Ten men are now at work preparing quarters for the men to be employed in running the slope. Mr. Wardner is a rustler and as the mine has every indication of proving first-class he is pushing the work. . ."

To develop the coal mines, Wardner searched for additional financing, lining up what became known as the "Helena Syndicate": A.M. and M.M. Holter, Peter Larson, John T. Murphy, M.K. Downs, S.T. Hauser, J.H. Bloedel and others. Wardner then sold his interest in the Blue Canyon Coal Mine Company (BCCMC) to the syndicate; Bloedel retained his shares and became secretary of the firm.

Recognizing the need for a town near the mine, Bloedel purchased acreage from Zobrist to form Blue Canyon Townsite Corporation in January, 1891. The investors included Bloedel (one-half interest), E.C. Gove (one-quarter interest), C.E. Rice (one-eighth interest), and C.L. Erwin (one-eighth interest).

The first mined coal was transported to tidewater in March, 1891, with much fanfare. A large placard on the side of the four-horse wagon proclaimed that Blue Canyon coal was now ready for purchase, and samples were left at several business places. In an interview in 1891, however, president Downs said: "A miner's business calls for a risk in capitol [sic] before it is possible to realize a profit and no one knows better than us the chances we take. One thing is for sure. If the coal peters out . . . and you can bet your pile it will NOT . . . we want to be in a position to haul logs, and get a

Blue Canyon Mine.

— From Galen Biery Collection

chance to get back the good gold we put in; coal, not logs, is what we are after."

J.J. Donovan, the engineer then building the Fairhaven and Southern Railroad, became the general superintendent of the mine, initially encountering some problems. Even though the coal admittedly was of the best quality, the formation was baffling to coal miners from the East because the earth's elements were mixed up through past volcanic action. No neat seams awaited pickaxes. When miners dug into the vein, rock was mixed into the vein or pierced it. When exposed, this rock swelled and tended to break supporting timbers. New ideas had to be conceived to stabilize the mine workings, an unanticipated expense.

Coal began to pour from the mine—about fifty tons per day by October, 1891. The first mine shaft was at an altitude of 1,122 feet, a half mile above the lake. Relatively unproductive, the site was abandoned and activities moved to a lower elevation about one-third mile west of the original. A tunnel accessed the seam, and coal came to the outside by mine cars, then down by tram to the lake for transport.

To avoid loading and unloading coal from a lake barge, a pressing matter was to put a railroad through directly to Lake Whatcom. Having first obtained a franchise to build a railroad along the north side of Lake Whatcom from the town of New Whatcom, the Bellingham Bay and Eastern Railroad (BB&E) was organized December 17, 1891. Edward Eldridge was President; S.T. Hauser, Vice-President; and J.J. Donovan, Secretary-Treasurer. Directors included Elwood Cosgrove and Peter Larson. The firm lost no time in securing trackage rights over existing street routes from Fairhaven and Northwest Street Railway, constructing a terminal at Silver Beach, and beginning to grade and lay tracks.

The *Fairhaven Herald* reported May 18, 1892, that work was progressing swiftly to build new tracks to connect with existing electric railway tracks that came near Lake Whatcom. Special signals were to be installed to prevent collisions between streetcars and the locomotives. The report went on to say:

"Engineer Donovan is now preparing plans for the improvements at the mine—rebuilding the tramway and building the bunkers. Between $30,000 and $40,000 will be expended in the next ninety days. The construction of the barge is progressing finely, and will be completed June 1. The company expects to begin the construction of a substantial office building, also an engine house, oil, sand and tool house on its property near the boundary Line between Fairhaven and New Whatcom. City coal bunkers for retail business will also be constructed here. . . . The company expects its new locomotive Friday."

The locomotive was to come over the Seattle, Lake Shore & Eastern (SLS&E) to Sumas, then over the Bellingham Bay and British Columbia (BB&BC) into Bellingham.

Meanwhile, construction crews ran into a snag when the Great Northern Railroad (GNR) took severe exception to the BB&E's building an overhead crossing of its rails. Earlier Donovan had submitted his crossing plan to Superintendent Neff of the GNR—forty feet above the tracks on a fourteen-degree curve supported by a bridge of two sixteen-foot arches. Neff did not approve it (some accounts say he required a sixty-foot span) and would not reply to Donovan's subsequent queries. Since the site was within the city limits and BB&E had a franchise from the city, Donovan commenced to bridge the crossing without waiting for sanction from the GNR.

Hearing of the decision, the GNR attempted unsuccessfully to get a restraining order on this, a Saturday evening. They summoned employees to the scene to tear out the timbers placed by BB&E May 21, 1892, at 5:00 PM. Donovan asked New Whatcom Marshal McIntosh for protection when he planned to begin again at 7:00 AM. The GNR kept a locomotive at the scene all night. On the next morning, a Sunday, P.C. McCormick, contractor for the job, brought seventy-five of his men to the job site, protected by four policemen. The GNR ran its locomotive back and forth over the crossing, effectively preventing the crew from erecting timbers. The *Herald* described the ensuing scene:

"Donovan then resorted to a clever strategy. He divided his men into two parties. One party would attempt to put a timber over the track and the locomotive would run past them, when the other party would get the timber over before the engine could get back to them. The Great Northern then sent to F&S Junction for a construction train and a crew of about fifty men. Before they arrived a bent of the bridge had been erected. Engineer Scurfield, of the Great Northern, ordered his men to fasten a chain to these timbers. The other end was attached to the train and the engine started. But a coupling pin had been drawn in some way and the cars parted. This was attempted several times with the same result. Chas. Geske, assistant bridge foreman, and J. Jarvis, of the Great Northern, were arrested during the skirmishing."

Frustrated the GNR's man then suggested that the company would agree to a thirty-foot clear span crossing, Donovan agreed to this, and an agreement was signed by noon. By this time the mayor and twenty special police had arrived prepared to protect BB&E's rights to cross, but no further "war" ensued. However, by 5:00 Sunday, a restraining order was issued against Donovan's crew and work stopped. The matter was cleared up in the next day or two, and the noontime agreement honored.

An excursion marked the completion of the railroad to Silver Beach, attended by about 150 people who "by the satisfied Cheshire grin on their faces when they returned, they had evidently enjoyed the trip and the lunch, and realized that the B.B.&E. road is a most valuable piece of property with fine deep water facilities. J.J. Donovan was master of ceremonies and welcomed the guests, giving them cigars and a little tract entitled, `How Blue Canyon Coal Came to New Whatcom.'"

A 2,200-foot tram was built to bring the coal down to the bunkers beside Lake Whatcom, where rail cars on barges were loaded and towed to the northwest end of the lake.

Henry "Captain Harry" Reasoner operated the ship *Ella* to tow one of the earliest railroad car barges, a barge capable of carrying twenty-four coal cars on three parallel tracks. (The *Ella* was remodeled and named the *Prentice* in 1906.) With the arrival of tracks at Silver Beach train crews could transfer the coal cars directly onto the new railroad bound for bunkers at Bellingham Bay. The first such direct shipment went over the rails in July 1892.

Until the BB&E made it around the north shore of Lake Whatcom, the coal continued to come from Blue Canyon by barge. Residents had good passenger service, too, with as many as seven boats on the lake in the early 1900s. One could travel on the *Adelaide* or the *Marguerite* from Silver Beach

The Ella, under Captain Henry Reasoner.

– From Galen Biery Collection

to Park (or Blue Canyon City) and return for fifty cents. Prior to the completion of the railroad, four passenger trips were available daily.

In 1891, the SLS&E was finished from Seattle to Sumas (through Wickersham). Ownership was transferred to the Seattle & International Railroad Co. in 1896, and sold to the Northern Pacific Railroad (NPR) in March, 1901. The same year the BB&E went through the foothills along Lake Whatcom all the way to Wickersham. In October 1902, the NPR took over operation of BB&E and bought the line in 1903 to gain direct access to Bellingham from Wickersham (a portion of the old NPR tracks is still in use by the Lake Whatcom Steam Railway, an excursion train).

The mine hummed. New machinery was added. On March 23, 1893, the Fairhaven Herald reported that: "Two cars of powerful hoisting machinery for the Blue Canyon Coal Co. are on the track in front of the Bellingham Bay and British Columbia depot. . . . The machinery will be used for hoisting cars of coal out of the mine, and consists of a very heavy drum upon which the wire rope will be coiled, and two engines to drive the machinery."

Another item on April 4 reported: ". . . a new vein, eight feet thick, has been struck, about 100 feet below the present slope, and 1,000 feet east of the present tunnel. . . . The output is now about 200 tons daily and this will be increased. The company has now a contract with San Francisco parties for the delivery of 3,000 tons per month, and another firm in the same city wish to arrange for the delivery of an additional 1,000 tons monthly. . . . The bark Theobald arrived yesterday for a second cargo for San Francisco and will begin loading on Thursday or Friday, or as soon as the Alaska, which is now at the bunkers, has received her cargo."

Unfortunately, the Alaska never made it to San Francisco. It sank on April 22 with 1,900 tons of coal on board. The crew was saved; the ship seems simply to have sprung a major leak.

Coal development and mining continued concurrent with railroad building. The coal bunkers were at the base of the mountain, as well as washers. Before washing the coal was put through a sieve, gleaning about a 50% usable product. It was loaded directly into the cars resting on barges.

The coal was worked from a tunnel nearly level with the lake during 1892-93, with a new approach probing the interior of the mountain underway, a tunnel almost a mile long. Downs praised the quality of the coal:

"Our fine coal is much better for steam than lignite. Lignite always remains in a pulverized condition; but Blue Canyon coal cokes, and the fine stuff has only to be stirred occasionally to be quite as good as the coarse coal."

Downs reported that the veins going east pinched out and no one knew where they picked up again. To the west they had a fifteen-foot vein, but it was "dirty." Therefore, they followed the incline downward from the mouth of the entry tunnel about 800 feet above lake level. Downs said:

"We are now down 600 feet where entry No. 3 is made. There are from six to seven feet of solid coal as far as we have gone. We shall sink further to the level of the lake. While the lake is 800 feet below the croppings where the incline commences, the vein dips at about 30 degrees. . . ."

Downs stated the firm intended to submit the coal to Secretary Tracy's agents (Navy or procurement) to be appointed a supplier for the United States vessels, if they got the chance. On April 27, 1894, the chance was there. Blue Canyon Coal secured a contract for coaling the Bering Sea fleet of eight warships, despite active competition from mines in Comox on Vancouver Island, another near Fairhaven, and at Black Diamond toward Mount Rainier. The special fleet was formed under Secretary of the Navy Herbert to enforce the international treaty on sealing and stop poaching while the seals were migrating and birthing. All were coal-burners. The *Yorktown* was the first to begin coaling followed by the *Mohican*. It was reported that the *Yorktown* steamed on Blue Canyon coal from Bellingham to Seattle in six hours, a remarkably fast trip.

Naturally, all this development sparked a real estate boom in Blue Canyon townsite and at nearby Park. By 1895, about 1,000 people lived in Blue Canyon. Through the memoirs of Olga E. Pattison, daughter of a mine supervisor, Andrew Ecklund, in the hands of her daughter, Elaine L. Zobrist, we get a picture of life in the isolated town. Pattison said that all travel to and from Blue Canyon in the early years was by boat; there were no practical roads or trails. A Masonic Lodge was organized as early as 1893, and the members traveled monthly to Silver Beach for a meeting. The town grew so fast that there was a considerable tent city, but eventually these gave way to neat houses landscaped with flowers and fruit trees. Most homes contained three rooms plus a lean-to for kitchen and washroom. Residents carried water from the lake or flumed it down from a mountain stream.

Important visitors to Blue Canyon often stayed with the Andrew Ecklunds. Pattison remembered J.J.

Pioneer Andrew Ecklund.
From Galen Biery Collection

Donovan, Peter Larson, and others as guests, even though there was a three-story hotel in the town.

Before Blue Canyon really became a town, a saloon enjoyed a brisk business but the 1889 mine superintendent, a Mr. Dalton, forced it to close. (This apparently was during the time when Wardner and cohorts were in charge.) Instead the building housed the Custer Brothers Store and the post office. On Saturday afternoons, the boat brought a barrel of beer as a treat for the men.

Social affairs usually were held in a private residence formerly a large boat house. Pattison remembered that families would gather and all would

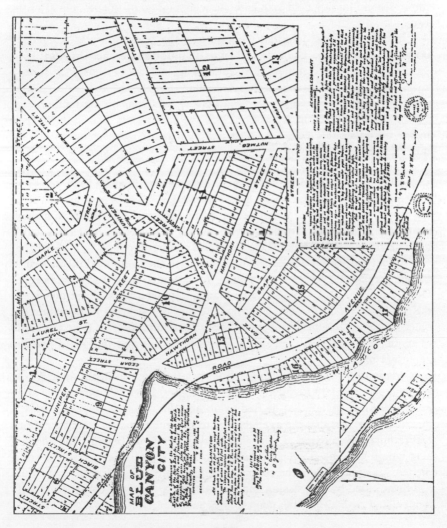

be peaceful until about nine o'clock. By that time, some of the men might have been drinking and, whether for that reason or sheer energy, a rousing fight would break out. On one occasion, Pattison's mother hid a fugitive from such a brawl and, brandishing a large stick, held off those who came after him to "get him." She courageously convinced the drunken mob that the law should handle whatever controversy existed.

In the late 1890s at least ninety children attended the local school four to six months each year, with the same teacher then going on to another community to teach for the balance of the year. The schoolhouse served as a church or meeting hall, as well. Baptisms in certain sects consisted of immersion in the icy cold lake and one woman died of pneumonia after the rite.

Since mining is inherently dangerous, the operation was nagged by occasional accidents. The year 1893 was an unfortunate one. On April 16, a gas explosion burned miner Otto Mullenberg, but not seriously. In June, a cave-in of a roof in a chute killed Alexander Grant, and in late July, some men were injured in leaping from a runaway cable car on the incline.

Two years later on April 11, 1895, the community was stunned by a major gas (accounts called it "dust and fire damp") explosion within the mine that killed twenty-three miners, becoming Washington's worst mine disaster. The blowup was soundless to those outside the mine. W.A. Telfer stated that he was working in the bunkers when he heard a loud yell from the entry to the mine, far above him. The worker, Tom Valentine, was waving and calling for help. When he reached the entry, Telfer found a disheveled, exhausted miner, James Kerns, sitting in a stupor where he had fallen after carrying a fellow miner to the mouth of the tunnel.

"Ecklund, Telfer and the others penetrated the tunnel. At the switch of the gangway 800 feet from the mouth of the tunnel, they found the body of George Roberts and, beyond, three loaded cars which had been blown off the tracks and a dead mule. . . . Ecklund and others tried to penetrate the other rooms and chutes but, beyond room 21, about 500 feet from the angle of tunnel and gangway, the safety lamps went out and the gas drove the explorers back."

Many of the dead were single, but six left widows and children. At the inquest, officials laid no blame on the operators. David Edmunds, the state mine inspector, stated that he had examined the mine on March 7, only a month earlier, and that the available air to the mine was three or four times that required. Explosion of "fire-damp" was ruled out, because the concussion would have been even worse and torn the entire mine apart. No comprehensive explosion in the rooms or digging areas had occurred; the men had been killed by concussion and after-damp. Men in the chambers or off-tunnels had rushed into the main tunnel and died. The theory was verified by the fact that one man dived behind some timbers and survived, while two others in the gangway were killed instantly. The conclusion was that men digging in the area known as the "breast" had encountered a pocket of gas which exploded, the resultant concussion rolling through the gangway and tunnel like an invisible blockbuster, killing everything in its path. A horse near the breast of the gangway was blown right out of his harness, retaining only his collar. A miner, James McAndrew was hurled with awful violence against the timbers and broke many bones, as was the fate of another. There was little or no fire after the explosion.

The bodies of the twenty-three victims were taken to the Blue Canyon schoolhouse for a common funeral service and, except for those shipped to known relatives, were transported by steamer and train to Bay View Cemetery. A cortege of about 1,000 silent spectators and relatives watched as the dead were interred with various religious rites performed over them. The eulogy written by Whatcom County journalist Frederick H. Adams dramatically described the scene in Roth's *History of Whatcom County*: "Twenty-three stalwart forms which had been full of intelligence and energy Monday, yesterday lay prostrate, like mown wheat stalks, before the coroner. They were the tenements, the shells, of the souls of a company of knights of labor which had received sudden orders and crossed the river of death in a body." At the time of death it mattered little whether their mates were Catholic, Protestant or atheists.

Another reporter had a different impression of the scene: "Doubtless if the ghosts of some of the dead miners were present they winked jocularly at one another at the nicety of the distinctions made between a K.P. or a Mason, or a Catholic, or a Methodist, and crowed over an extra honor, when their mortal shell received it."

After cleanup and inspection of the mine, and after the period of numb grief was over, the men went back to work at the mine a week later. The largest output for any one day was recorded a month later. Business continued to be brisk, with ships lying in the harbor to await coaling. The earth, however, continued to fight back; one miner said it was not a mine, but a series of several mines in its fragmentation of veins. However, by 1898, a five-year recession took its toll on industries and the mine company was not able to sell its coal as readily. Particularly damaging to the mine's economy was that the Navy was now converting to oil as a fuel. Reportedly the mine had produced 8,200 tons in 1901, and 6,010 tons in 1902. The mine ceased operating briefly in 1903, and some people moved on.

In 1904, the mine was leased to William Lawton, who operated it for two or three years. In 1907, J.M. Walter leased it personally, only to go into receivership after a year. Then a company was organized as the Whatcom County Mining Company, with J.M. Walters as President, and Andrew

Ecklund the Mine Superintendent. The mine produced steadily for twelve more years, closing in 1919. In 1920, the bunkers and other structures near the railway tracks, caught fire from a locomotive spark, and burned entirely. During the latter period, most of the coal went to the Seattle Lighting Company to be used for coal gas lighting. Refinement of electric lighting put an end to that market, too.

The nearby town of Park, established by the Zobrists, had grown during building of the railroad. Many of Blue Canyon townsite's original homes were in the way along the narrow buildable ledge of level ground, so owners moved the structures southeast to Park and continued to live in them. As a virtual twin town to Blue Canyon and its coal-miner families, Park ben-

efited, too, from the rapidly growing logging industry. The first need was for timbers for the mine and buildings for the workers. J.H. Bloedel, who owned the Samish Bay Logging Company with Wardner, started a logging camp somewhere near Blue Canyon, complete with bunkhouses for about twenty men, cook shack, blacksmith shop, and some family homes. By 1898, the original camp discontinued work and workers moved on to other local camps, with logging activity at its zenith. That year of 1898, J.J. Donovan, an inactive partner in the logging company, became chief engineer and general superintendent of the BB&BC that entered Bellingham from Sumas. He also became involved in a substantial development firm, the Bellingham Bay Improvement Company, with principals that in-

Executives of Bloedel-Donovan Lumber Mills, L-R: (Top) J.H. Bloedel, President, J.J. Donovan, Vice President, (Middle) C.W. Mason, Peter Larson, Jack Donovan, (Bottom) F.C. Faust, C.L. Flynn, and J.H. Prentice.
— From Galen Biery Collection

222

cluded Pierre Cornwall. Bloedel saw logging as the economic salvation of the area, organizing the Lake Whatcom Logging Company (LWLC) on August 11, 1898, in conjunction with J.J. Donovan and Peter Larson, and in 1901 the Larson Lumber Company.

The LWLC started its operations with eighteen men and one horse "Queen." Two steam-driven donkey engines were used to yard the logs, with the mare Queen pulling the cable back into the woods for the yarding crew.

LWLC soon was operating on a large scale in heavy timber from near Blue Canyon and Park all the way to Alger and Lake Samish. Top quality fir and cedar logs were delivered to the Geneva Lumber Company at the west end of Lake Whatcom in 1898. At the same time, the E.K. Wood Lumber Company and Knight Timber Company operated camps and mills between Blue Canyon City, Park and Wickersham. Farming and logging spread into the Acme Valley, with settlements developing at Wickersham, Acme, and Saxon—all just a few miles away from Park and Blue Canyon, and Van Zandt and Clipper toward the north end of the valley. A small town called Standard north of Acme bloomed to be the largest of the lot in 1910, population 375. Then it faded away to 100 by 1920; today the only trace of the town is a forlorn derelict building in the middle of a pasture.

Settlement in the Acme Valley was facilitated by the completion of the SLS&E, acquired by the NPR, as mentioned before. The fate of the Acme towns was bound up with the history of Park and the LWLC. Just a small collection of homes today, Saxon was surrounded by mills between the 1890s and 1917, including: Dahlen Brothers shingle mill, with several workers; Empire Lumber Company with eight men working in 1897 to produce over twelve million shingles; Ferguson Camp, a substantial operation opening in 1905; Key City Logging Company, no information; Knight Brothers with twenty-one loggers; B.E. Lynch, a shingle bolt cutter and lumber mill of the 1890s; Fenton and True Merrill, no information; Osgood and Wheeler Company, shingle mill operators of 1911; Reichert Brothers shingle mill around 1907; L.D. Reynolds with a saw mill in 1893 and after; Tofel Brothers shingle mill, later owned by Yorksten, no information; and Truettle Tie Mill making railroad ties in 1913. All of these operations were small and somewhat temporary, largely working on the remains of timber logged off by larger firms like LWLC. Many cut shingle bolts from the stumps remaining after first cuttings.

Logging of the area completely eclipsed the brief glory of the Blue Canyon coal mine. Within two or three decades the LWLC alone had 1,400 loggers in the woods living in six camps, and employed another 1,600 in four sawmills, three planing mills, three shingle mills, a sash and door factory, and a box manufacturing plant.

The town of Park was a lively crossroads for the NPR and a private woods-access railroad owned by the LWLC. From there, the logs could be shipped by NPR to Wickersham and on south, or be dumped into the lake for booming and towing to the mills on Lake Whatcom. The logging railways were notoriously unreliable and inspired colorful language from their crews. One of the worst was a two-mile section built by the BCCMC in 1896, and later used for logging. A crew member said that there were five different kinds of rail on that stretch, some six by six timbers with flat steel strips bolted on top. When the summer sun beat down on the wood, it shrank and caused the rails to come loose and derail the trains. Trains then did not have air brakes, either, and the steep grades and heavy loads governed only by hand brakes caused the wheels to develop significant flat spots from skidding on the rails.

When the logging crews moved farther from the lake, the town of Park declined in importance. For years Park was the starting point for the Lake Whatcom Railway, a steam train excursion line. In the late 1980s, however, a squabble over rights-of-way caused it to move operations to Wickersham. Blue Canyon townsite was largely deserted after the mine closed and today a handful of homes, old and new, straggle along the steep slope. The Blue Canyon Foundation, largely a halfway house and recovery center for alcoholics and substance abuse victims, thrived for a time. After it closed, the main structure, remodeled from an old mine building, was burned by the fire department. A Bellingham group financed a "fat farm" near Park, but it flopped. All that remain at Park are the old store building and a shed housing some rail cars, now disconnected from the tourist railroad. Wickersham and Saxon are mere collections of homes and farms, but Acme made it into the late century as a thriving small village of 500-600.

Chapter 25
GLACIER

Only thirty-five to forty people remain in the once-bustling town of Glacier, situated on the Mount Baker Highway at the 2,000-foot level of the North Cascades Mountains. Estimates of the unincorporated (but platted) town's population during the 1890s and early 1900s were about 400. From an official census of 1930, the township's population had declined to 119, but population boomed during the Depression years to perhaps 700-1,000 residents in and around the town.

Glacier had an enviable position during the gold rush days; it was the jumping-off place for the gold mines—the Lone Jack, Boundary Red Mountain, Gargett, Excelsior, and dozens of others that were little more than holes in the mountain or staked streamside lots. The State Trail began at Cornell's, later to become Glacier, and mile posts were marked from there.

Glacier, too, was the center of a rough trail building effort in 1893 that ended twenty miles short of Hannegan Pass, at which time all work was halted. Perhaps the surveyors who had entered the mountains beyond Glacier, first in 1886 for a railroad, and in 1893 for a connector wagon road to the Slate Creek Mining Area said "I told you so." They had warned builders of the overwhelming barriers to transportation through the precipitous North Cascades mountains.

Chester C. Cornell is credited with being the first homesteader of Cornell, renamed Glacier in 1904. An ex-miner, he came in 1888. Perhaps he looked for gold, but he staked his claim at today's Glacier after he noticed the coal deposits near Glacier (Cornell) Creek. Curiously, he did only minor development on the mine. Instead, he raised vegetables and hay during the summer months to sell to the miners probing for gold. He expanded this service to include a crude hotel in 1889, and was the area's first postmaster, 1889-1904.

No town existed, though. Homesteader Albert Vaughn settled on the site in 1889, then platted the town and filed the plat nine years later in 1898. A shack ten feet by twelve feet served as a schoolhouse for a handful of children. A road or trail was completed to Glacier over the Warnick Bridge across the Nooksack River, in September, 1899. With all the prospecting in the mountains, though, a means of hauling heavy equipment had to be devised.

This meant a railroad, of course, and the rails moved closer every day as the Bellingham Bay and British Columbia (BB&BC) extended east, first to Maple Falls and in June, 1904 to Glacier. The BB&BC was designed to haul passengers and freight from Sumas, where a connection could be made to Bellingham. The railroad later was acquired by the Chicago, Milwaukee and St. Paul and was heavily used until 1943, after which the tracks were taken up.

A special excursion party came from Bellingham to celebrate the completion of rail service to Glacier. After Frank Boucher, railroad agent, greeted them, they hiked, fished and ate their basket lunches. The scenery was grand, but few manmade attractions had yet come to Glacier. A roundhouse at Glacier catered to minor problems of the locomotives and cars. A Wells Fargo telegraph office served the prospectors. Sherman Jones and George A. Gray opened the Logs Hotel in 1902, operating on the south side of today's highway, about two blocks west of today's Graham Store. It was sold to Mrs. M.E. Branin in about 1904, the only hostelry in Glacier for a few years. Henry Boettiger started a hotel in 1906, later operated by Harvey Haggard. That was about it at the time of the excursion.

However, the needs of tourists and prospectors, plus a fledgling group of logging companies, sparked growth of a business district. Whit Jacobs built the Mountain Home Hotel shortly after the arrival of the railroad at Glacier, chiefly to accommodate the railroad crews for overnight stays. He turned its operation over to his wife Blanche and ran a new general store, selling it to John F. Drake in 1910. The Mountain Home burned down in 1915, along with a collection of original shacks and buildings in the area. All Jacobs had left of his investments was a tourist camp on Church Mountain at about 7,000 feet altitude that W.H. Lawson and he had constructed in 1907 near a small glacier. Sometime before 1910 George McLaughlin built the Mount Baker Inn across from the Mountain Home Hotel, running a general store, garage and gas station at street level and renting rooms on the second floor. Later Earl McLaughlin ran the Mount Baker, which burned in about 1948.

A person traveling to Glacier was subject to the vagaries of weather and machinery. In 1907, a winter storm involving torrential rains loosened a bank near the Warnick bridge and sent a slide of earth and rock over the tracks, one to three feet deep for about a quarter mile. No trains ran for almost a month. During the same period even the wagon road was closed for awhile from an earthslide.

In 1915, the town still boasted three hotels, a store, at least one saloon, postoffice, the town hall, William Martineau's pool hall and bike shop, a card room, George A. Hall's candy store, barber shop, and Charlie Bourn's livery stable, perhaps a couple of quietly operated brothels. Perhaps 200 residents lived there permanently, a population greatly amplified in summer by prospectors that came and went during the first two decades of 1900. In summer the hotel space was grossly inadequate and prospectors often gathered moss to spread beneath their bedrolls among the trees. A doctor and dentist came. Lawyer James L. Sligh, an assayer, and several companies set up business offices in Glacier related to the logging and mining industries. A fraternal lodge served to foster comradeship in the isolated town.

In 1906, the townsite of Glacier became part of the National Forest Reserve, but squatters or homesteaders settled on agricultural land before January 1, 1906, were given deeds to their homesteads and mining claims were honored, although the government thereafter asked for a royalty on production of minerals.

The closest gold mine was the Glacier Mining Company, located a few miles east at the site occupied now by Snowater, a resort community. Residents in the 1990s still remember a a tunnel, mine carts, and equipment at the site.

Whit and Blanche Jacobs began The Mountain Home Hotel.
— Photo courtesy of Mike Impero

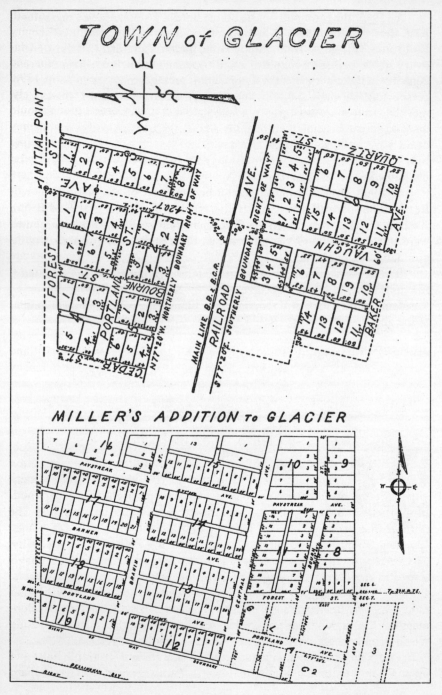

TOWN of GLACIER

MILLER'S ADDITION TO GLACIER

Coal mining sporadically created excitement in the community. Cornell, who started it all, formed the Cornell Creek Coal Company with Henry Wiggins, working along a shallow seam virtually on the outskirts of Glacier. Cornell had filed his claim as a *homesteader*, so S.C. Anderson and John Barber are credited with registering the first two *coal* claims in 1898. As drilling proceeded, the coal seam appeared to pitch downward severely. After the railroad arrived, an expert suggested that the Cornell group should start a tunnel at railside and, when they intercepted the coal seam, they could bring the coal directly to the rail cars. Unfortunately, the tunneling failed to intercept any seams. Cornell died suddenly in 1909, but several others had developed small coal mines along Cornell Creek and elsewhere near Glacier. They bored tunnels into the recognized coal deposit, including the Smith tunnel, Bellingham Bay tunnel (drilled by Alexander Polson), Palmer tunnel, and the first known producing site—the Discovery tunnel. Three hundred people came to see the Discovery Mine tunnel at the southern edge of the coal field and bring home samples of the good anthracite coal. A group of hunters in 1907 are credited by some pioneers with discovering another segment of the extensive coal deposits on Coal Creek.

Coal prices left financiers lukewarm about the prospects, but in that year of 1907, a group of people holding coal claims sought financing for development. The group included: H.S. and W.M. Yarrow of Fergus Falls, Minnesota; G.A. and Ethel A. Alexander; J.M. and E.M. Alexander; H.P. and Carrie Hagler; and Lewis and Lucy Darrow (Washingtonians). The company hired A.L. Black, Sr., to travel to the East Coast and seek financiers in exchange for an option on their lands—containing an estimated thirty-three million tons of coal. Leading the investors was A.G. Bennett of Scranton, Pennsylvania. The Washington Anthracite Coal Company (WAC) was incorporated September 30, 1907, by A.G. Bennett, Lincoln Davis, F.D. Wilson, Thomas H. Cavanaugh, and H.D. Watrous. The Articles of Incorporation called for the firm to "acquire, own, lease, use or develop any lands containing coal, iron, or other ores or minerals, stone, water rights, and any woodlands or other lands required or useful for the purposes of the company." The Articles also included mining, building facilities such as railroads, trams, telephone lines, etc. The patented claim holders were to receive a royalty. The WAC apparently purchased land near the railroad, at the south of today's townsite, plus property in the bed of Cornell Creek for crushers and bunkers. Possibly it was at this time that a short railroad spur was laid toward their mine entrance. Bennett placed a limit of one and a half years on the development work; if a mine was not producing coal by then, the financial backing would have to cease. WAC did not make the deadline.

Prospectors found coal seams at Slide Mountain near Maple Falls and up on Church Mountain, a spire that looms sharply beyond Glacier. Richard

Shields, a geologist?, said that the Church Mountain vein was twenty-four feet wide and possibly seven miles long, slanting off to the northwest. Four men explored the feasibility of mining this seam but apparently gave up in 1909.

In 1908, William F. Dodge, mining and consulting engineer from the anthracite region of Pennsylvania, said the "coal is bright in appearance and ignites freely, being fully as lasting in duty as the better grades of Pennsylvania anthracite coal," and that when properly manufactured could equal the best in Pennsylvania. The field was examined by E.G. Woodruff of the U.S. Geological Survey, who gained a different impression: "The coal is mostly anthracite or high-grade bituminous, but some of it is lower grade. Generally, the percentage of ash in the coal is very high, . . ." He concluded that prospecting to date did not show the likelihood of commercial development. Later analysts concluded that there were 4.8 million tons of coal in the reserve, but that the cost of producing coke from the coal was considerable higher than production of petroleum coke.

Nonetheless, Senator Alexander Polson of Olympia, Washington, leased 2,500 acres of coal lands in September, 1908 (much of the land now was in the National Forest Reserve). The *American Reveille* of May 31, 1911, stated that Polson was bringing drills down from his other claims in the mountains to mark the limits of the coal-bearing strata. He staked claims, applied for patents and, while he was waiting for them, built a nice home and office building in Glacier. Polson completed a five-mile tramway and a thousand-foot chute to bring out the coal. Coal seams in the strata were identified as seam 1, seam 2, etc., as they ran through a large area in which several claimants were working.

Polson estimated possible production at 1,500 tons daily from his claims, but the rail executives protested they did not have the capacity to haul that much. However, the coal was yet to be seen.

Around 1915, Polson had dug a tunnel at the 4,200-foot elevation, contacting coal seam #2 (south of seam #1), an eight-foot seam of good anthracite. Later the tunnel also touched seam #1, and Polson's firm mined and shipped coal. According to a later-day coal prospector, Gary Graham of Glacier, seam #2 is about ninety-five feet thick of mixed quality anthracite—a bit more sulphur than seam #1, varying from low quality ash to high quality anthracite. "Parts are very good," he says.

Encouraged by the extent and quality of the coal, Polson installed a big steam generator outside the mine entrance, using coal to run the plant, the steam being used to operate jack hammers.

Mary DeBorde, U.S. Forest Service cultural resource technician, said that Polson also attempted to intercept the seams at elevation 950. This required a self-draining adit to be driven in excess of 15,000 feet toward the

The Polson Coal Mine.

— Photo courtesy of Mike Impero

seams. Polson succeeded in the attempt, but World War I intervened, bringing his operations to a halt until 1919. The Tozier Tunnel was then drilled and worked until 1932, when the Great Depression of the 1930s brought all activities to a halt.

Since the United Collieries (UC) was incorporated December 21, 1909, perhaps this firm took up where Washington Anthracite left off with its claims, but the author can find no indication of any actual mining by this firm after that date. The incorporators were John W. Langdon, Dorsey F. Baker, and Everett Smith, with offices in Seattle and capital stock of $1,500,750. A firm of the same name—United Collieries—was incorporated on March 24, 1930, by Leslie H. Dills and H.W. Broenkow, and appeared to have acquired portions or all of the former Polson claims.

Probably because of the Depression, nothing significant was achieved by the later United Collieries, and in 1940, Consolidated Coal Mines, Inc., organized and began to acquire some of the scattered patented claims from many different people.

According to Fraser Madill of Glacier Land Company, Richard Randall, a developer, was fairly successful in purchasing or settling numerous claims on coal lands and putting them together. Henry J. Madill was able to pur-

231

chase this package, joining a very tangled conglomeration of private claims and government lands (also purchased) into a sizable chunk of real estate. Having acquired a controlling interest in Consolidated's operation, Madill brought his collection of lands into the assets of the Glacier Land Company (GLC) when it was incorporated in 1949. Despite the proven existence and excellence of the coal, economic and environmental factors inhibited further development of the coal.

Around 1957, the GLC leased the timber rights, reportedly for $200,000, to Puget Sound Pulp & Timber Company. The latter was purchased by Georgia-Pacific Corporation, a major wood products firm in 1963. The rights permitted logging until about the year 2020. In turn, the 5,000 acres of timber rights were purchased by the Trillium Corporation in 1991.

Below-ground or mineral lease rights had been acquired by the Canadian-American Mining Company headed by Chris Palzer, and in October, 1975, Al Firchau of Whatcom County, Washington, bought the lease rights. He proceeded to mine about 5,000 tons of excellent anthracite coal and sold it chiefly to the Portland Cement plant of Bellingham. Firchau—with the collaboration of Gary Graham of Glacier—planned to sell more coal for charcoal briquets, used not just for barbecuing but for major home heating in some countries. The two men embarked on an international quest for good markets, also visiting mines in the Orient and Europe to educate themselves on modern mining methods. South Korean firms expressed keen interest in the coal, but the cost of shipping was not cost effective. Another idea Firchau and Graham conceived was using the carbon for anodes in aluminum products, but other products did the job better. Finally, Firchau considered obtaining a permit to do strip mining, to see once and for all what exactly was in that Glacier coal field. At this time, some members of the community objected. Whether for this or other reasons, the latest effort at coal mining in Glacier was suspended. Al Firchau died, and Graham went back to his engineering design enterprise and the operation of the landmark restaurant and store, Graham's store.

Graham's ownership of the store evolved from George McLaughlin's Mount Baker Inn and store of the early 1900s. The business was operated for years by George Hinton, then Earl Graham and his wife, who leased it to Clint and Joe Nunamaker, then Charles and Shirley Graham. Earl Graham's grandson Gary, forsaking an engineering career at Boeing Aircraft, took over its operation from the early 1970s until it closed in 1995. The zany promotions of Graham kept the restaurant and store in newspaper headlines for years.

Logging and shingle mills periodically swelled the population in and around the townsite of Glacier. As early as 1901, the Angus McDonald Shingle Company near Glacier was filling orders for new residents of the town. McDonald teamed up with Reginald Nestos to operate a pack train service for miners, as well. A West Virginia corporation, the West Coast Lumber Company bought several sections of timberland in June, 1901, not far from Glacier. Art and Jess Knight, the Knight Brothers Logging, worked on the North Fork of the Nooksack River in 1905, then moved their operation near Boulder Creek east of Maple Falls, to access the BB&BC tracks. They built a spur line that merely crossed the Nooksack plus a few additional hundred feet to enable an engine to pull logs down the tracks and across the bridge. In 1909, the Balcom-Vanderhoof Logging Company logged off eight to ten carloads a day from a site just east of Glacier. Allen and McRae, later Allen and Nolte logged in 1921 and 1922. In 1911, the Lake Mill Lumber Company operated near Glacier, and the A.H. Campbell Lumber Manufacturing Company in 1917. At Warnick, originally a separate small community, but considered a part of Glacier later (only two miles away), were the Ferguson Brothers Logging Camp in 1903, and the Elder Brothers log camp and railroad spur in 1904. From 1907-08 poor economic conditions nationwide slowed the growth of the logging and lumber industries, but in 1909, things improved again.

A little later, two significant lumber mills helped to support the town: Miller & Sons (M&S), about a mile west of town, and Warnick Lumber Company (WLC), another mile or so.

The M&S shingle mill was originally built by Elmer & Merle Little, who sold the mill to Frank Boettiger in 1936, but it was unprofitable. In 1939, Leon Miller, who had operated successful mills at Sumas and Shuksan, bought the operation. Using the method that had proven profitable, he converted the mill to using logs instead of shingle bolts and manufactured boxcars of shingles until 1952, shipping them by rail all over the nation. M&S employed about twenty men at the mill and another fifteen to twenty men as loggers. M&S built five cabins across the highway from the mill, and four families (besides the Millers) lived there.

Warnick and its WLC, located just east of the Warnick bridge about two miles west of Glacier, also may be considered a part of Glacier, although the settlement there was first named Warnick for a chainman who helped to build the Warnick Bridge in 1899, and early Warnick residents were very adamant about their separate-ness. The WLC was established in 1919 by Frank M. Brooks and Nathan P. Carver. During initial operation, the company installed a long chute to bring down logs from the mountains above. A massive donkey engine eased them down the slope. Some workers lived in Glacier or drove to their homes elsewhere, but others lived at the site; all were fed at the company cookhouse. The WLC operated briskly with about thirty employees (probably an equal number in the woods to provide logs) until the camp burned down in 1924. It was promptly rebuilt but abandoned after 1935, when the Depression made the plant unprofitable. A Japanese company bought and dismantled the camp structures for scrap metal.

A ever-growing industry in Glacier was tourism. The tourists came by train to stay in the hotels, roam the forests and fish the streams. Outdoor enthusiasts ranged from families interested in weekend hikes to dedicated climbers. Mazamas, a renowned Portland mountaineering club, came to Glacier as a jumping-off spot from which to climb Mount Baker itself. The trail forged by such climbers still is heavily used today, *only now the Glacier Creek road provides auto access to the trailhead that leads to the Coleman Glacier. Until 1986, the Kulshan Cabin on the trail provided shelter for climbers heading onto the snow-and-ice portion of the climb.

To emphasize the charms of Whatcom County, Bellingham's Mount Baker Club and Chamber of Commerce organized the Mount Baker Marathon in 1911. Fourteen hardy athletes registered for this first event, a demanding and free-wheeling race, a round trip of seventy-six to 112 miles, depending on whether one chose the Glacier Trail or the Deming Trail. The contestant started from downtown Bellingham, made his way any way he could (on foot, horseback, train, or car) to Mount Baker and back—of course, the mountain portion was entirely on foot. Huddled in tents, judges actually awaited the contestants at the summit.

This first race was both incredibly challenging and hysterically funny. Only five contestants were still contending at the snowfields. Of these, Joe Galbraith had reached the Deming Trail in Hugh Diehl's stripped-down Ford racing car, made it over the summit of Mount Baker, and returned to the car, so weary he had to be strapped into the vehicle for the return trip. In and out of the ditches and potholes of the crude road, Diehl and Galbraith made it back to Bellingham in twelve hours, twenty-eight minutes to seize first place. Meanwhile, those choosing the Glacier Trail made it to the town of Glacier by train and set off. Harvey Haggard, a Glacier resident, bounded up and down Mount Baker in ten hours, one minute (Galbraith's over-the-mountain portion took ten hours, forty-six minutes), then threw himself onto the train. Rules decreed that the first runner to arrive in Glacier could commandeer the train, leaving subsequent contestants to fend for themselves. Haggard was resting, stark naked, on a cot in the train when the locomotive hit a 1300-pound bull on the tracks and was derailed along with the passenger car. Haggard came out of the car dazed but, after dressing, he hopped into a willing passerby's buggy for the ongoing trip. At Maple Falls the driver's horse was spent, so Haggard jumped on a nervous horse that bucked him off at Kendall. Spectators piled him into a car for the balance of the trip to Bellingham. He fainted twice enroute but managed to walk into the Chamber of Commerce building to claim second.

This wild race was cancelled after a runner fell into a crevasse in the 1913 race. Even though he was miraculously discovered and rescued, the race was deemed too dangerous. Its successor, the popular Ski-to-Sea Race held annually since 1973 is a relay race. It starts with downhill and cross-country skiing, goes on with a runner, biker, kayaker on the Nooksack River, and sea kayaker across Bellingham Bay to Marine Park. As many as 200 teams compete—and the race still finds contestants rushing down the main street of Glacier as original marathoners did.

When the BB&BC cancelled most passenger service to Glacier by 1911, Ole Hanson provided stage service with a new Model T Ford from 1912-18. Jim Yelton established a scheduled bus service to Glacier around 1915, and also chartered his bus for Mazamas and other organized groups to haul their gear and members from Bellingham. Inevitably, climbers were lost on the slopes of the treacherous mountain. The worst accident occurred July 22, 1939, when an avalanche swept the entire party of twenty-five students and guides from Western Washington College of Education (Western Washington University) hundreds of feet down the Deming Glacier. The trip always had been well-organized, an annual outing since 1917, but when the slide stopped, seven people were unaccounted for. One was found quickly and survived. Another was located within three hours but was dead. Searchers found a third body the following day, but four others claim the Deming Glacier as their tomb.

A live volcanic crater has belched steam from the south side of Mount Baker as long as the recording of local history. Glacier mountaineer, Doug Hamilton, says local people have hiked into and camped right on the edge of the fumarole, although within the crater were the carcasses of birds killed by the sulphurous fumes.

In the early 1920s a group of financiers from Bellingham formed the Mount Baker Development Company, intending to build facilities for tourists. In February, 1923, the group purchased five acres to set up a camp of fifteen tents in Austin Pass Meadows, plus a cookhouse in a tent. Tourists came as far as Shuksan by car, then transferred to horses.

Work began in 1924 at the Meadows, site-clearing and initial construction work for Heather Inn. An inn accommodating fifty people plus several two-room cabins was built at Shuksan (several miles below the ski area) on a site that had been John Broyles homestead. To finance all the construction, the Mount Baker Development Company principals sold stock in the company.

Convinced that the resort would be completed, the federal government completed construction of the Mount Baker Highway to Austin Pass in 1926. The gravel road was only one-way in places, and must have been a thrill to travel.

235

Mt. Baker Lodge.

Interior of Lodge.

— Photos courtesy of Doug Hamilton

The handsome Mount Baker Lodge opened on July 14, 1927, an L-shaped building 210 feet long and from fifty to 130 feet wide with a Swiss architectural appearance. At one end a viewing tower soared seventy feet above the structure, giving wonderful views of surrounding mountain scenery. The lobby was 130 feet long and fifty feet wide; it had a "walk-in" fireplace at one end. A polished oak floor invited dancing in the lobby. According to Ray Heller, author of a pictorial history of Mount Baker:

"The ceiling was supported by fir pillars. An Alaskan Indian theme done by Ross Gill of Seattle in gray and red decorated the lobby and continued into the main dining room where it was accented with gold. The lobby, dining room and corridors were lined with cedar shakes. Around the lobby were electric lamps with shades painted in the Indian motif. There were dozens of comfortable chairs and lounges and twelve writing desks held a supply of the lodge's stationery."

Near the lobby was a fountain, as well as a gift shop and a lovely dining room to serve the guests in the one hundred rooms. In its first year of operation, over 11,000 guests stayed at the Mount Baker Lodge, a first-class lodge with special horse and burro trips, dancing, movies, and campfire programs. From mid-August to closing on September 19, 1927, a movie crew stayed at the lodge while shooting the film, "Wolf Fangs," starring Charles Morton, Caryl Lincoln, James Gordon, and a dog named Thunder. The lodge bulged with tourists who came to watch the filming, as well, and in 1928, the Mount Baker Development Company built a two-story addition to the lodge. Business boomed.

As early as 1927, also, a group of ski enthusiasts began climbing the slopes near the lodge (closed in winter) to ski down on crude wooden skis, often home-made or barrel staves with broom-handle poles. A jump was prepared for a contest in 1930. Skiers either returned from the mountain daily or sometimes stayed in a stone cabin at the Meadows. Investors discussed the feasibility of keeping the Mount Baker Lodge open in winter.

Unfortunately, at sunrise on August 5, 1931, a fire broke out near the kitchen of the lodge and spread rapidly. All of the guests were routed out and escaped safely, but most lost all their gear. One guest jumped twenty feet from his second story room, clad only in pajamas, pants and a coat. As the flames raced through the building, an oil tank blew up to add volatile fuel to the conflagration. A guest described the noise of the fire as a shriek from a steam whistle. The lodge was leveled in two and a half hours. All that remained were the stone chimneys and fireplace, the foundation and heaps of melted glass. Volunteers, including a crew working on the highway, managed to keep the fire from turning into a major forest fire, though the forest was burned within a short radius of the structure. Sadly the lodge was never rebuilt. Only the annex served guests as Heather Inn after being remodeled.

Glacier received international renown in 1934, when the movie, *Call of the Wild*, was filmed in and around the town and at a special set at the Mount Baker ski area. The movie starred Clark Gable, Jack Oakie, and

Loretta Young. Enroute to the Heather Inn, the stars were marooned at Glacier, and Loretta Young boarded for a time at Aleen and Earl Graham's home across from Graham's store. Gable, Oakie and other movie people were parceled out to other residents, and from time to time during the movie production were guests at Grahams' restaurant. The Nooksack River near Hannegan Pass became the "Yukon River," and during a filming of Gable and others coming downriver on a raft, all aboard fell into the river.

Graham's restaurant and bar next to the store gained further movie fame in 1975, when it became the bar for the film, *The Deer Hunter*, starring Robert DeNiro. Local citizens served as extras in both films.

After World War II, the Heather Inn was changed to a dormitory for skiers and a rather primitive two-story wing added. Up to 800 sailors from the Whidbey Island Naval Base came for recreation at times, accommodated in triple-deck bunks. The structure became unsafe and was burned intentionally in 1952.

However, the excellent ski potential was developed by investors over the next decades and today a Mount Baker Day Lodge serves skiers and those simply playing in the snow.

Since the only access road to Mount Baker leads through Glacier, it continued to be an important jumping-off point, just as it had been in the gold rush period. Its population declined sharply, though, as surrounding logging businesses pulled out, the coal mining was suspended, and fast autos made it possible to go to Mount Baker and return to Bellingham or Vancouver, B.C., on the same day. Today the only businesses are a store, bar, a couple of restaurants, a motel and a few small ski-related shops—fewer than fifty permanent residents supplying the labor. It is so quiet that, in the 1950s, a pet deer wandered the streets, bumming morsels and tidbits. It had been raised by two boys when its mother was killed. To prevent hunters from shooting it, the residents placed a big red ribbon around its neck. Concerned for its health, authorities removed it to Silver Lake to revert to the wild. Life continues at a sleepy pace in Glacier except during holiday weekends and ski season.

Loretta Young and others at Graham's during filming of Call of the Wild.

— Photos courtesy of Doug Hamilton

Chapter 26

MAPLE FALLS

On the Mount Baker Highway twenty-six miles from Bellingham, Maple Falls today is merely a crossroads community of about 300 people serving tourists and skiers. Some summer people or retirees have built new homes that grace the side streets, but like respectable dowagers, most homes are showing their age—a few dowdy, many powdered and rouged to be neat dwellings. It is hard to believe that the town once was an important railroad stop and a center of logging and milling activity. Around 1920, about 1,200 people lived in Maple Falls; even in 1901, when the country had just opened up, the town had 150 (it was said half of them were in brothels).

The search for gold in Canada that began in the late 1850s spread into the North Cascades, but the heavily forested foothills were almost impenetrable and numerous rushing streams sometimes dangerous. The Nooksack River rampaged over its banks during the spring snow melt.

Prospectors bound for the Fraser River and Barkerville originally chose the Nooksack Trail from today's Bellingham to near Everson, then north across the border to connect with the Fraser around Chilliwack, British Columbia. Earliest travel into the Cascades was by or on the Nooksack River. Intrigued by the stories of gold prospects as close as Sumas Mountain, in August, 1860, five men, John Tennant, John Bennett, Frederick F. Lane, William Wood, and George Cagey left Whatcom (Bellingham) to explore upriver. They spent an unpleasant five days trekking eastward beyond today's Acme valley, then hired two Indians to transport them to the junction of the north and middle forks of the river east of today's Deming. It was a fruitless and dangerous trip for seven men and a dog in an overloaded dugout canoe. A brief exploration of the middle fork of the Nooksack yielded no promise of gold.

In 1873, J.J. Parker and a Mr. Farwood set out from Lynden and Everson in an Indian canoe, turning into the South Fork of the river where it winds through the Acme Valley. Parker reported that the two found sparse "color" on some of the bars but that he felt the geology of the area was not promising for major gold strikes.

The next known person to explore the country toward Mount Baker was the lively and courageous Lynden pioneer, Phoebe Judson. She and a small party climbed Mount Nooksack, twelve miles east of Lynden, during a pleasurable outing in August, 1874.

More homesteaders than prospectors found the valleys east of Lynden pleasant and settled down to farm. Adventurers pushed up the North Fork of the Nooksack River to Loop's Ranch, the end of the known trail, which lay just beyond today's Maple Falls, then bushwhacked their way to climb Mount Baker. The trail became a wagon road of sorts after gold was discovered near Twin Lakes and Ruby Creek, mentioned in other chapters. The wagon road later was extended to Glacier, but definitely ended at Shuksan. From there, one could work his way up to Mount Baker or veer northward into the gold fields.

A West Virginian, Carthage Kendall, was the first to homestead about three miles west of Maple Falls at today's hamlet of Kendall in 1884. Carl, Norman, and other Caulkins families settled a mile or so north toward Silver Lake, then called Fish Lake. John and Minnie Hardan received a patented claim west of Maple Falls on the north bank of the river. Today's townsite seems to have been swampy and disdained at first.

The town of Maple Falls.

– Photo courtesy of Mike Impero

Hardan built a rough cabin of hand-split timbers with a lean-to as extra sleeping space. He opened a small store, applied for a postoffice as Hardan and the postmaster's job.

George Albert King and his wife Caroline were the first to settle on today's townsite in 1889 or 1890, building a cabin near the crossroads of the Silver Lake Road and the Mount Baker gold trail. They were quick to realize the potential for a lumber mill, the eventual impetus for the community's development. Maple Creek Falls was a series of cascades totaling about thirty-five feet, sufficient to provide water power. King built a flume to lead the rushing water to his new mill and, when disillusioned prospectors returned from the Mount Baker Gold Rush of the 1890s and 1900s, he was there with lumber with which to build homesteaders' homes. King renamed his mill the Maple Falls Lumber Company, turning out rough lumber, then added a planing mill in 1901 to produce smooth boards. Eleven years later the mill burned.

The canny King reacted swiftly when he learned that the Bellingham Bay & British Columbia Railway (BB&BC) was to build an extension from Sumas toward Mount Baker. He set aside ten acres of his land for a townsite near the site of a proposed depot, platted and recorded the plat June 29, 1901. He planned for the future, designating streets sixty-six feet wide, although at first only a trail wound through the brush. The main thoroughfare then called Lake Street is today's Silver Lake Road. When John Hardan moved away from his homestead in 1895, King gained the post office, and the name was changed to Maple Falls in June, 1901, as well.

The railroad roughed out its route in 1901 and completed trackage and a depot by April 15, 1902, operational except for a bridge between Kendall and Maple Falls. The extension in 1904 to Glacier permitted loggers to construct short rail spurs along the line to access the towering timber. Industries had an access to the outside world, and the town began to enjoy a real estate boom.

Although the town enjoyed supply business during the gold rushes to Mount Baker, it was timber that made the town. It was timber that also destroyed much of the town in the guise of timber fires that repeatedly threatened or invaded Maple Falls.

Limited tourism also fed the town's coffers as soon as the rails came. Outdoor enthusiasts came to Maple Falls, where early settler, Embret Gerdrum, met them at the depot with a team and wagon for the trip to Silver Lake, three miles north. A livery stable provided rental horses for those who wanted to go on horseback. Guests stayed at the Gerdrums' home, ate well, and enjoyed guided hiking trips, horseback rides, and fishing. Later the Gerdrums built a plain, serviceable hotel/resort building near the lake, a square building with numerous bedrooms on the second floor, kitchen facilities on the first, and a wide porch encircling the structure—a pleasant place from which to contemplate nature. Gerdrums sold this, the Silver Lake Resort, to Mr. and Mrs. Ruby Alexander in 1923.

By about 1906, Maple Falls had a complete business district, including such luxuries as a public bath house. The town even had an opera house managed by J.P. Asplund, also the supervisor of the Bellingham Bay Shingle Company mill. An immigrant, Justus Schmidel, described his arrival at night in the fall, 1906 for friends in Europe:

"As I looked around me I saw lights here and there. With the snow gently falling, it looked like a bewitched fairy-tale town in the middle of a primitive forest. On both sides of the broad street stood two rows of wooden buildings. One was beside the other with protective roofs resting partially on posts. These extended over the sidewalk. It gave the sidewalk an appearance of an arcade." (*Seattle Times*, February 14, 1965, translated from a German book written by Schmidel.)

He reported livery barns, a tobacco shop that had a card room for poker and blackjack at the rear, a liquor store, restaurant, saloon, stores, and the two-story Boulder Hotel. Schmidel's further impressions were ethereal:

"Men with slouch hats filled the streets like legendary charcoal burners and bandits. This was a Saturday night and all the men from the surrounding camps had come to town to relax. People were everywhere. They stood in dense groups before the houses. The men passed me in the fresh fallen snow, silent as ghosts."

Roll Bates had the first barber shop, and M.V. Murray was an early blacksmith. Herbert Leavitt, Sr., from Quebec built the Mt. Baker Hotel and Saloon in 1901 and the Bellingham Bay Chop House. J.J. Stocker built the Greenwood Hotel in 1901 sporting a bar and billard parlor. In 1902, John W. Groves opened a boot and shoe repair shop, and Mrs. Jesse Wheeler used her glassed-in front porch as a bakery. The Beckwith and Griffith store also known as O.K. Department Store opened in 1904. The Maple Falls Pool Hall and Cigar Store opened in 1915, and E.H. Mohler an ice cream parlor about the same time. Other hotels were Maple Falls Hotel, Boulder Hotel, and Silver Lake Hotel. Doctors came, a Modern Woodmen of America Lodge as early as 1902, and a lawyer James Henderson Cannon came in 1906 to become known later as Judge Cannon. Residents bragged that their town would be a major metropolitan center before long.

A manufacturing plant opened in 1913, producing shoes, harness and gloves, primarily for those working in the shingle and logging businesses that ringed the community and shipped their products by train to the outside world.

The tangled saga of the mills includes the following firms: (The list was largely provided by Maple Falls resident and writer, Frances E. Todd.)

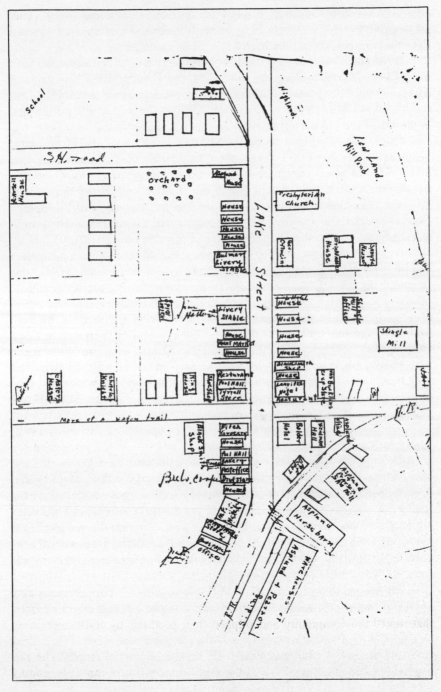

School

S.H. road.

Orchard

Lake Street

Highland

Low Land.
Mill Pond.

Presbyterian Church

More of a wagon trail

Buch. cooper

243

The Caulkins-Gerdrum Mill (CGM) operated from about 1898 to 1926 in the valley north of Maple Falls toward Silver Lake. The families ran it themselves until 1906, then leased it to E.L. Connor.

Fred D. Fobes, a solid pioneer of Maple Falls, obtained financing from a St. Louis, Missouri, company called Chicago Lumber and Coal Company (CLCC), and incorporated Maple Falls Shingle Company (MFSC) in 1901 on leased land just north of the CGM. On the site of today's public boat ramp on Silver Lake, Fobes built a skidway. Loggers cut shingle bolts (cedar chunks four feet four inches long) from forests near the lake, floated them to the skidway and removed them to the mill on skid sleds pulled by oxen. An additional source of transportation was provided by building a small dam at the entry to Maple Creek and floating bolts down the creek to be held there. When sufficient pressure had built up against the dam, a worker opened the gate and the logs plummeted downstream into a millpond adjacent to the shingle mill. After the dry kiln burned in 1905, MFSC and its contracts were sold to the Silver Lake Manufacturing Company (SLMC), controlled by CLCC and managed by Fobes. In 1906, SLMC also acquired the old CGM and built an entirely new, larger, four-engine mill. The company built a two-story structure at the site for its offices on the first floor and, on the second, housing for single workers and visitors. Married men occupied four cottages nearby. Fred Fobes and C.H. Wilson purchased the company in February, 1920, continuing as SLMC. This firm also logged near Glacier for several years, loading the logs on the BB&BC and transferring them onto a spur at Maple Falls for the mill, two miles distant. After losing most of the extensive millsite to fire, Fobes shut down the SLMC mill between 1928 and 1930.

Campbell Slough Shingle Company began operations in 1902, and ran under various ownerships only two years.

Bellingham Bay Shingle Company was formed by Charles E. Lind and Thomas S. Dalquist in April, 1903, and operated a mill in Maple Falls. The company installed a large power plant in 1905 to provide electricity for their mill, and, in the process, provided the townsite of Maple Falls with electricity, a task taken over later by Puget Sound Traction, Power and Light Company (PSTP&L). In 1906, the firm leased a millsite from MFLC, apparently timberland agents, and enjoyed a brisk business until 1912, when the plant was totally destroyed by fire.

Fire also claimed the Bigelow Mill, along with a boarding house and cookhouse less than two miles southwest of Maple Falls. It operated from 1906 to 1912.

One of the larger operations was Chinn Brothers and Bryan (CB&B), a company that acquired title to almost 700 acres of timber adjacent to Maple Falls along the Nooksack River. Their first camp was across the river from

Maple Falls on a flat spot at the base of a steep incline near the railroad bridge spanning the river. The company built several rail spurs to access timberlands and constructed bunkhouses, workers' cabins, a school, and a large work camp.

CB&B built an unusual rail spur with a 46% grade from the steeper hills down to the railroad bridge across the river and on into Maple Falls at a Y near the depot. The method of transporting logs was this: A donkey engine and spar tree or pole at the top of the incline track loaded logs onto the cars, and also controlled the speed of descent for the cars. On one occasion, a mixup occurred in the whistle signals and loaded cars plummeted down the track, hitting the end of the line with such force that the spar pole above snapped in two. Surprisingly, that was the only casualty.

Another dramatic incident took place in 1917, when the rampaging river had washed out a number of supports for the railroad trestle. A train crossing the bridge stalled out in the middle of the sagging span. The engineer scrambled out of his cab to safety, whereupon the superintendent of the firm asked if—for a quart of whiskey—anyone would volunteer to run the teetering engine on to safety. Oscar Knight did so without harm, except maybe later if he drank all that whiskey!

– Photo courtesy of Mike Impero

Jake and Dave Erb moved their shingle business from Everson to a new site three-fourths of a mile east of Maple Falls in May, 1912. The brothers built a neat camp that included cabins for married workers, and built the millsite and log yard across the river from camp. The company logged and cut shingle bolts far upriver, then floated them down to the mill—a method also employed by the United Shingle Mill far downriver. The latter floated logs and bolts all the way from Glacier down the North Fork of the Nooksack to Deming.

The Baeten Lumber Company, owned by Henry J. Baeten, less than two miles north of the Maple Falls, manufactured railroad ties from 1917 to 1925.

Other mills in or near Maple Falls included the short-lived McRea and Hardeman mill that operated from 1901 to about 1903, when it moved to Kendall; and Cline and Wood shingle mill that started in 1912. Davey's Shingle Mill may have had a brief life; the local newspaper reported a fire June 13, 1902, that burned the kiln and destroyed completed shingles, but not the mill building itself. The Heaton Mill was purchased from founder J.D. Miller in December, 1901, and created shingles in Maple Falls until 1910 or later. Ranier Cedar Shingle Company operated in 1901, owned by R.E. Callahan and Frank Kelley. Dozens of other small operations struggled along between 1900 and 1925.

Some of the earliest shingle weavers or sawyers were experienced tradesmen from New Brunswick, Canada, who demanded good wages for the times. In the early 1900s they were paid $2.50 for ten hours work, whereas a supply packer made $1.50 per day. By the mid-1930s the daily wage was $8 to $10 and in 1954, $20 to $24 for a six-hour day, all based on piece-work. The weavers worked on what was called a flat machine first, then an upright machine. The work was hazardous for fingers and hands; few escaped whole. Missing digits became virtually a weaver's trademark.

The weavers, like other specialists, tended to develop their own distinctive mode of dress, such as bell-bottom trousers twenty-two inches wide that snapped as they walked. In the early days weavers were a rough lot with a reputation of being braggarts, but single loggers cooped up in bunkhouses or tent camps were hardly cultured, either. Maple Falls simply was a rough, tough town on weekends when the woodsmen came to celebrate. Brothels and saloons thrived. Physical prowess counted in this setting, and fighting was common.

Justus Schmidel recounts witnessing a battle in January, 1901, between a tame bear (who intensely disliked loggers, for they teased him) and a brawny logger Timidy. Spectators made bets on the outcome. The bear was routed from hibernation in his stout shed. He ambled out snarling, and Timidy struck the first blow against his neck. The bear and man exchanged a few punches; then the bear seized the lumberjack and hugged him murderously, clawing at him with his back feet. Just as spectators thought the man was finished, Timidy stood on the bear's paws with his spiked shoes. Distracted the bear squirmed around and Timidy managed to get his hands around the bear's neck and throttled him.

"Without paying any attention to the applause of the crowd, the lumberjack followed by a swarm of admiring worshipers, headed for the bar and disappeared inside. The bear got up slowly, growling as if ashamed of its defeat, and crawled into the shed," wrote Schmidel.

But more substantial companies came to employ less nomadic laborers to work at harvesting large logs from Kendall to Glacier. Among the outfits operating near Maple Falls was the Lake Whatcom Logging Company (the same firm that logged around Park) working southwest of town as early as 1901. Perhaps the very earliest *logging*, not milling concern was the McCush Logging Company (MLC) under William McCush. The company arrived simultaneously with the railroad—even before, perhaps—and employed at least fifty men to log and build a skidway to drag logs to the end of the rails. Later MLC built a railroad spur to access its lands. MLC went into a partnership with George Christy and operated as Christy Timber Company.

A major logging outfit was Knight Brothers (KB), owned by Jesse and Art Knight, who started near Glacier in 1905 under contract to CB&B to log the south side of the Nooksack River. They collaborated again with CB&B to log the timber from Slide Mountain, so steep that the logs were simply cut and rolled down the mountainside. After that major contract was completed, KB logged near Silver Lake. The firm moved on to Nicolay in 1925.

Fires plagued all of the timber companies. At that time, locomotives were prone to spit out sparks and, in the dry summer seasons, fires erupted. In 1904, about 100 acres burned adjacent to Maple Falls, including the Alsop Brothers' timber company camp building and machinery. In July of the same year, a fire swept down the riverbank east of Maple Falls and burned a trestle of CB&B's rail spur and logs stacked for loading. An entire city block of Maple Falls burned August 6, 1925, starting with a house fire.

Nature provided other surprises. A spectacular electrical storm, not very common in the Northwest, especially in winter, entertained Maple Falls residents on December 3, 1915. A lightning bolt struck the transformer of the PSTLP, setting the internal oil on fire. Flames and smoke spewed into the air, but all that was damaged was that transformer; of course, the town was darkened until the system could be repaired.

Around 1924, the BB&BC raised the freight rates for hauling logs to market, causing several timber companies to fail. CB&B was able to continue for awhile, then it, too, closed down permanently.

Soon thereafter a derelict set up camp in the deserted CB&B office building. Despite the pleas of social workers that he should move, Carl Jon or "Hermit Jon" stayed put. He came regularly to buy groceries at Haggard's store with the proceeds of his welfare check and collected old newspapers and magazines that locals saved for him. Apparently he never took a bath; he and his clothes were sooty and black. A visitor to his camp found that he baked his bread in an old blacksmith's forge. He kneaded the bread with his unwashed hands and, if his nose ran, he tucked the dough under his arm and wiped it. Before Jon could ask him to lunch, the visitor thought of a prior engagement. Hermit Jon died in 1935, as alone as he lived, his body undiscovered for some days.

In later years Puget Sound Pulp & Timber logged off large areas of the forest between Maple Falls and Glacier, using trucks after the railroad ceased its operations. The mills became larger and moved to towns and cities like Bellingham, served by the mainline railroads. Loggers could drive to Bellingham and truck in supplies cheaper than purchasing them in the small town of Maple Falls. A couple of sawmills continued through the Depression years and later; in fact, the Clinard and Knight sawmill still operated in 1946. But the town sharply declined to become merely a crossroads settlement.

Clausen Lime Company opened in the early 1950s to tap the limestone deposits near Silver Lake, offering a few jobs to Maple Falls residents. The firm quarried large pieces of rock four to twelve inches in diameter and sold them to Georgia-Pacific Corporation until 1988. GPC "cooked" the rock in an acid bath that dissolved it to produce calcium carbonate used in paper processing. Since 1988, Clausen hauls rip-rap or quarries crushed lime, used mostly for decorative gardening.

Back in 1900, at a different location on the western slope above Kendall (a few miles west of Maple Falls), huge deposits of excellent quality limestone also sparked interest from an English firm, Balfour and Guthrie, doing business in the United States as Western Estates Company. As they acquired and developed the property, they talked of building homes for several hundred people. Kendall promoters visualized a community of 3,000 to 4,000 people. The deposits were mined but, outside of the original and temporary construction crew, Kendall only gained ten or fifteen families. The materials were shipped by rail to Bellingham for the Olympic Portland Cement Company.

Today Maple Falls is a sleepy place. A veterinarian occupies the old railroad depot building, the library and townsite offices occupy a building on the site of Boulder Hotel, and a handsome new store graces the site where Leavitt's Hotel & Restaurant once was located. Vacationers living at nearby time share resorts and transient tourists (skiers in winter) fuel the handful of businesses that remain from the town that expected to be a metropolis.

Chapter 27

SEMIAHMOO

The Semiahmoo Spit, a spindly band of beach and sand, embraces Drayton Harbor just south of the international border between Canada and the extreme northwestern United States mainland. At this prime maritime location, seagoing Indians based their fishing and trading activities in times past. Unfortunately, other native people from what is now southeast Alaska frequently swept down in masterful forays to take booty and slaves. Suffering near decimation from such attacks, the Semiahmoo band was forced to move away from the exposed spit.

During his explorations of the Northwest coast in 1841, Lt. Charles Wilkes charted the area, calling the spit "Tongue Point" and the circular bay to the south "Drayton's Cove" after the ship's artist, Joseph Drayton, and so they appear on Wilkes' map. However, the spit usually has been known as Semiahmoo, an Indian word that may mean "sunshine and shadow," or perhaps "half-moon" because of the curving bay. The spit is about a mile long and contains around 125 acres of land. At the point of its connection to the headland marking the northwest corner of the United States (except for the appendage called Point Roberts), the spit is only about 200 feet wide but at its terminus, a long stone's throw across the water from Blaine's own spit, it widens to about a quarter mile.

A few hundred feet north on the 49th parallel is the invisible line forming the international border, as decreed by treaty between Great Britain and the United States on June 15, 1846. That same year the United States Government formed the U.S. Boundary Survey Commission, charging it with the formidable task of marking the border at intervals across the entire continent. Archibald Campbell was appointed head of the American crew and Capt. John Summerfield Hawkins of the British Royal Engineers. Campbell arrived in midsummer 1857 to establish a camp just north of the 49th parallel on British soil at Campbell Creek, not far from today's Peace Arch Park.

On November 18, 1857, then Lt. Richard C. Mayne on *H.M.S. Plumper*, Capt. George H. Richards commanding, wrote of entering Semiahmoo Bay.

251

The first duty of the expedition was to determine exactly where the 49th parallel met the sea, so the point could be used to accurately carry that line across the continent. Mayne mentioned that the spit then was covered with grass, drift-timber and a few pine trees. The British expedition's surveys differed only eight feet from that marked by the American Commissioners. Mayne wrote that the American party included Mr. Campbell, the Commissioner; Lt. G.G. Parke of the U.S. Topographical Engineers, astronomer; two or three other astronomers, a doctor, naturalist, botanist, and the captain and subaltern in charge of the military escort. Some of the party were veterans of the marking of the Mexico-United States boundary. Upon completing the survey, the *Plumper* moved on to work at various assignments out of Victoria.

In July, 1858, Richards was given the task of taking Major Hawkins of the Royal Engineers and a professional group similar to that of the Americans to Semiahmoo Bay as the British half of the boundary commission. Estimated cost to the British of marking the boundary with a thirty-foot cleared strip to the Rocky Mountains ranged from 32,000 pounds to 45,000 pounds, and proved closer to the latter figure.

On this trip, Mayne commented that most of Semiahmoo spit and also Point Roberts had been pre-empted, and that shacks had been built at both sites.

The American escort, Company F, Ninth Infantry, about seventy men, was commanded by Capt. D. Woodruff and had its own surgeon. Several of the men were detached to a small post at Chilliwack to guard the supplies of the Commission. Lt. Parke utilized mostly civilian employees. During a visit to the camp December, 1858, Inspector Gen. Joseph Mansfield included in his report a rough sketch of the post, showing quarters for men and officers, hospital, blockhouse, and other buildings. The hospital was merely a corner of a supply shed equipped with basic medical supplies. The soldiers had no bunks but did have a mess room and kitchen with a cooking stove and a good bakery. Morale may have been poor, because records showed twenty-two desertions during three years and, in the guardhouse at the time of the report, one of four imprisoned deserters said he would desert again for he had been badly treated.

Living peacefully in lodges a hundred yards from camp were about fifty Indians, but Mansfield disapproved of socializing with them, writing that an amorous soldier who had been warned not to bother a young Indian woman had been shot (wounded) by a Commission employee for merely conversing with her.

Mansfield concluded his report with the statement: "I do not regard the discipline of this command, as what it should be, & I think this company should have the advantage of further instruction at some post like

252

Steilacoom. I will suggest to the Commanding Officer of this Department the propriety of a change."

However, the men seemed to get the job done. Crews cleared a boundary forty feet wide along the 49th parallel leading eastward from Semiahmoo, installing sturdy iron posts at intervals. At times, as many as 150 men lived at the camp—astonomers, engineers, infantrymen, teamsters, packers, lumberjacks, and hunters James Bertrand and John Harris.

Gold-seekers streamed into the area about the same time, bound for the Fraser River and beyond; Semiahmoo Spit seemed a logical camp from which to launch into the wilderness. Hoping to cash in on the migration, William King Lear opened a small trading post on the spit in 1858 and platted the town of Semiahmoo City. He expected it to become a boom town, because the British government issued orders that all prospectors were to obtain a license at Victoria before heading to the Frasier River gold digs, Semiahmoo seemed a good departure point.

Editor William Bausman of the short-lived Whatcom (Bellingham) newspaper, *The Northern Light*, visited Semiahmoo in September 11, 1858, reporting that the town on the spit contained eight or ten comfortable residences, smaller outbuildings, tents, and a population of about twenty people. An early resident of Semiahmoo and former member of the California legislature, Judge Tuttle, lived in a tent. Editor Bausman says of him that "The last glance we had of him, he was standing in front of his canvas domicil[sic], amid a halo of steam, arising from a heated frying-pan, which he had just removed from the fire, redolent with the compound odor of numerous palatable ingredients." A pamphlet compiled by the Immigration Aid Society, Port Townscnd, no datc, asscrts that at a timc shortly after Bausman's trip, 1,500 miners were camped at Semiahmoo Spit, awaiting opening of the trail to "Frazer river, the latter having this bay for its southern terminus." The author believes this was a gross exaggeration, but it is reasonable to assume a few hundred. The miners found few public facilities at Semiahmoo. A Mr. Mitchell, also a former member of the California legislature, opened a crude hotel. A provision and grocery store was operated by a Mr. Gilmore, representing the Sacramento, California, firm of Sneath, Arnold & Co. Lear amplified the income from his trading post by running a ferry to the Boundary Commission Camp across the channel.

Other settlers straggled into the area now known as Blaine, platting land as "Semiahmoo," also. According to Roth's *History of Whatcom County*, the first recorded property transaction was the deed by John Shaw to Augustus Hibbard on June 26, 1858, of eight-ninths of 160 acres along Semiahmoo Bay. The sizeable tract was platted but never filed, evidenced by a power of attorney given on July 19, 1858, by six men to sell lots in the town of Semiahmoo on the preemption claim of John Shaw. They were: W.W.

253

Wallace, John Shaw, Augustus Hibbard, W.T. Grissim, C.A. Sears and A.C. Tryon. There followed interlocking and complex transfers of interest among the six, sometimes through intermediaries, seemingly a sort of real estate syndicate. Hibbard and Shaw sold out their interests within a month and went on to new pursuits.

The remaining developers cut a street from the clearing and started to build a wharf out to deep water from the mud flats. Capt. William Dennis and James Godfrey acquired a pile driver for the construction work. Another man, George W. Gift, cut a crude trail to Fort Langley on the Fraser River, almost twenty miles distant. In a newspaper report, editor Bausman wrote that there were two or three substantial frame buildings in this town

SEMIAHMOO CITY
AND
HARBOR

SCALE 300 feet to one inch

LEGEND
Streets are 60 feet wide
Main Street is 70 feet wide
Lots are 50 by 125 feet
Blocks East of 2nd Street are
266 by 250 feet
Blocks West of 2nd Street are
266 by 300 feet
Alleys are 16 feet

DESCRIPTION
Lot 1 of Section 2 T 40 North of
Range 1 West

Irregular solid lines are Government
Meander lines

VOL. 1 PAGE 12 C.O.
W.P.A.
674-1937

and three crude homes, plus a few tents and log houses. Of the six or eight buildings, two were saloons. The burying ground of the Semiahmoo Indians was surrounded by a palisade of some kind and contained carvings. Only three white women lived in the settlement. Bausman declared in *The Reveille,* "May these separate towns flourish, is our sincere wish! If the goldfields are ample enough, there is hope for them. . . ."

The International Boundary Commission's camp sustained the spit and its neighbor town for a year or two. When the work camp moved on to Chilliwack, as the clearing progressed, both Semiahmoo of the spit and Semiahmoo on the site of today's Blaine fell into complete ruin.

A decade later, the spit came to life with the settling of California Creek at the south of Drayton Cove or Harbor. Earliest pioneer farmers were Edward and Lois Boblett, Daniel and Sarah Richards, and Amos and Eliza Dexter. These adventurers had come by wagon train to Oregon and on to Seattle by ship, searching for a new life on their own land. Having heard that land was available near the international border, Richards and Stanley built a boat to make the trip from Seattle. After making their claims, the two returned to gather up their wives and, with Dexters, traveled to their new

Part of the boundary line between The United States and British Columbia, with Mount Baker in the distance.
— March 1, 1868, Illustrated London News

home by chartered steamer, the *J.B. Libby*. With no wharf the small steamer merely put in close to the gentle Semiahmoo spit. In her diary Lois Boblett wrote: "They had to push the cows overboard and let them swim ashore. We got down in small boats and were put ashore that way. When we got our stuff all landed, there was an old house [believed to be the old hotel of 1858] that we all moved into 'til we got our own places located and got ready to move on them. It was beautiful weather and Mrs. Richards, my sister [Eliza Dexter], and I went for a walk and we picked a big bouquet of wild roses and wild strawberries in October. We thought we were in a new world."

The following year Aretas and Lydia Whitcomb, Lois and Eliza's parents, moved up from Seattle to Semiahmoo, and other immigrants settled between Dakota Creek and California Creek. Among them were John Frederick Tarte, his wife Rebecca, and their five children, who came from England in 1872 to purchase and farm a large homestead on California Creek. Brothers Ed and Lewis Holzheimer homesteaded 160 acres and acquired the first cow, first mowing machine, and first wagon and team in the area. Encouraged by the activity, Sylvester Clark, a schooner peddler of drygoods, dropped anchor and started a store on the spit in February, 1871, reviving that old Semiahmoo City.

For the first settlers, a banquet of seafood and wild fruits and berries was there for the taking, but cash money was hard to come by. Some split shakes by hand and hauled them to the spit for loading aboard steamers that took products to market. Others raised potatoes and cabbages for shipment. The steamer *Evangel* made regular stops at Semiahmoo until the completion of a bridge over California Creek in 1888, making land travel possible over a crude road from Whatcom to today's Blaine and on into New Westminster, Canada.

In her diary, Boblett mentioned that the settlers celebrated Fourth of July of the centennial year 1876 with a grand picnic on the spit, where there were a few large fir trees, a gravel beach, and dry, grassy picnic grounds. A very active church and a new school contributed stability to the community around California Creek. Amos Dexter started a sawmill on Drayton Harbor, followed by other mill entrepreneurs. New resident R.H. Roper operated a hotel.

The son of Doctor C.B.R. Kennerly of the Boundary Survey Commission and Cecilia Chanique of the Semiahmoos, George Kinley (a free spelling of Kennerly's name) worked frequently for the Elwood and Murne store. He told author Percival Jeffcott (see bibliography) that black bears were numerous around California Creek and that, during a foray to provide meat for a lumber camp, he almost met his doom:

[At California Creek and tidewater] "Salmon berries grew in great thickets along the stream, and at that time were heavy with fruit. . . . the head and shoulders of a big bear came into view as he reached to pull the bushes toward his mouth to strip the berries. . . . I was somewhat careless, and failed to drop my game instantly when I fired for his heart. Usually the black bear does not turn on his enemy when wounded, but makes off through the brush in his effort to escape, but this one proved the exception. With a roar, he started towards me, mouth open and his beady eyes afire with rage. I had neither time to reload nor a chance to regain my paddle and swing the canoe out of the shallow water before the oncoming beast would attack me. Grasping my knife, I prepared to defend myself as best I could . . . [but] he suddenly slumped and rolled down to the water's edge stone dead."

Not only bears were killed in this pioneer land, but on Christmas Day, 1883, Roper shot dead a transient named Daniel Shea. It seems that loggers Tom O'Brian, Daniel Shea, and others were drinking to celebrate the holiday at Roper's hotel. The following day, when the loggers returned to continue their spree, Roper objected. In the ensuing argument, Shea insisted that Roper should drink with them and thrust the bottle into his hands. When Roper went outside and threw the bottle over the fence, Shea started kicking and hitting Roper. The innkeeper went inside, grabbed a double-barrelled shotgun and shot Shea as he was being removed from the scene by his cohorts. Another account said that Roper went into the hotel or house in an attempt to avoid further violence, that Shea forced his way into the house, where Roper shot him in self-defense. Roper was bedridden for several days as a result of Shea's pummeling.

A married man with twelve children, Roper was characterized as a good, quiet man of temperate habits, not a drinker. A jury absolved him of criminal intent, ruling that he acted in self-defense of his family and home. According to *The Reveille* of February 15, 1884, the verdict met with almost universal approval.

In 1887, Semiahmoo storekeeper and postmaster Murne was murdered by a desperado on the New Westminster wharf over an argument about minor wages due the perpetrator, William Shearer. Shearer stabbed Murne eleven times, then tossed the knife into the river. He was convicted and was to be hanged but he was ruled insane, instead, spending his life in the penitentiary.

Heralding a change in the lifestyle of the community, Mason B. Clark and Charles Jones opened a salmon packing operation in 1877. The short-lived business of salting and packing fish in barrels, also the smoking and processing of herring, suffered from lack of easy markets. J.A. Martin and James Tarte (John the innkeeper's oldest son) opened a cannery in 1881. After a year's operation, Tarte turned to steamboating, transferring his in-

Alaska Packers cannery.
– Photo courtesy of Semiahmoo Park, Whatcom County

terest to John Elwood and his partner James G. Murne (relative of the murdered storekeeper), who continued to ship about 400 cases of salmon a day to Seattle and San Francisco that year. Tarte also opened a hotel at Semiahmoo, which burned in 1886. He rebuilt and continued to operate it until his retirement in 1894. Murne and Elwood acquired Sylvester Clark's store, and later Elwood operated a boarding house that served the canneries.

Semiahmoo on the east side of Drayton Harbor had gradually assumed the new name of Blaine and was incorporated in 1890. Semiahmoo on the spit was merely an unincorporated settlement, not officially annexed to Blaine until 1974. The spit retained its "working" identity due to its separation from Blaine by the entry channel to Drayton Harbor. Adding to the coffers of Semiahmoo in the late 1880s Steward Shumway, a resident of the spit, did considerable logging on the adjacent headland. Probably he and other loggers benefited from the escalating need for lumber by cannery companies.

D. Drysdale of New Westminster, British Columbia, purchased the Martin and Elwood cannery interest in 1891, renamed it the Point Roberts Canning Company, and installed modern machinery. Work on the facility moved ahead full speed so that the company could take advantage of the July 1891 salmon run. (Drysdale had acquired a prime fish trap site near Point Roberts.) On the spit, the new buildings included a cannery, forty feet by forty feet with sheds on either side, and a boiler room almost as large. That year the cannery packed 7,369 cases of sockeye and 1,457 cases of coho salmon. In 1893, the firm packed 36,244 cases of sockeye. By 1917, the pack was 94,624 cases of salmon.

A veritable river of salmon flowed by the spit and through the creeks and the Nooksack River. Governmental authorities made some effort to control the growing fish trade. Back in 1856, the fledgling legislature had authorized county commissioners to appoint a county inspector of salmon and to destroy any product found to be unfit for consumption. In 1877, the Washington Territorial Legislature outlawed the practice of dynamiting fish to stun them and bring them to the surface, restricted fish traps or weirs from covering more than three-fourths of the diameter of a stream, and required all exported salmon packages to be marked "P.S. Salmon" in two-inch letters.

Like other cannerymen, though, Drysdale did place fish traps along perceived salmon migration paths in salt water. Then as today fish streamed around Point Roberts on their way to the Fraser River and other streams. Indians, Chinese and Caucasians worked elbow to elbow to ready the fish for canning. Drysdale's competitor at Point Roberts, A.E. Wadhams, installed a setup similar to that of Drysdale, and the two soon became rivals for the salmon.

Meantime, far north in Alaska, that same year of 1893 marked the incorporation of a powerful corporation, the Alaska Packers Association (APA). The first canneries in Alaska had been built in 1878 at Old Sitka and Klawock; by 1889 there were thirty-seven Alaskan canneries operating; and

Brailing Salmon from traps. Puget Sound, Washington.
— Photo courtesy of Semiahmoo Park, Whatcom County

in 1892 only fifteen, adjusting to a glut of canned salmon that required a search for new markets. A selling agreement was concluded among various packers in 1891, but incorporation of twenty-two pioneer companies, some large, some very small, into APA was concluded February 9, 1893.

Noting the brisk activity at Semiahmoo and Point Roberts, the APA purchased Drysdale and Wadhams' canneries in 1894, as well as several other smaller packers in the area. Drysdale and Wadhams accepted APA stock as part payment for their firms; indeed, Drysdale became a vice-president and manager of the Semiahmoo site for APA. The company's properties then included nine other canneries in Alaska. At one time, the company held an interest in fifty-three canneries.

In the earlier days, APA's office was in Alameda, California, near San Francisco. For the first half century, it remained the staging area for the far-flung salmon empire; and most maintenance of ships and scows was performed there, too. After World War II, the offices were moved to Seattle, and Semiahmoo became the staging and maintenance area.

In 1896, Peter J. Waage was appointed manager of the fish traps for APA around Puget Sound and became superintendent of the company's Puget Sound fishing and packing divisions three years later. In addition to Semiahmoo and Point Roberts on Puget Sound, APA's realm included a cannery at Anacortes, Washington, purchased in 1901.

The Semiahmoo cannery expanded. By 1903 there were two large warehouses, several bunkhouses for workers, dining halls, and a two-story office building. As far as "downtown" businesses, the town buildings and residences of the original Semiahmoo were abandoned or wrecked; the burgeoning commercial district of Blaine took over most needs.

Most of the butchering of salmon was done by Oriental crews, and the fishermen tended to be from Scandinavian countries, Portugal, and Slavic countries. APA honored the diverse nationalities by naming its ships after their countries.

In the early decades, most workers were recruited and housed on the spit in bunkhouses, including a crew of "cannery girls." Marjorie Reichardt of Blaine interviewed three women who were cannery veterans. They said the "girls" were housed in neat bunkhouses, six to a room, with a matron governing the dormitories. The female workers ate in their own messhall, the meals served family-style in pleasant surroundings. Garbed in cotton blouses, bib overalls, socks and rubber boots, the women worked on "filler lines," packing fish into cans prior to the steam process. After the cans were processed, the women worked on the labeling line. Life there was not all work; there was time for beach picnics or trips into Blaine on the small ferry that operated between the spit and town.

At mid-century fishing and canning were seasonal and, except for storage crews, the APA facility at Semiahmoo operated only four or five months annually. Thus, most laborers were hired from the local area. They lived in bunkhouses at the spit during working days, returning home whenever possible to tend their farms and homes. They ate most of their workday meals in the company messhall and, when the season ended, the company permitted employees to buy surplus supplies at low prices.

There were only a few small houses on the spit. A notable exception was the mansion constructed after 1891 by Daniel Drysdale near today's marina site, a seven-bedroom house dubbed the "White House." During ensuing years, the superintendents and families usually lived there in relative luxury, and the home also housed visiting executives and sometimes their vacationing families.

Ketchikan, Alaska, was the "salmon capitol of the world," with large fleets of fishing boats raking in the salmon to supply canneries such as APA. Dozens of other canneries and fleets operated throughout Southeast Alaska and northward around Bristol Bay, the Alaska Peninsula, and Kodiak Island.

As the activities of APA escalated, the firm acquired its own fleet of ships to serve the remote Alaskan locations, Anacortes, Point Roberts and Semiahmoo. By 1901, the firm owned sixty-six vessels, including sixteen steam launches, nineteen steamers, eight large ships and four barkentines. In 1913 the company operated eighteen "star" ships, three and four-masted sailing vessels with iron or steel hulls (the 19th had been wrecked in 1908). Ships such as *Star of Scotland* and *Euterpe* (later named the *Star of India*) hauled milled lumber, workmen, supervisors, and supplies from California and Washington to Alaska. They returned, stuffed to the gunwales with canned salmon;

A "Star" ship.
— Photo courtesy of Semiahmoo Park, Whatcom County

in fact, the company used the spacious ships as floating warehouses, retaining the cases of salmon until the product was sold. Then the cases of forty-eight one-pound cans could be transferred directly from a Star ship to an ocean freighter or to wagons and trucks for placement in rail cars.

Probably influenced by the increasing traffic, the U.S. Government installed a Semiahmoo Harbor light in 1905. It was built on pilings in shoal water offshore of the spit in Semiahmoo Bay, a Victorian-style octagonal one and a half story structure topped by a cylindrical lamphouse. According to Jim Gibbs in *West Coast Lighthouses*, the installation displayed a fixed red light with a dark sector between west and north from a fourth order French-made lens by Barnier, Benard and Turenne of Paris. The lens was lit by an oil lamp. The fog signal was a third class Daboll horn powered by steam boilers. Gibbs said that lightkeeper Ed Durgan had a fatal heart attack in March, 1920, while manhandling a boat onto davits, so his wife Estelle became a full-fledged lighthouse keeper, one of only three women on the West Coast. After 1944, the big lighthouse was dismantled, replaced for several years by a pyramidal light station. That, too was demolished and replaced in 1971 by a light and daymark.

The enormous power wielded by APA and other cannery firms in Alaska did not go unnoticed by the federal authorities who, as early as 1913, began to worry about conservation of fish. Runs were threatened not only by American fishing practices but also by the catches by foreigners in offshore waters. Recognizing the important economic impact of the industry on jobs and commerce, the government moved discreetly, however. Their chief weapon in curbing excessive catches in Washington was the passage by the people of Initiative No. 77, making fish traps illegal, phased out between 1934 and 1936.

In 1916, California Packing Corporation (which later became Del Monte) entered negotiations to purchase APA, continuing to permit near autonomy to APA as a subsidiary. About 1948, the parent company asserted more control over the company.

Postwar years found the Northwest and Alaskan fishing industries in disarray. It was necessary to settle with the U.S. Navy for the cost of ships appropriated for Navy use during World War II (some sunk). APA no longer maintained its own fleet of steamers (which had eventually replaced the sailing ships), accepting only one ship back from the Navy and soon selling that one, the *S.S. Chirikof*. Instead APA moved the cans by Liberty ships until about 1968, and container cargo barges thereafter. Gillnet fishermen energetically returned to seek salmon, joined by larger purse seine boats and small reefnet operations to supply APA.

Canning operations at Semiahmoo ceased in 1965, because of the poor salmon runs in Puget Sound and the Fraser River. Machinery repair and scow maintenance continued at Semiahmoo until 1982. APA had acquired World War II surplus, self-powered, flat-bottom scows for conversion to fish tenders. The tenders, eighty to 100 feet long and painted a bright orange with black trim, went off to Alaska, where the operators bought fish, storing them in huge brine tanks for transport to canneries. The name of a tender was painted in large letters on the sides of the tender and the APA flag on the smokestack, making them easily recognizable to Northwest mariners. During off season the tenders came to Semiahmoo to await maintenance.

The spacious warehouses at the spit continued to be used to store canned salmon until sale requests came in. A workman of the 1950s described the commotion when an Alaskan ship arrived. "Speed was the word," he said in a 1984 *Bellingham Herald* article, "The salmon kept coming off the ship, and had to go somewhere. You'd start in one corner and fill that all the way to the rafters. You'd build kind of a stairstep affair. Each step would be nine cases high, about as high as an average man could reach. . . . Working in just a T-shirt you would come off the job soaking wet in cold weather [but] we made a comfortable living. . . ."

From 1946 to 1975, the cases were loaded onto Puget Sound Freight Line barges, the *Lovejoy, Indian, Warrior,* for transport to railside in Bellingham, as orders warranted. Later trucks took over this task.

Curiously, in the 1980s, the old barge *Warrior* returned to Semiahmoo Spit, this time to the new marina. Romantics said she came home to die. Owned by a Minnesota man, Art Aymes, the boat was awaiting conversion to a self-propelled fishing boat. One night she sprang a mysterious leak and sank, releasing a small quantity of dark oil. A lively battle ensued as to who actually owned the craft, who was to remove the hulk, who was responsible

S.S. Chirikof.

– Photo courtesy of Semiahmoo Park, Whatcom County

263

for damage to the environment, if any. It all got resolved and the *Warrior* was removed.

With the decline of business in the north, the office of APA was removed to Bellevue in 1975, and the salmon storage was assigned to a Del Monte warehouse in Vancouver, Washington. John Cuthill, formerly the cannery superintendent at Clark's Point, Bristol Bay, Alaska, became the director of real estate for APA in 1981, assisting in the sales of APA sites. In 1983, the APA name and its three labels were sold to Con-Agra (the "Banquet" label), a firm that never was in the salmon or fisheries business. As the activities at Semiahmoo had wound down to practically nothing, Del Monte sold the APA property to the Trillium Corporation, Bellingham, on April 15, 1980.

Primarily a land development corporation, Trillium leased part of the original site of Semiahmoo (City) to the Atlas Hotels in late 1985 to build the four-star hotel, The Inn at Semiahmoo. Trillium and others developed the 900 acres of headland lying between Semiahmoo Bay and Birch Bay into lots for homes, a lovely golf course designed by Arnold Palmer, and condominium properties.

Today the entire spit and headland form a pleasant community, officially a part of Blaine. However, the community and homes around the western side of Drayton Harbor continue to be referred to as simply "Semiahmoo." The original city may have died, but the sense of community survives.

Whatcom County Parks obtained land near the neck of the spit for public use, and Trillium moved the former APA bunkhouses to the park site for conversion to an interpretive center focusing on the salmon industry and local history. Several original APA buildings remain on the site of the Inn at Semiahmoo; indeed, a shopping center is planned for one large structure. Rusty tracks and powerful dollies for moving scows into maintenance facilities weave and twist on the shore, and a forest of old pilings, cut knee-high, are like gravestones for the old Semiahmoo businesses.

Remains of pilings.
— JoAnn Roe Photo

Chapter 28
SHUKSAN
Shuksan, the Lone Jack and Red Mountain Mines

The mine tunnels and rubble still are there, covered by the forest ferns. The stunning scenery remains untrammeled. But today few realize that, before 1898, possibly 2,000 people inhabited towns, largely tent cities, a short distance east of Glacier below the Twin Lakes near Mount Baker. Largest by far of the settlements was Shuksan with about 1,500 people, marked today only by a modern highway maintenance center for the United States Forest Service at the junction of Twin Lakes trail and the Mount Baker Highway.

North Cascades gold fever was sparked by the rich finds of British Columbia's Fraser Canyon and Barkerville three decades earlier. After all, British Columbia and Washington shared the same mountain range, even if it was given a different name south of the border. When prospectors headed for British Canada in the 1850s and 1860s, they struck out northward from Bellingham. Some returned to the Cascades in the 1880s and 1890s to comb the ridges and streams for gold and silver. The three forks of the Nooksack River looked especially promising.

In 1885, a party led by L.L. Bales verified that there were gold signs on the South Fork of the Nooksack, mountain-ward from today's village of Acme. The interest centered around the mouth of Skookum Creek, where a townsite called Livewood was laid out to accommodate the prospectors moving in to squat and stake claims. Prospectors found free gold, placer gold, shining in their pans. However, the returns were so sparse that the rush was over within a year, and searchers moved deeper into the mountains. Giving wings to their feet were the very real finds in extreme eastern Whatcom County beyond today's Ross Lake—Barron, the Azurite and others.

In 1897, Jack Post, Russell S. Lambert, and L.G. Van Valkenburg made a big strike in the high country near Twin Lakes, where just the scenery was worth the exploration trip—the mine known as the Lone Jack Mine, consisting of several claims. Their finds triggered a gold rush to Mount Baker country.

265

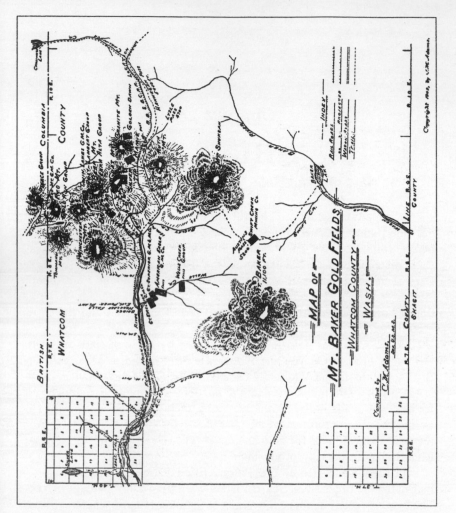

The three good friends were an unlikely trio. Post had wandered the area for years searching, probing and filing on unworthy prospects. Lambert was an attorney from Sumas. Van Valkenburg was a successful logger and farmer from near today's Nooksack and, while historical accounts speak of Post and Lambert, little is said about Van Valkenburg. The men were bound together by a camaraderie of the outdoors and the adventure of prospecting. About two years after the three started to tramp the hills as a group, they were camped at the foot of Winchester Mountain near Twin Lakes on August 22, 1897, where the snowy shoulders of Mount Baker and its neighbors reflected the waning light. They vowed to split up the next day and follow their hunches; all agreed that the lode was somewhere near for the streams yielded color. As the 23rd came to a close, Lambert and Van Valkenburg returned wearily to start dinner. Post did not appear until so late that his friends feared for his safety. Then, according to historian P.R. Jeffcott in *Chechaco and Sourdough*, the two men heard Post yelling, "I've found it! I've found it!" He "came into sight around the shoulder of Bear Mountain, the picture of a wild man, and at a speed very suggestive that a bear really WAS after him."

When he calmed down enough to talk coherently, he said he had ascended almost to the top of Bear Mountain, when he spied an outcropping in plain view with gold sprinkled throughout, a belt extending some distance. On the crisp morning of the 24th, the three staked out their claims on what became known as the Post-Lambert or the Lone Jack Ledge. Jack Post staked Discovery Claim No. 1, the "Lone Jack;" Van Valkenburg No. 2, the "Jenny;" and Lambert No. 3, adjoining Lone Jack on the north, the "Sidney." The men jointly staked the other two claims, "Whist" and "Lulu."

The Post-Lambert or Lone Jack stamp mill.

– From Galen Biery Collection

Someone had to trek out to Sumas to file the claims, buy supplies, and take samples of ore to be assayed. Lambert drew the short straw. When he arrived in Sumas, he found the assayer moving his house; it was in the middle of the street on wheels. Quite understandably, he was not eager to stop work and assay the gold right away, especially since he had grown accustomed to the meager assays previously booked by the trio. After persuading the man, John Knuehmann, to do the work, Lambert took the train to New Whatcom (part of today's Bellingham) to file the claims. When he returned to Sumas, Knuehmann—his eyes bugged out—announced that the assay ran $10,750 to the ton, an incomprehensible richness in an era when $20 to the ton was worth working. Indeed, as soon as he concluded his business with Lambert, he left his house in the street and rushed off to Twin Lakes along with every other able-bodied man in the area. Within days the Twin Lakes and Swamp Creek area teemed with prospectors, the activity spilling over into the Ruth Creek drainage across the ridge.

Tent cities sprang up like gray toadstools: (using today's designations) Union City on the Twin Lakes trail from Mount Baker Highway, just short of the lakes; Trail City, originally Herman, where Swamp Creek runs into the North Fork of the Nooksack (a *Seattle Times* article of September 25, 1897, said there were 300 inhabitants in tents there); Wilson's Townsite a little farther east at Ruth Creek and North Fork; Gold City in the Ruth Creek Valley toward Hannegan Pass; and Gold Hill where the Highway Maintenance Station stands today at the Twin Lakes road or trail and Mount Baker Highway. Gold Hill soon became known as Shuksan and, especially after the State Trail (going through Gold Hill) was recognized as the best approach to Lone Jack, it overshadowed its neighboring settlements and became a real town of 1,500 residents, most of them first living in tents. Others built cabins, just dugouts with cribbed-up doorways of logs. Typical furnishings were a crude bed and chair, a stove or open fire pit, a kerosene lamp or candles, and shelves.

The population was volatile, of course, as prospectors tend to come and go. Judge John Broyles at Trail City was the first permanent settler of the area, his property remaining privately owned long after the gold rush had ebbed. Mary de Borde, Cultural Resource Technician in the Glacier Ranger District, said that rival developers tried to evict Broyles at the time, even threatening violence and leading him off the site with a rope around his neck. However, Broyles received support from the authorities and remained possessor of his claim. Earlier prospectors had built a one-room shack on the site, Broyles built a two-room home twenty feet by thirty feet. Later a claim squatter built a large barn and outbuildings. However, no real town ever grew up at this point. A foot log placed across the chilly Swamp Creek helped miners on their way along State Trail.

By 1898, the town of Shuksan was growing daily. Two stores and a post office were established, plus thirty new cabins. Storekeeper John Treutle's chief problem was keeping his shelves stocked with merchandise brought in by pack train. In the nearby towns, entrepreneurs were quick to seize the opportunity of supplying the camps. Since freight and passengers came to Bellingham by ship, the city was in a key position to outfit prospectors. By spring of 1898, a stage line ran as far as Boulder Creek; after that point, it was afoot or horseback. The Northern Pacific Railroad served Sumas from Seattle, so travelers could ride that far in comfort, then take to the hills. Deming also was mentioned as a good starting point up the Nooksack River. Once beyond Glacier, a very steep wagon road existed through Saar Creek Canyon, but pack trains for Red Mountain claims and the Lone Jack often preferred to travel another gentler grade from Chilliwack, B.C., past Cultus Lake, the Chilliwack River and Silesia Creek. Heavy equipment for the Lone Jack often came in by this northern road, despite its greater length.

Assays from claims near the Lone Jack were running steadily from $1,000 to $4,000 a ton. *The State* said ten assays showed gold from 2.32 oz. of gold per ton to 28.40 oz. in three cases and that there were small amounts of silver, too.

P.R. Jeffcott wrote that mining experts soon came to the mountains to assess the real worth of claims, primarily to provide fodder for brochures encouraging investment in claims. One Fred W. Fox spent considerable time around the Twin Lakes area and pointed out in an interview with the *Reveille* the promise of prospects other than Lone Jack in the district, including the Barber Claim on Ruth Creek, and findings on Red Mountain. He also noted that placer gold in paying quantities existed in Boulder Creek.

Whether sparked by further prospecting fever or just reluctant to get into the hard work of mining, Post and Lambert soon sold their rights to a Portland syndicate that included men named Hahn and Friede, November 27, 1897, for $100,000. (The March, 1901, edition of a magazine, *The State*, asserts that Post and Lambert sold claims almost immediately for $60,000 and again, shortly thereafter, more claims for $350,000, a considerably different total.) Spokesman and mining engineer for the syndicate, Henry Staneslawyski, announced that the group would install a ten-stamp mill and machinery in the spring of 1898 and forge ahead in developing the ledge. A newspaper item a year later stated that a ten-stamp mill awaited transportation from Chilliwack, according to company representative, William J. Conners, and that fifteen men were employed building cabins at the mine.

The gold ledge was struck in the Lulu tunnel 118 feet down, and the ledge continued down to 250 feet, seven feet wide. Once the stamp mill finally arrived on site, it was placed about a mile below the mine entrance and plans were made to supply it with a tram.

The Portland syndicate went to work improving the trails and dragging in equipment, using a donkey engine and tractor to pull sleds over the rough trail from Glacier to Shuksan. The chief impediment to swift development was the altitude of the Lone Jack. The property ranged over a steep slope from about 3,700 feet to 5,850 feet altitude, comprising 88.76 acres. Near the timber line it was snowbound for all but two or three months of the year. The proposed tram to the mill required power, and one first had to build a power plant on Silesia Creek. Perhaps the Portland syndicate viewed all this as a big hole into which they would pour money, as they sold their interests in October, 1899, for $150,000 to English & Son of the Golconda

Mine, Sumpter, Oregon. Seventy-five men were working at the mine in 1900.

English & Son went right to work on the power plant and tram, bringing the one-inch cable to the site on the backs of a series of pack horses—all in one piece—a prodigious feat.

By 1902, Lone Jack Mine was in brisk production. The mine consisted of three levels with tunnels of less than a mile in total length and still are in relatively good order. In this rugged part of the North Cascades the tunnels were drilled through virtually solid rock and needed only two wooden timbers in the whole mine. During drilling the miners left rock pillars to stabilize the roofs of the tunnels.

The mine at that time used the mercury extraction method after crushing the ore. A stable vein of quartz contained the gold, in places visible to the naked eye. These obvious rich veins were given priority and, it is asserted, at least one "hi-jacker" went into the mine during off-season and "high-graded" the best vein illegally.

As the Lone Jack began to yield gold, a critical task was getting the refined product out of the mountains into banks. Andrew Ecklund, that intrepid pioneer who was connected with the Blue Canyon Coal Mining Company, became assistant to Staneslawyski at the Lone Jack and was assigned the task of transporting the gold. With only one guard, usually John Cress, who lagged behind or forged in front some distance to watch for danger, Ecklund tramped out of the mountains. Ecklund varied his times and dates of departure and, learning of a potential robbery threat on one occasion, hid within the mine for a few hours, then set out. He arrived at civilization behind those suspected of waylaying him. On another occasion, Ecklund and Cress were traveling into the dusk and sensed danger where the trail went through a narrow defile. Looking up, they found a would-be robber on a rock fast asleep with gun in hand. Ecklund and Cress tiptoed past and continued their journey.

Ecklund continued to work for English & Son, even after losing the fingers off one hand in a mine accident (his jacket sleeve caught in a cable and dragged his hand into machinery). During winter time, when the snows made it impossible to work at the high elevation, the Lone Jack was monitored by caretakers who received winter supplies plus the right to keep any gold they could mine. In 1916, one of the two caretakers murdered the other and threw his body down a watery mine shaft, escaping with the gold dust and fading into oblivion undetected.

The mine continued to yield significant returns until 1920, despite a mill fire in 1906 that necessitated replacement of building and equipment. Perhaps a million dollars in gold was realized. In 1920, the steep terrain took its toll; a violent snow slide overran the mill and wiped out the workings. Despite the setback, the mill was rebuilt again at a less slide-prone location.

According to the best information, Josephine Brooks purchased the mine around 1920 as a property for her son Phillip to manage (Phillip was just graduating as a mining engineer). Unfortunately, Phillip died suddenly shortly after the purchase. Brooks' nephew Harry Bullene was the foreman of the mill and inherited the mine. Descendants still owned it in the 1990s.

In a report on the mine by Francis J. Crossland, surveyor, given to Phillip Brooks on November 10, 1922, the Portland Syndicate including Hahn and Friede had taken out $192,000 of bullion during their five years under management of Andrew Ecklund. Subsequent lessees may not have been so fortunate. A list of equipment used at that time included:

A "Willis" Mill with 30-ton capacity per 24 hours with amalgamating plates, a Dodge crusher, and two especially constructed oil flotation tanks.

Power plant consisting of an impulse Pelton water wheel driving a 50 KW Westinghouse 60-cycle generator.

Pipes, flumes, etc. as needed.

No. 1 North American sawmill of 5,000 foot capacity.

Electric installations and lighting plants for the mine, bunkhouse and offices.

Telephone system including 7-1/2 miles of wire connecting the mine with the town of Shuksan. An intercom system in the mine, mill, powerhouse, sawmill and office.

Ingersol Rand compressors and accessories.

Assay facilities, blacksmith shops, mine cars, 650 feet of track, aerial tram line that ran 696 feet from tunnel to terminal with buckets, living facilities and equipment including a bunkhouse for 100 men. The latter was built as a long structure into the hill, so that—if a slide came down—presumably it would go right over the living quarters. The Lone Jack ran three shifts of men during the early 1920s.

Supplies still had to come on the so-called State Trail which came up the south side of the North Fork

Harry Bullene.
– From Galen Biery Collection

271

of the Nooksack River from Nooksack Falls, crossed the river at Treutle's Bridge near Shuksan, then continued to Twin Lakes. The mine could not then nor yet today be accessed directly from Twin Lakes, because of the steep terrain, but the road/trail continued north, then east around the mountain and down to the mine. Everything came on strings of pack mules and horses. In later years, designated employees brought the gold out on pack horses, instead of on foot as Ecklund had done.

Disaster struck again during the winter of 1925. A huge snow slide roared down the mountainside and destroyed the entire set of buildings and equipment listed above. Fortunately, no one was there, since the reinforced bunkhouse did not withstand the avalanche, either. With the price of gold at a low ebb, it was impractical to rebuild the facilities. Harry Bullene did not reopen the mine.

When trespassing hikers in the 1960s discovered unexploded dynamite about 400 feet within the Lulu tunnel, John Bullene (inheritor of the mine) gave the National Park Service permission to destroy the dynamite (which was actually not dangerous, he said). Bullene told the author that a demolition team from Fort Lewis did the job October, 1963, with plastic explosives and rolled the ore carts and tracks, mixed with rock, into a big ball. The mine tunnel was not entirely closed, but the offending dynamite was destroyed, indeed. Bullene leased the mine in 1992, and it might reopen.

Other minor gold discoveries from time to time near the sharply declining settlements like Shuksan brought new and wistful searchers into the area. Two small mines that did ship ore were the Gold Run and the Excelsior, both in the same district as the Lone Jack, near the town of Shuksan. A Sumas group that included the Gargett brothers had promising diggings at Gold Run Pass above timber line near Twin Lakes and incorporated the Gold Run Mining & Milling Company on January 4, 1911. L.R. Gargett was named president, C.L. Gargett secretary, and John M. Saar as general manager. At least eight years earlier the individual claims that made up the company had been worked sporadically. The site was developed laboriously by toting engines and lumber on horseback up a steep trail. The miners packed in an old Buick engine to operate a sawmill and an air compressor to be run by water power. Despite the backbreaking labor, the partners managed to build cabins, a mill and a small tram, lay rails and extract ore. Between late May and September, 1911, they took out sufficient ore to send to the Tacoma Smelter. When the returns did not warrant the effort, Saar turned over his stock to the Gargetts. It seems that the mine was worked intermittently thereafter by the two brothers with disappointing results. The mine was closed in the late 1930s.

It is amazing to the author that anyone ever noticed the outcropping on Wells Creek called The Great Excelsior Gold Mine. The Great Excelsior was on the west side of Wells Creek a short distance south of Nooksack Falls off the Mount Baker Highway, five miles west of Shuksan. It lies in a most gloomy and inaccessible gorge above the point where Wells Creek empties into the North Fork of Nooksack River, below the formidable and beautiful twin cascades of Nooksack Falls. Perhaps the rushing waters had uncovered the outcropping of quartz over centuries.

There in 1900, W.H. Norton and others staked claims. The Great Excelsior Mining Company was incorporated in 1902, and a sawmill dragged in over a precipitous trail. Forty men worked to set up a four-stamp mill and tunneled into the mountain to bring out the ore. However, according to Jeffcott, the water-concentration process used by this company resulted in only a 50% recovery of available gold, which was insufficient in the first place. The Great Excelsior Mine was sold to The President Group Mining Company, which spent another quarter million dollars of fruitless development, substituting the customary cyanide process of recovery for the water method. The ore simply did not seem to warrant any investment, and no further efforts were made to work the extremely remote and difficult site, but in 1966, the deposit was restaked by American Smelting and Refining Company.

Great Excelsior Mine campsite and power station.
— From Galen Biery Collection

The mining effort was only a part of the activity around Nooksack Falls. At the turn of the century, if one wanted to develop water power for electricity, it was cheaper to file lode claims on the river and acquire title than it was to file water rights and pay for permits and fees. Hence, Stone and Webster acquired five lode claims in 1902 with the river as a lode line and including the falls, then obtained a patent for mining purposes. The firm did assessment work but, according to early forest ranger C.C. McGuire, " . . . by fortunate chance the tunnel driven in the search for gold was just in the right place to lay the pipe line from the top of the falls to the later location of the power house." McGuire also claimed that an assayer's report showed $164.56 per ton of gold and silver, whereas no mining was ever done on the claims. One wonders, he added . . .

Anyway, the combination of mining and power plant development . . . or whatever was going on . . . led to the establishment of a small settlement on the south side of the North Fork that included a few homes and the Excelsior Hotel, more company housing than hotel, although it did accept transients. Jeffcott relates in his book, *Chechaco and Sourdough* the tale told by Leona McClimans, daughter of the hydroelectric operator at the Falls:

The Excelsior Hotel cook received a stipulated amount with which to buy groceries for the employees. When miners had abandoned their cabins after failure of the mine, they often left behind pet cats, which multiplied relentlessly. To save money and line his own pockets, the cook began to boil up cat stew, which the employees ate unknowingly for some time. When the duped diners learned of the cook's antics, they were horrified and talked of hanging him, but he escaped camp one jump ahead of them.

In this area of ragged terrain below Nooksack Falls, along a stream to be called Dead Horse Creek, prospectors in the early stage of the gold rush found the skeleton of a horse tied firmly to a tree. No owner, dead or alive, was listed as missing. Perhaps he fell to his death off some precipice, leaving the poor beast to die of starvation and thirst.

Part of Excelsior remains, because the power plant still operates and in 1994 was being monitored by Doug Hamilton of Glacier on a twenty-four-hour basis; he worked ten days on, four off, during which time a licensed replacement took over.

Concurrent with the Lone Jack, however, was another profitable mine, not far north. It was located in 1902 near the Canadian border, high in the heights of Red Mountain (called Mount Larrabee today), by Thomas Braithwait of Licking or Lawrence, a crossroads near Sumas. Braithwait and companions were goat hunting and the mortally wounded quarry tumbled into a steep canyon. After Braithwait's party worked its way into the defile, the men were electrified to notice a vertical ledge with specks of gold shin-

274

Stamp mill, Boundary Red Mountain steepness assists handling of heavy blocks.   *– From Galen Biery Collection*

ing from it. From this grew the Boundary Red Mountain Mining Company (BRMMC). Conflicting reports credit the Red Mountain discovery to C.W. Roth Associates in 1897 or 1898.

Even more mysterious is a mention in the *American Reveille* of July 19, 1892, that Judge Elmon Scott's claims on Red Mountain received patents: Climax, Climax Extension, Rocky Draw, Glacier, Klondike, Mountain Boy, and Golden Beaver. Perhaps they were in a different location on Red Mountain. At any rate, the Red Mountain Gold Mining Company was organized by Judge Scott, and in November, 1907, the BRMMC was incorporated and took over the assets of the former firm.

Since the location was at a much lower elevation than Lone Jack, it could be worked more months of the year. The mine was most conveniently accessed through Canada via the Chilliwack River and Silesia Creek, so the Canadian town of Chilliwack probably benefited the most from supply business. The BRMMC built a dam on Silesia Creek, a sawmill to provide lumber for mine buildings and supports, and a five-stamp mill and workers' buildings to be operational by 1913. Facilities included a bunkhouse and cookhouse for seventy-five workers, a commissary or warehouse for groceries and supplies, a machine shop, blacksmith shop, and assay office. Electricity came to the site from the Silesia Creek plant and a telephone service was installed.

In 1914, the mine was the leading producer of gold in the county with an output of about $15,000. The following year George Wingfield of Nevada was manager. He completed the power plant and some building expansion, securing over $68,000 in gold that year. The outbreak of World War I caused the prices of supplies and machinery to rise and a scarcity of labor; despite these factors, the number three tunnel was lengthened. But the mine closed in 1918, when the power plant burned.

The company resumed operations in 1922 after rebuilding the power plant, operating twenty-four hours a day with a maximum daily output of fifty tons. A 1600-foot tram carried ore from mine to mill. From a company brochure, the operation was described:

"Tram buckets dump into a bin, whence the ore is drawn over a grizzly set to one inch and coarse rock is broken to one inch by a 7" x 10" Blake crusher. Two Challenge feeders deliver the crushed ore to a battery of ten stamps, each weighing 1000 pounds, where it is reduced to pass a 12-mesh battery screen. A classifier delivers the sands to a Marathon mill for regrinding and the entire product is then amalgamated. The mill has an established recovery of 90 per cent."

Late in the 1930s, according to P.R. Jeffcott in his book, *Chechaco and Sourdough*, the stamp mill burned. Then the chief stockholder of the mine, Tom Bourne, a veteran Mount Baker area packer, rebuilt the mill and added modern machinery, only to have it all swept away by an avalanche of ice and rocks from the glacier above in 1942. Bourne apparently mined the tailings until 1946. Until its closure in 1946, almost a million dollars of gold was realized from the mine, the greater part mined during the first ten years of operation.

The mine has never reopened, although presumably the gold still exists and the mine has been leased a few times. In the 1950s it was acquired by a Chicago Syndicate amidst speculation of redevelopment, but nothing has happened to this day.

The mining legends live on; the Lone Jack may become active, but Shuksan (except for the highway maintenance building), Trail City, Gold Hill and Union City have long since been covered by the lush forest vegetation or their relics hauled away by souvenir-seekers. Only the spirits of those 2,000 hopefuls inhabit the diggings these days.

BIBLIOGRAPHY.

"Abandoned Still is Discovered," *The Clear Lake News*, February, 1922.

Alaska State Library & Archives records on Alaska Packers Association, various.

Anderson, Linda; Win Williams, Sr.; and James Hermanson. "Irondale, A Town that might have been an industrial giant," *Port Hadlock Days*, pamphlet, June 7, 1977 and rev. 1979.

Andrews, Ralph. *Glory Days of Logging*. Seattle: Superior Publishing Company, 1956.

Arbuckle, Marie. *The Old Fir Tree*. Lynden: Profile Publications, Inc., 1984.

Barnes-Hinds, Lillian; Carol Ann Post; and Marjorie Reichardt. "Pioneers of Peace," pamphlet, Diamond Jubilee Committee of Blaine, 1959; reprinted and index added, Whatcom Genealogical Society, Bellingham, 1976.

Barrett, Helen O'Brien; Anne Summers Carlson; Margaret Willis, editors. *Skagit County Grows Up*. Mount Vernon, Washington: Skagit County Historical Society.

Bennett, Eben. Oral history tape, Skagit County Historical Museum, LaConner, Washington.

Binns, Archie. *The Roaring Land*. New York: Robert M. McBride & Company, 1942.

"Birchport," *Washington Magazine*, June, 1890.

Blanchard Centennial Album. Blanchard, Washington, 1985.

Blonk, Hu. "Gold at Hart's Pass," *Wenatchee Daily World*, October 22, 1959.

Boblett, Lois. "A Pioneer Woman of the Great West," typescript, Semiahmoo Park.

Booth, T. William. "Design for a Lumber Town by Bebb and Gould, Architects," *Pacific Northwest Quarterly*, vol. 82, no. 4, October, 1991, pp. 132-39.

"Boundary Red Mountain Mine," unpublished brochure, 1922, Special Collections, University of Washington, Seattle.

"Brick and Tile Factory," *Skagit County Times*, December 28, 1911.

Britton, Diane F. *Irondale, Washington*. Niwot, Colorado: University Press of Colorado, 1991.

Bullene, John. Personal papers, Bellingham, Washington.

Campbell, Patricia. *A History of the North Olympic Peninsula*. Port Angeles: Peninsula Publishing, Inc., 1980.

Carson, Rob."Hadlock's Green Spot held this vision of the future . . ." *Port Townsend Leader*, Summer, 1979.

"The Cascade Mining District," *Northwest Mining Journal*, 1909.

"Centennial of Pope & Talbot Sawmill Celebrated by More than 5,000," *Portland Oregonian*, September 11, 1953.

Chechacos All. Mount Vernon, Washington: Skagit County Historical Society, 1973.

Clallam County Library, Port Angeles, Washington. Miscellaneous files, clippings, unpublished manuscripts, articles.

Clallam County Museum, Port Angeles, Washington. Research files and miscellaneous data.

Clark, Donald H. *18 Men and a Horse*. Bellingham, Washington: Whatcom Museum of History and Art, 1969.

Clark, Donald H. "Ship Sinking Changed Northwest History," *Tacoma Ledger-News Tribune*, July 31, 1949.

"Classen Plant Will Soon Start," *Port Townsend Leader*, March 29, 1911.

Clear Lake Historical Association. Clippings, sketches, articles.

"Clear Lake is an Active Community," *The Courier-Times*, May 26, 1960.

The Clear Lake News, Centennial Edition, June 9, 1991.

"The Cokedale Coal Mine," *Fairhaven Herald*, June 21, 1893.

Coman, Edwin Thurman. *Time, Tide and Timber*. Palo Alto: Stanford University Press, 1949.

Committee. *Jimmy Come Lately*. Port Angeles: Clallam County Historical Society, 1971.

Committee. *Pride in Heritage.* Port Townsend, Washington: Jefferson County Historical Society, 1966.

Corson, Donald L. "When Coal was King in Washington," *Pacific Search,* December-January, 1975-76, pp. 18-19.

Crossland, Francis J. Report on Lone Jack Mine prepared for Phillip Brooks, November 10, 1922.

Davidson, Mrs. Percy E. Unpublished, typed reminiscences at Jefferson County Museum, Port Townsend, Washington, October 5, 1959.

DeBorde, Mary. *Glacier, a History.* Glacier: U.S. Forest Service, 1981.

Defunct corporations, computerized files. Washington State Archives, Olympia.

Dietz, Laura. "The old towns: etc."; *Skagit Valley Herald,* no date (from files of Skagit County Historical Museum).

Dungeness, The Lure of a River, Bicentennial 1976 special project, *Sequim Gazette.*

Dynes, Violet Eldred. "Dear Old Sedro-Woolley. Clear Lake—Giant of Industry, Asleep," *Sedro-Woolley Courier-Times,* August 10, 1967.

"An early resident looks at Dungeness history," *Jimmy Come Lately Gazette,* May 5, 1976, pp. 11-12.

Edson, Lelah Jackson. *The Fourth Corner.* Bellingham, Washington: Whatcom Museum of History and Art, 1968.

Eklund, Don. *Bay View: Pioneer City of the Sound.* Bellingham, Washington: Western Washington University, Center for Pacific Northwest Studies, March, 1987.

Erickson, Beth. "Digging for gold in the Lone Jack Mine," *Bellingham Herald.*

Evans, Gail E. H. and Gerald W. Williams. *Over Here, Over Here* (U. S. Army's Spruce Production Division in World War I). Pamphlet prepared for National Park Service, Port Angeles, and Willamette National Forest, Eugene, 1984. See Clallam County Library, Port Angeles, Washington.

Evans, Lynette, and George Burley. *Roche Harbor.* Everett, Washington: B&E Enterprises, 1972.

Field, Newton, compiler. Mt. Baker Almanac, U.S. Forest Service, 1950.

Fish, Harriet U. "Carlsborg, Hamlet in Change," Carlsborg: Harriet U. Fish, September 18, 1984.

_____. "Gettysburg, Wash.," *The Daily News,* Section C, Port Angeles, Washington, February 28, 1982.

_____. *Tracks, Trails and Tales.* Sequim, Washington: Harriet U. Fish, 1983.

Forwood, Margaret R. "Historic Port Hadlock: Prosperity to Poverty," *Port Townsend Leader,* March 21, 1974.

Franzen, Sue. "Maple Falls Once Was Busy Sawmill Center," *Everson News,* July 30, 1964.

Gibbs, Jim. *West Coast Lighthouses.* Seattle: Superior Publishing Company, 1974.

Gray, Rodney E. Typed reminiscences at Skagit County Historical Museum, LaConner, Washington.

"The Great Silver-Lead District of the Cascade Range in Washington," *Northwest Mining Journal,* June, 1907.

Greenberg, Ellen, "Historic Note on the Alaska Packers Association and the Company Records," typed report, Alaska State Library & Archives, Juneau.

Gregory, V.J. *Keepers at the Gate.* Port Townsend, Washington: Port Townsend Publishing Co., Inc., 1976.

"Hadlock Bay Nominated for National Register," *Port Townsend Leader,* May 7, 1980.

Hall, Ada. "Avon * * The Town," typed reminiscences, March 7, 1957, Skagit County Historical Museum, LaConner, Washington.

Hall, Harry. "Early Days at Pysht, Washington," unpublished manuscript at Clallam County Library, Port Angeles, Washington.

Hanify, Mary Lou. "Dungeness site of early massacre," Dungeness Visitors Guide, *Port Angeles Evening News,* 1971, page 28.

Haro, Lee. "Concern, criticism over North Cascades park mining plan," *Bellingham Herald*, October 12, 1975.

Hein, Myrtle. Oral history tape, Skagit County Historical Museum, LaConner, Washington.

Henson, Jack. "Carlsborg Mill Crew Consists of Many Old Time Sawmill Men," *Port Angeles Evening News*, July 25, 1945.

_____. "One Time Boom Town of Port Crescent," *Port Angeles Evening News*, October 16, 1952.

"High Lights in a Modern West Coast Operation," *American Lumberman*, September 8, 1923.

Hodges, L. K. *Mining in the Pacific Northwest*. Seattle: *The Post-Intelligencer*, 1897.

Holbrook, Stewart. *Green Commonwealth*. Seattle: Dogwood Press, 1945.

"Hospitality is another post office service," *Sequim Gazette*, May 5, 1970.

Hult, Ruby El. *Lost Mines and Treasures*. Portland: Binfords & Mort, 1957.

_____. *Untamed Olympics*. Portland: Binfords & Mort, 1971.

Huntting, Marshall T. *Inventory of Washington Minerals*, Vol. 1. Olympia, Washington: Division of Mines and Geology, 1956.

_____. "Mineral Wealth in the Cascades," *Seattle Post-Intelligencer*, April 14, 1968.

An Illustrated History of Skagit and Snohomish Counties. Interstate Publishing Company, 1906.

"Inspector General Mansfield's Report of Inspection of the Post of Semiahmoo, December, 1858," Bellingham Public Library.

"The Irondale Proposition," "The Coming of Steel," and other articles, *Pacific Builder and Engineer*, August 6, 1910.

Irondale Steel Company prospectus, Jefferson County Historical Society, Port Townsend, Washington.

Jeffcott, Percival. *Nooksack Tales and Trails*. Ferndale: Whatcom County Pioneer Association, 1949.

_____. *Chechacho and Sourdough*. Ferndale: Percival Jeffcott, 1963.

Jefferson County Historical Museum, Port Townsend, Washington. Research files, clippings, and miscellaneous data.

Jenkins, Olaf P. *Geological Investigation of the Coal Fields of Western Whatcom County, Washington*. State of Washington, Department of Conservation and Development, Division of Geology, Bulletin No. 28, 1923.

_____. *Geological Investigation of the Coal Fields of Skagit County Washington*. State of Washington, Department of Conservation and Development, Division of Geology, Bulletin No. 29, 1924.

Jenkins, Will D. *Last Frontier in the North Cascades*. Mount Vernon, Washington: Skagit County Historical Society, 1984.

Jones, Roy Franklin. *Boundary Town*. Vancouver, Washington: Roy Franklin Jones, 1958.

Kenady, Mary. *Barron*, a typewritten summary prepared for United States Forest Service (USFS). USFS office, Winthrop, Washington.

Kerr, Gordon. Unpublished, typed personal reminiscences, Clallam County Library, Port Angeles, Washington.

Kivley, Melvin. *Hadlock Hill*. Port Hadlock: Melvin Kivley, 1981.

Koert, Dorothy, and Galen Biery. *Looking Back*. Bellingham, Washington: Koert and Biery, 1980.

Krause, Fayette F. "Dungeness Spit: World's Largest Natural Sandspit," *Pacific Search*, pp. 16-17.

Krenmayr, Janice. Article in *Seattle Times*, November 1, 1964.

Landes, Henry. "The Non-Metalliferous Resources of Washington, Except Coal," *Washington Geological Survey*, Vol. I, Part 3, 1902, pp. 24-27.

_____. *Washington Geological Survey*. Washington State Geologist, Volume II, Annual Report for 1902, 1903.

Latteier, Carolyn. *From Wood Alcohol to Beach-side Fun*, etc.," *Port Townsend Leader*, August 20, 1986.

LeWarne, Charles P. *Utopias on Puget Sound, 1885-1915*. Seattle: University of Washington Press, 1975.

"Limestone," typed manuscript, Todd collection at M. Impero, Bellingham, Washington.

Lindemood, Lee J. Oral history tape, Skagit County Historical Museum, LaConner, Washington.

"Logging proposed to open mining claims in North Cascades Park," *Seattle Times*, October 16, 1975.

Lotzegell, Mrs. George. "Pioneer Days at Old Dungeness," *Washington Historical Quarterly*, vol. 24, p. 264.

McBride, Debbie. "Steel Rolling Mill was Economic Foundation . . . ," *Port Townsend Leader*, June 29, 1983.

McCurdy, James G. *By Juan de Fuca's Strait*. Portland: Binfords & Mort, 1937.

McDonald, Lucile. "Bessie Luton—Former Town Marshal," *The Seattle Times*, Sunday, November 21, 1965. pp. 5-6.

_____. "Disappearance of a Lumber Town," *The Seattle Times*, November 16, 1958.

_____. "Gold-Mining Years in the North Cascades," *The Seattle Times*.

_____. "New Life Comes to Quarantine Station at Diamond Point," *The Seattle Times*, January 27, 1963.

_____. "Port Crescent . . . Only a Memory," *The Seattle Times*, September 17, 1961.

_____. "Port Gamble Takes a New Lease on Life," *Seattle Times*, September 14, 1947.

_____. "Sequim Was `Hunter's Paradise' Century Ago," *The Seattle Times*, January 22, 1961, pp. 1-2.

McDonald, P.A. "Coast's Own Fore & Afters . . . ," *Marine Digest*, December 14, 1940 and January 18, 1941.

McGinnis, Verna L. "Port Ludlow," *Hood Canal Kitchen Capers*, 1949.

McGuire, C.C. Typed memoirs from Mount Baker Snoqualmie National Forest files, copy at author's office, Bellingham, Washington.

McLellan, Roy Davidson. *The Geology of the San Juan Islands*. Seattle: University of Washington Press, 1927.

Markel, Dan B. "Iron Factory Built on Port Townsend Bay before Statehood," *Seattle Post-Intelligencer*, January 7, 1940.

Mayne, R.C., Commander R.N., F.R.G.S. *Four Years in British Columbia and Vancouver Island*. London: John Murray, 1862.

Meany, Edmond S., ed. *Vancouver's Discovery of Puget Sound*, etc., particularly chapter "Three Years at Shoal-water Bay," 1915.

Meany, Edmond S. "Western Spruce and the War," *Washington Historical Quarterly*, vol. 9, no. 4, 1918, pp. 255-58.

"Mining Claims Still Occupy North Cascades," *Daily Olympian*, April 6, 1976.

Moen, Wayne S. *Mines and Mineral Deposits of Whatcom County, Washington*. Olympia, Washington: Department of Natural Resources, 1969.

Monson, Ken. "Avon Once Busy River Town," *Mount Vernon Daily Herald*, December 23, 1955.

Moore, F. Stanley. "An Historical Geography of the Settlement around Lake Whatcom prior to 1920," Technical Report No. 21, Western Washington State College Institute for Freshwater Studies, June, 1973.

Morgan, C.T. *The San Juan Story*. Friday Harbor: San Juan Industries, 1962-1966.

Morgan, Murray. *The Last Wilderness*. New York: Viking Press, 1955.

"New Dungeness grew, then came Carlsborg," *Sequim Gazette*, Sequim History Section, May 7, 1968.

New Washington Writers Program. Portland: Binfords & Mort, 1941.

Newspapers, various issues, including *Bellingham Bay Mail, Bellingham Herald, Bellingham Buyer, Blaine Journal, Burlington Farm Journal* including several columns by Ray Jordan, *Carlsborg Review, Fairhaven Herald, Mount Vernon Argus, Mount Vernon Daily News, Methow Valley News, Northern Light, Northern Star, Port Angeles Evening News, Port*

Townsend Leader, Puget Sound Herald, Puget Sound Mail, The Reveille, Seattle Post-Intelligencer, Seattle Times, Sebring's Skagit County Illustrated, Sequim Press, Skagit News (later the *Skagit News Herald* and then *Skagit Valley Herald, Wenatchee Daily World.*

Northwest Mining Journal, 1906-1910, from Washington State Library, Olympia.

"North-Western Washington," pamphlet compiled by Immigration Aid Society, Port Townsend, no date.

O'Hara, Maggie. "The old Alcohol Factory," *Sequim Gazette*, November 7, 1979.

Okanogan County Heritage. Various editions, esp. 1974-75 and 1984-85. Okanogan, Washington: Okanogan County Historical Society.

"Old Dungeness: first county seat of Clallam County," *Sequim Gazette*, Sequim History Section, May 7, 1968.

Paxson, Don. "Timber!" *The Daily News*, Port Angeles, Wash., Summer, 1975.

Pilcher, Gilbert. "The Rise and Fall of Irondale," for Washington Pioneer Project, typed manuscript, Jefferson County Historical Society, Port Townsend, Washington.

Port Angeles Evening News, editions containing "Peninsula Profiles." Also special edition, "Pysht Tree Farm Edition," October 31, 1952.

Port Crescent Leader. Selected editions, esp. "To Hunt for Cannibals," March, 1892.

"Port Ludlow—Mill Town Memories," *Port Townsend Leader*, Summer, 1974.

Rabins, Erick S. "The Changing Economic Functions of Settlements along the Northern Pacific and Milwaukee Railroads in the Nooksack Basin 1900 through 1960," master's thesis, May 20, 1983, Western Washington University.

Reichardt, Marjorie. Private scrapbook of articles authored for various publications 1980-84 on behalf of Semiahmoo Park.

Resort at Port Ludlow, various public relations materials.

Rice, Charles. "A Steel Ghost Haunts Irondale, etc.," *Tacoma News Tribune*, June 1, 1968.

Richardson, David. *Magic Islands.* Eastsound, Washington: Orcas Publishing Company, 1964-1973.

_____, *Pig War Islands.* Eastsound, Washington: Orcas Publishing Company, 1971.

Roe, JoAnn. "Bellingham's Daring Dash from Snow to Sea," *American West*, May/June, 1986.

_____. *The North Cascadians.* Seattle: Madrona Publishers, Inc., 1980.

Roth, Lottie Roeder. *History of Whatcom County.* Chicago: Pioneer Historical Publishing Company, 1926.

Royer, Marie Hamel. *The Saxon Story.* Bellingham: Whatcom County Historical Society, 1982.

Schmidel, Justus. Translated by Robert E. Pike from German book, *Die Harte Schule*, in article, "Experiencing the 'Hard School' in Maple Falls," *Seattle Times*, February 14, 1965, and in book by Frances E. Todd.

Schmierer, Alan C. *Northings up the Nooksack.* Seattle: Pacific Northwest National Parks and Forests Association, 1983.

Scott, James W. and Daniel E. Turbeville III. *Early Industries of Bellingham Bay* etc. Bellingham, Washington: Fourth Corner Registry, Center for Pacific Northwest Studies, 1980.

_____. *Whatcom County in Maps 1832-1937.* Bellingham, Washington: Center for Pacific Northwest Studies & The Fourth Corner Registry, 1983.

Sequim Dungeness Museum, Sequim, Washington. Papers.

Simmons, Dick. "Lone Jack Mine Dies Like Queen She Was," *Bellingham Herald*, August 30, 1964.

"Skagit and San Juan Counties," *Northwest Mining Journal*, October, 1907.

Skagit County Historical Museum, LaConner, Washington, miscellaneous data in files.

The Skagit River Post, Centennial Edition, June 9, 1991.

Skagit Settlers. Mount Vernon, Washington: Skagit County Historical Society, 1975.

Skaling, P.E. Letter and excerpts of old letters, Skagit County Historical Museum, LaConner, Washington.

Smith, Norman. "Victory," a series of articles in the *Port Angeles Evening News*, 1950.

Steele, E.N. *The Immigrant Oyster.* Olympia, Washington: E.N. Steele, 1964.

Swan, James G. Diaries 1871-72, Special Collections, University of Washington, Seattle.

_____. "Sequim Prairie, Washington Territory," *Washington Standard*, February 23, 1861.

Swaney, Homer H. Obituary, *Seattle Times*, January 22, 1904.

Taylor, Eva Cook. *The Lure of Tubal-Cain.* Port Townsend: Jefferson County Historical Society, 1972.

Thompson, Dennis Blake. *Logging Railroads in Skagit County.* Seattle: Northwest Short Line, 1989.

Thompson, Erwin N. *North Cascades N.P.* etc. Washington, D.C.: U.S. Department of the Interior, National Park Service, Office of History and Historic Architecture, March, 1970.

Thompson, Lawrence L. "United States Marine Hospital No. 17, Port Townsend, Washington, 1855-1933," Master's thesis, Western Washington University, August 19, 1988.

"Thunder Creek," "Skagit County, Skagit Queen Consolidated Mining Company," "Mining Notes, The Standard Reduction and Development Company," and other news notes and short articles in *Northwest Mining Journal*, various editions 1907-10. Washington State Library, Olympia.

Todd, Frances E. Clippings from her files, M. Impero Collection, Bellingham, Washington.

_____. *The Trail Through The Woods.* Maple Falls, Washington: Frances B. Todd, 1982.

Told by the Pioneers, 3 vols. Olympia: Secretary of State, 1934-38.

United States v. *Glenn Widing* etc., and a comprehensive file about the contesting of Widing's development of Skagit Queen claims, in National Park Service files, Sedro-Woolley, Washington.

United States of America vs. *Jess Sapp, Robert A. Rukke*, et. al. Transcript of contest hearings for Valumines, Inc., holdings, in National Park Service files, Sedro-Woolley, Washington.

Washington Resources, vol. 1, no. 1, April, 1893.

Washington State Archives, Olympia, Washington. Files.

Washington State Library files, various. Olympia, Washington.

Weir, Allen. "Early Dungeness Valley History," speech before Washington State Historical Society, 1892. Copy at the Museum of the Clallam County Historical Society, Port Angeles, Washington.

Wells, John. List of excerpts from lumber magazines about Clear Lake, Clear Lake Historical Society.

Western Steel Corporation stock prospectus, from files of Jefferson County Historical Society, Port Townsend, Washington.

"Whatcom County, the Klondike of Washington," pamphlet, Bellingham Public Library.

Widrig, Charlotte. Article in *Seattle Times*, December 24, 1961.

Wilkes, Charles. *Narrative of the United States Exploring Expedition.* Philadelphia: Lea and Blanchard, 1845.

Wilkie, Rosemary. *A Broad Bold Ledge of Gold.* Monte Cristo, Washington: Rosemary Wilkie, 1958.

Wright, E.W., ed. *Lewis and Dryden's Marine History of the Northwest.* Portland: Lewis & Dryden Printing Co., 1895.

Zobrist, Elaine. *Ghost Towns of Lake Whatcom.* Typescript at Bellingham Public Library, 1979.

Useful interviews with: Jim and Carol Bates, Tim Bates, Wayne and Danna Beech, Galen Biery, Sr., Steward Blythe, John Byrd, James Cannon, Verna Carter, May Caryl, John Cuthill, Richard "Slug" Davis, Harriet U. Fish, John Gosset, Gary Graham, Ernie Gross, Doug Hamilton, Steve Hauff, James Hermanson, Harold Hobson, Thad Hodgins, Frederick W. Hubbard, Beth Kautz, Dave Lambert, Ernie Larson, Muriel Larson, Frances Leander, Joy McCarter, George McCush, Fraser Madill, Clarence Miller, Helen Mitchell, Wayne Moen, James Moore, Charles Novak, John R. Pankratz, Blanche Peeples, August Radke, Henry Reasoner, Wayne Rouleau, Robert Rukke, Louise Schumacher, James Scott, John Soderberg, William Soren, Jake Steiner, Morrie Tarte, Neil Tarte, Eva Cook Taylor, John Werner, Win Williams, Sr., Mae Wray, Ralph and June Zoberst.